Pages from the
Harlem Renaissance

Studies in African and African-American Culture

James L. Hill
General Editor

Vol. 6

PETER LANG
New York • Washington, D.C./Baltimore
Bern • Frankfurt am Main • Berlin • Vienna • Paris

Anthony D. Hill

Pages from the Harlem Renaissance

A Chronicle of Performance

PETER LANG
New York • Washington, D.C./Baltimore
Bern • Frankfurt am Main • Berlin • Vienna • Paris

Library of Congress Cataloging-in-Publication Data

Hill, Anthony D.
Pages from the Harlem Renaissance: a chronicle of performance /
Anthony D. Hill.
p. cm. — (Studies in African and African-American culture; vol. 6)
Includes bibliographical references and index.
1. Jackson, James Albert. 2. Theater critics—United States—Biography.
3. Afro-Americans in the performing arts. 4. Harlem Renaissance.
I. Title. II. Series.
PN1708.J28H56   791'.092—dc20   [B]   95-31999
ISBN 0-8204-2864-7
ISSN 0890-4847

Die Deutsche Bibliothek-CIP-Einheitsaufnahme

Hill, Anthony D.:
Pages from the Harlem renaissance: a chronicle of performance /
Anthony D. Hill. –New York; Washington, D.C./Baltimore; Bern;
Frankfurt am Main; Berlin; Vienna; Paris: Lang.
(Studies in African and African American culture; Vol. 6)
ISBN 0-8204-2864-7
NE: GT

Cover design by Jeff Nisbet.

Illustrations, as enumerated on page ix, were provided courtesy of Manuscripts,
Archives and Rare Books Division, Schomburg Center for Research in Black
Culture, The New York Public Library, Astor, Lenox and Tilden Foundations;
Billboard Publications; Beverly Jaenson; and The Anthony D. Hill Collection.

The paper in this book meets the guidelines for permanence and durability
of the Committee on Production Guidelines for Book Longevity
of the Council of Library Resources.

Printed in the United States of America.

To my parents,

    Leroy
        and
            Flavor,

my family and loved ones;
and to the memory of my "brother,"

    Jon
        Ron
            Buren

Contents

Illustrations

All illustrations unless indicated below are photographed by Chuck Pulin, courtesy of *Billboard* Publications. Special thanks to Tim White, Editor-in-Chief and Darren Hartley, *Billboard* archivist.

Cover, Jeff Nisbet.

Maps, Beverly Jaenson 69, 71, 74, 77, 78, 83.

The Anthony D. Hill Collection 14, 15, 16, 32, 33, 40, 41, 42, 43 44, 47, 48, 70, 73, 81, 82, 103.

Courtesy of Schomburg Center For Research in Black Culture. Special thanks to Diana Lachatanere, head:

Foreword

The news in last month's issue of *Billboard* may hold little interest for us, but really old "news," written seventy years ago, absorbs us, whisking us back to Jackson's Page and the days of The Theater Owners' Association (TOBA), the booking agency that sent African Americans (colored then) on sweepingly long tours. Traveling by train, rattling along in segregated coaches coupled directly behind the steam engine which belched coal gas and dirt into the car, those actors, dancers comedians, and aerialists lurched toward one night stands in Memphis, or two nights in New Orleans, or, if lucky, a week in Chicago. For the Colored audiences outside of Harlem, these traveling talents were Saturday night's entertainment.

Appearing in theaters segregated either by seating or by performance hours, the performers' salaries, like their dressing rooms, were small and shabby. A producer often absconded with the box office take, leaving the talent stranded without funds or union recourse. (Colored were not yet admitted to white vaudeville and equity unions).

As Black show business grew, *Billboard*, the national show business tabloid, saw an opportunity to increase its circulation. Who better to report the burgeoning African American show business than James Albert Jackson, a former journalist, a conservative republican, and a railroad detective who knew the itinerant life. The logo on Jackson's column read "J. A. Jackson's Page in the interest of the Colored Actor, Showman, and Musician of America," and he did just that. Not only did Jackson review vaudeville, film, fairs, circuses, and legitimate drama, but he used his position at *Billboard* to confront abuses, one of which, the midnight show, often required performers to perform without any additional salary. These late night revels appealed to rowdy crowds who demanded music, dance and laughter sparked by bawdy jokes. Family audiences stayed home. Jackson campaigned for family entertainment, which would build audiences for Colored performers who, in turn, would drop their "blue" material. He demanded that producers meet their obligations to performers, and in return, actors fulfill their contracts. He supported unions which would offer death and illness benefits to show people.

A glance at Jackson's Page of October 21, 1922 reveals wonderfully diverse creative talents—an announcement for Jesse Shipp's film, *Shadows and Sunshine*, featured America's only colored aviatrix—Bessie Coleman; the right hand column discussed the performers at the county fair at Asheville, North Carolina; Jackson saluted an opening of a new musical *Step Along*, and published a photo of Mae Brown, "a woman director"; he praised a white show at the Greenwich Theater, and gave a puff review to Maharajah the Mystic; then he thanked a white Masonic Lodge for including

Colored talent in its shows. The reader may recognize none of the artists named (except the most famous like Ethel Waters), however, "Lesser-knowns," most of whom never played in Harlem itself, were the life and root of "show biz," and Jackson's Page was their ticket to immortality.

In writing about Jackson's Page (1920-25), Professor Hill provides insight into an amazing man, who wrote about a world and time that is now recognized as a seminal period of American performance history. Anthony Hill has made *Billboard's* "old new," very new indeed.

Professor James V. Hatch
Hatch / Billops Collection

Acknowledgments

I owe thanks to many people who helped me with this book for their advice and support. In particular, I thank my mentors: Professor James V. Hatch of the Hatch/Billips Collection for his long discussions, endless suggestions, and for always being there for me; Professor Cedric Robinson, a remarkable scholar and individual for the fellowship at the Center for Black Studies at The University of California at Santa Barbara. Dr. Robinson, as a teacher and friend, helped me to understand what the erudite W. E. B. Du Bois echoed early in the twentieth century, that "Everything is Political"; Professor Douglas Daniels, former Chair of The Department of Black Studies at The University of California and Santa Barbara for his expertiese and for opening my eyes to "what is relevant"; and Professor Sam Hay for always lending an ear.

I wish to thank Dean Donald Harris of The College of the Arts and The Department of Theatre at The Ohio State University for the Level II grant and the SRA that afforded me the time and means to work on the book. Also, I thank Gail Peters of The Academic Computing Services at The Ohio State University for the countless hours she consulted me on the index, and for her patience. Dorothy, many thanks for the moral support and for relieving me of other important matters. Many others deserve praise who helped me with this book or were inspirational. I also thank you.

James Albert "Billboard" Jackson

James Albert Jackson
Profile of a Renaissance Man

J ames Albert Jackson was the first black writer to edit a column in *Billboard* magazine, a white newspaper. He challenged the false and exaggerated appraisals of black performers as always being "great," and insisted that black theater and black artists be taken seriously. During the Harlem Renaissance, between 1920 to 1929, Jackson, a conservative, worked within the hegemonic[1] culture to make changes in the black show business industry. He documented black entertainment for five years to boost, illuminate, and advance the field. He also influenced public opinion and provided recognition for black performers on a national level.

The twenties were a time of ragtime and jazz, the Black bottom and the Charleston, and bootleg whiskey; it was a time of change and creativity in Harlem, the black entertainment capital of America. Whites and blacks who lived "uptown" were living in the midst of the Harlem Renaissance; and those who lived "downtown" came uptown. The performers of that time have become bywords in the history of black entertainment: Bert Williams, Charles Gilpin, Ethel Waters, W. C. Handy, Bessie Smith, Ma Rainey, Fats Waller, Rose McClendon, Paul Robeson, and Josephine Baker. But the man who helped to legitimize black performance in the American show business industry faded to an historical footnote.

J. A. Jackson, editor and columnist for *Billboard,* had a career as varied as those of the people he wrote about. He was a minstrel performer, a military man, a government and private industry employee, as well as a feature and theatrical writer, and a pioneer in the entertainment industry. Jackson was important as a progenitor of black performance news reporting and booster for black entertainment. "Jackson's Page" in

Billboard (as the column was finally titled on January 8, 1921) recorded the progress of black performance during the middle stages of the Harlem Renaissance—one of the most productive and creative periods in the history of African-American show business. The column served as a vital line of communication for members of the profession, providing a weekly chronology of artists, theatrical productions and organizations and affording greater opportunities for black performers. As editor of "The Page" for five years (1920-25), Jackson compiled and wrote most of his own material. According to *Billboard*, it discontinued the column because of retrenchment and a lack of advertisement.

Today, we rely on Jackson's writings for important information on this vital and significant period in black entertainment. The question then becomes: What was Jackson's role as a theatrical critic in advancing African-American show business during the Harlem Renaissance? To address the question, this historical study will investigate the nature and significance of Jackson's column; and of his vision of black performance as seen through "The Page" against the larger framework of national and cultural concerns of the 1920s. I will document and analyze the column from its founding in 1920 to its disappearance in 1925, focusing on Jackson as writer, reporter, spokesman, and observer of black entertainment.

Billboard, the *Variety* of its day, was the first white publication to offer a column on black performance. Founded in Cincinnati, Ohio as *Billboard Advertising* on November 1, 1894 by publishers William H. Donaldson and James Hennigan, it changed its name to *Billboard* three years later. The trade paper catered to the interests of the billposting,[2] poster printing, and advertising agencies. In 1900 Donaldson acquired Hennigan's shares and expanded the magazine from a monthly to a weekly publication. He broadened the paper to include many entertainment departments: burlesque, circuses, carnivals, street fairs and amusements, operas, dance, music, minstrelsy, and theater. "For the first several years, Donaldson wrote practically every word of the paper himself, sold ads, laid it out, and took it through production."[3] *Billboard* became a popular and prosperous show business paper. The central office in Cincinnati extended its operations to branches in New York, San Francisco, St. Louis and Chicago; but not without competition; *Variety* began in 1905 and the *Clipper* in 1907. By 1909, *Billboard* had ventured into music, becoming the first trade paper to publish reproductions of sheet music (both words and music) of leading songs of the day as a new editorial feature. The magazine covered a broad range and became so entrenched in the areas of carnivals, circuses, and fairs, vaudeville shows, legitimate theatrical advertising of dramatic stock and repertory companies, that no other trade paper seriously challenged them for the next several years.

As *Billboard* prospered and became the leading trade paper, Donaldson's editorial commentaries gained notoriety. He fought against whatever he thought would harm American entertainment and supported what he thought was in the best interest of show business. For example, union actors cited the publications for its great contribution to their victory in the 1919 Actor Equity-Producers strike. Frank Gilmore, Executive Secretary and Treasurer of Actors' Equity Association, wrote of Donaldson's support for the actors, "Not for a moment did he hesitate (to support the actors) because of his possible loss of managerial advertising. His principles meant more to him than his pocketbook."⁴ This kind of determination motivated Donaldson to initiate a department devoted to black performers. Before then, *Billboard*, as well as other white publications, limited reports on black show business to advertising and an occasional brief commentary.

With the boom in the entertainment industry after the war, whites discovered that blacks could sing, dance, and act. The in-roads they were making in the music, drama, motion picture, vaudeville, out-of-doors, and concert fields indicated that they were potential money makers. The possibility of large profits prompted a plethora of managers, agents, recording companies, theater owners, and motion picture producers, blacks and whites, to take a more vested interest in black show business.

Historically, the American entertainment profession discriminated against black performers. It stereotyped them as lazy, shuffling, oversexed, watermelon-eating, razor-carrying, illiterate buffoons. To gain acceptance, the industry needed a vehicle to advertise and promote black entertainers, one that could transcend racial boundaries and reach the largest possible audience. The inception of "Jackson's Page" in *Billboard* was, in its own way, as dramatic as the performances Jackson critiqued. On October 30, 1920, *Billboard* provided that breakthrough by announcing that it will inaugurate a department devoted to black show business:

> Beginning on November 6, 1920, a new feature section, written by a black man and devoted to black performers, artists, managers, and agents, will appear . . . weekly. . . . We feel that the professional artists and entertainers of the race have fairly won this recognition. . . . We are according the representation gladly even enthusiastically.⁵

Joseph and June Bundy Csida wrote in *American Entertainment* that

Donaldson "was acutely conscious of the discrimination against blacks and other minority groups."[6] They went on to say that his "attitude about them is based on basic principles of humanity, [he] feels that . . . every person needs a 'home base,' a 'place' he may share with others of like interests."[7] Furthermore, they concluded that Donaldson's idea was in keeping with his philosophy of helping entertainers on all levels and fostering the growth of the entertainment industry. The column was to appear on a trial basis, for a "reasonable time." If it engendered sufficient advertising to pay for itself, it would become a feature of *Billboard*. As the editor of the new department, Donaldson gave J. A. Jackson a personal vote of confidence as a "Negro writer of attainment and distinction."[8]

At age 42, Jackson was an imposing figure: a tall, clean shaven, full-faced, fair-complexioned man with a receding hair-line. His stout body fit neatly in his usual professional attire—a dark suit, white shirt, and a tie that exuded the air of a distinguished gentleman. His background was extraordinary. A group of Quakers had brought his family to America in 1753 after buying the family's freedom from Portuguese traders in the harbor of Portsmouth, England and had settled in what is now Centre County, Pennsylvania.[9] Jackson himself was born on June 20, 1878, in Bellefonte, Pennsylvania, the eldest son of Abraham Valentine and Nannie (Lee) Jackson and part of the fifth generation of Jacksons to be born in the same county.[10] Jackson's father, Abe, was in show business as a member of a commercial singing group, the McMillen and Sour Beck Jubilee Singers, organized in Belfonte, Ohio. It was the celebrated Fisk and Hampton Jubilee Singers who popularized this form of entertainment that was in vogue at the time.[11] The McMillen organization later became more widely known as Stinson's Singers. By this time, however, Abe had given up show business to return home to marry. Incidentally, William (Billy) Mills, the grandfather of the famous Mills Brothers' Quartet, was a member of this group.[12]

The oldest son of fourteen children, Jackson left home at an early age to ease the economic strain that burdened many large black households. He traveled extensively with minstrel shows and the railroad; hence enabling him to form acquaintances in every state in the union as well as in several foreign countries. He acquired statistics about the black profession that made him one of the more informed writers of his time. In addition, he collaborated with several well-known authors in national magazines and foreign papers.[13]

At age 15, Jackson was already honing his writing skills by working as a cub reporter for the Bellefonte *Daily Gazette* and the *Daily News*, two hometown newspapers.[14] On leaving Bellefonte circa 1896, the ambitious young Jackson continued to write while working as a bellboy and dining-room employee. During his stint as a dining room employee, a fellow workman, Richard B. Harrison, taught him elocution. Harrison would later be a dramatic arts instructor at Greensboro, North Carolina, but is best known for his powerful portrayal of De Lord in the stage version of *The Green Pastures*.[15] Experience in minstrel shows familiarized Jackson with the plight of race performers and the rigors of show business. Tom Fletcher, in his book *100 Years of the Negro in Show Business* (1954), writes about the first time he met Jackson in New York City at the turn of the century. Jackson, then an agent for Ed Winn's Big Novelty Minstrels (his first such job), was looking for feature players.[16] Fletcher, a "star comedian" with the big Novelty Minstrels who doubled as a trap drummer in the band and orchestra, said "Jackson was accumulating funds . . . to complete his college studies. . . . After the Ed Winn show closed, Jackson was still bitten with the show bug. He wanted to finish his education, but saw no reason why he couldn't make enough money in the winter to take up the courses he desired in the summertime. He had picked up considerable knowledge of show business and with his educational background, figured to become a good interlocutor."[17] Fletcher notes that Jackson . . .

> . . . got the nod from Richard and Pringle's Georgia Minstrels, starring Billy Kersands. The money wasn't much, but a fellow like J. A., or anyone else who didn't gamble, could save a nice little nest egg by the end of a season. And at the end of each season he would go back to school until he had finished his courses.[18]

Fletcher did not mention where Jackson went to college or when he worked as a minstrel performer. Nevertheless, it is most likely that Jackson toured with the minstrel troupes between 1896 and 1900, because he left home around 1896. To further substantiate this notion, C. T. Magill writing in the Chicago *Defender* in 1921 indicated that Jackson worked as a journalist for *Today*, an afternoon daily in Detroit around 1900.[19] After his one-year stint as a journalist, he migrated to Chicago, where he took a civil-service examination. Tom Fletcher states that while waiting for the test results, Jackson "hung out in Daddy Love's place, on the corner of 27th and State Street, where the actors all gathered in Chicago between seasons, or when laying off. There were a great many in show business who couldn't read or write, and those that could usually charged ten cents for writing a letter. Jack was always glad to oblige, but he would never accept a penny."[20]

Meanwhile, the versatile Jackson landed a year-long position as a bank clerk in 1902 with the Chicago Jennings Real Estate and Loan Company. According to Magill, Jackson was the first person of color to hold such a position in Illinois and the first black admitted to the American Marketing Association.[21] During his off hours, Jackson worked part-time as an usher at the famous Pekin Theater; he was present for its historic opening in 1904. This was home to the first black theatrical stock company. It became the most important venue for black theater since the days of the African Grove Theater in New York and the Hyer Sisters' touring troupe.[22]

After passing the Civil-Service examination, Jackson joined the U. S. Railroad police as a road officer, traveling the country investigating cases. One assignment of note involved his participation in the capture of the infamous Harrison Gang, headed by Jeff Harrison, closing the books on "The World's Greatest Train Robbery." Jackson remained with the railroad police for twelve years until World War I.[23] He married Gabriele Belle Hill on April 6, 1909. Although Jackson spent a great deal of his time on the road, he was a devoted family man—his wife often accompanied him in his travels.[24] During the War, Jackson's intelligence training with the railroad enabled him to land a position as a commissioned adjutant of The First Colored Provisional Regiment. (This was the original name of the 15th regiment.) Jackson was one of only two blacks during the war ranked as Agent-in-Charge for the United States Military Intelligence Service, General Staff, according to Magill.[25]

Throughout his pioneering efforts in varied occupations, Jackson never lost his proclivity for writing. The black press considered two of his articles to be among his best serial works; the *Globe* syndicated "The Negro at Large" (1912) and "The Underlying Case of Race Riots" (1919). Other publications throughout the country quoted excerpts from his articles extensively. The New York *Sun* and the New York *Herald* published several of his feature stories in the Sunday edition of the magazine section.[26] After the war, Jackson joined the staff of *Billboard*. Reprints of his *Billboard* editorials often appeared in black publications, such as the *Messenger*, New York *Amsterdam News*, Chicago *Defender*, and New York *Age*.

The history of black entertainment news reporting naturally involves the history of black newspapers. The emergence of black publications was due to many social changes. After the Civil War, from 1875 to 1895, masses of blacks migrated from the South to major Northern cities. Forced to live in ghettos, blacks still faced many of the same social attitudes from which they had fled. Recognizing the value of widespread exposure to this new populace, social services, religious and political organizations, and enterprising businesses began to use the black press to advertise.

The black press modeled its format after European publications. Whether they were newspapers or magazines, the physical patterns were the same. Both informed readers, provided critical interpretation, and promoted entertainment. Cultural illusions, however, distinguished the black press from its white counterparts. Informed criticism was essential for the growth of black show business. Theatrical news helped to culturally educate the illiterate working class as well as the illuminati. As literacy increased and blacks began to earn more money, a lower-middle income class emerged. This group began to buy more newspapers. Black newspapers catered to the needs of the increasing black readership by providing sensitive insights into cultural, social, and political issues that affected the industry. This point-of-view, before the 1900s had been otherwise unavailable to the black entertainment community.[27]

Due to the popularity of minstrel shows and musical comedies, George L. Knox seized the opportunity to tap into this burgeoning black entertainment industry. In 1897, the innovative pioneer race journalist founded the Indianapolis *Freeman* weekly newspaper. Three years after its successful launch, he installed J. Harry Jackson (no relation to J. A. Jackson) on the staff to report show business news. Shortly thereafter, he hired Sylvester Russellto edit a theater column entitled "The Stage." The audacious Russell "anointed himself. . . . The First Theater Critic."[28] The *Freeman* was the first recognized black newspaper to carry an entertainment page in each edition and to distribute black theatrical news nationally. The proprietors or managers of various shows would mail-in to the column news from acts appearing in local attractions or in other cities.[29] Russell reveled in his role as a theater critic, insisting that actors and entertainers respect his assessments of the industry; addressing issues of morality on the stage; setting expectations for performers, audiences, and theaters; and giving opinions on the merits of writing comical versus serious dramas. This pioneer critic was the forerunner of constructive criticism of black performers. He and J. Harry Jackson were prototypes for black performance news reporters. Their legacy of highlighting black achievement and setting standards in the industry was noticeable during the Harlem Renaissance.

By the early 1900s, blacks had launched almost 100 newspapers across the United States, beginning a sustained period of growth. Leading the way were the pioneer publications: the Indianapolis *Freeman*, the Chicago *Defender*, the New York *Age*, the Baltimore *Afro-American*, the Kansas City *Call*, the Denver *Star*, and the New York *Amsterdam News*.

Early on during the 1920s, an important booster of black show was theater critic Tony Langston of the Chicago *Defender*. The editor of a two-page theater column believed that the illumination of the black artist through mass exposure would foster growth in the black arts industry. With a circulation of 225,000, the publication had a larger distribution than any other black newspaper in the early 1920s. Langston wrote mini-reviews, made anecdotal comments, and informed the industry about theatrical activities in New York and on the touring circuits. He listed shows at local theaters and movie houses, noted new song hits, and kept a letter file for performers to inform the industry as to their whereabouts. Managers and agents wanted to be in the know about hit shows as well as promising and established artists.

Lester A. Walton of the New York *Age* and Romeo Dougherty of the New York *Amsterdam News* were two dramatic critics who helped strengthen the morale of black entertainers and cultivate an appreciation for entertainers.[30] They were quick to react to white reviews of black shows when they thought criticism was racist or based on ignorance of black culture. Occasionally, they would sharply criticize black shows and performers who did not "measure up." Dougherty and Walton were the most vocal regarding economic, political, and racial issues.[31]

The most notable patron of the black creative and performing arts during the 1920s was William Edward Burghardt Du Bois, the founder and editor of the *Crisis*, a Harlem-based publication. Earlier in 1916, Du Bois stated that he wanted to "teach the 'colored people' the meaning of their history and of their rich emotional life . . . and to use theater to reveal the Negro to the white world as 'a human, feeling thing.' "[32] By 1921, he declared "All art is propaganda and without propaganda there is no true art." Du Bois advocated "race" or "propaganda" plays. He saw theater as a political tool for social change. He also believed that, "New theater must consist of characters and situations that depict the struggle of African-Americans against racism [and] show people not only as they . . . were but also as they wished to be." [33]

Although Du Bois felt that black art often "lacked careful finish" and needed refining, he encouraged the race to write plays about the black experience and to support black theater. He distinguished himself from his contemporaries in two important ways. First, he sponsored annual playwriting contests in the *Crisis*, and awarded prizes for the best one-act play between 1925-27. Thus, he proclaimed the *Crisis* as the Negro's chief talent scout and encouraged readers to identify dramatic talent. The play contest not only provided scripts for Negro universities and the little theater movement, it also encouraged black playwrights to write about the black experience in a new and creative way. Even though the plays were diverse in subject matter, Harlem Renaissance writers defined them in two categories: "folk" plays or "race and propaganda" plays.

Theophilus Lewis was yet another Harlem writer and advocate of "race" or "propaganda" theater. In 1917, A. Philip Randolph and Chandler Owens, both college-trained Southerners, founded the *Messenger* that gained the reputation as the most vibrant and controversial black journal in the nation. The team added a theater column in 1923, and Lewis joined the staff as a part-time drama critic. From September 1923 to July 1927, he wrote a monthly column entitled "The Theater, The Soul of Black Folks." Lewis preferred folk art for its appeal to lower-income black audiences. He believed that it was this audience that kept theater alive. He also envisioned that the black middle class chose white productions over the black ones. Like Du Bois, Lewis called for indigenous black theater that "embodies the whole spiritual life of a people; their aspirations and manners, their ideas and ideals, their fantasies and philosophies, the music and dignity of their speech in a word, their essential character, and it carries this likeness of . . . people down the centuries for the enlightenment of remote times and races."[34] In his own way, Lewis was advocating a repository system to preserve cultural representation for posterity.

While Russell, Du Bois, Walton, Dougherty, and Lewis' works helped to advance black show business during the 1920s, J. A. Jackson's work reflects an appreciation of performance. Richard Schechner defines it as a "broad and deep . . . field . . . that includes performative behavior of all kinds ritual, aesthetic, sportive, playful; and in all contexts from everyday life to high ceremony in a variety of circumstances and cultures . . . along with familiar forms such as dance, theater, and ritual."[35]

J. A. Jackson stood apart from his contemporaries in several distinct ways. Like Sylvester Russell, he celebrated black achievement in the entertainment industry. Unlike Russell's contemptuous reactions to "actors, prima donnas, and aspiring critics,"[36] Jackson tempered his critiques with sensitivity. At this time, *Billboard* was the oldest and largest American entertainment trade paper. Like Sylvester Russell, Jackson set high moral standards for the industry. He was as quick to criticize profanity, vulgarity, and unprofessional attitudes, as he was to challenge unfit working conditions on black touring circuits, particularly The Theater Owners and Booking Association (TOBA).

Jackson's method of collecting information on the black entertainment field was unlike other Harlem theatrical critics. Most of these journalists printed material sent-in by members of the profession in addition to covering the sport and amusement field. Jackson's column was the first in a major show business publication to search out, report on, and promote the various types of Negro entertainment. It covered all aspects of the colored entertainment industry: music and opera, minstrelsy, vaudeville, burlesque, circuses, carnivals, street fairs, and amusement parks. Theater practitioners considered "The Page" a regular source of information because of the vast amount of data Jackson collected, compiled, and published in his annual survey on the industry.

Jackson also stood apart for his effectiveness in getting artists organized to protect their rights. Additionally, he encouraged performers to belong to a theatrical organization so that it would be easier for agents, managers, and producers to locate them. Editorials in "The Page" played an active part in the formation of the Colored Actors' Union, the National Association of Colored Fairs, and the Deacons.

Finally, Jackson stood apart because he "went behind the curtain to highlight activities and interactions of figures from all aspects of the business side of the trade: music publishers (like Clarence Williams or Maude Nooks, 'The only woman publisher of the race'), theater owners, talent bookers. . . ."[37] Jackson published several surveys related to the state of the black entertainment business. In the first survey in 1921, he pointed to the many economic opportunities in theaters, parks, fairgrounds, show properties, and musical instruments that ran far into the millions. Moreover, he reminded readers that the Negro professional musician made astounding weekly wages, which found their way into virtually every channel of business in the black community. Charles T. McGill, a black journalist for the Chicago *Defender*, classified Jackson as the best-known of black writers among white publications.

When white business interests discovered the economic potential of the black show business industry, they hired someone of color to discover the breadth and diversity of this field. Jackson was the viable candidate for the job in that he knew the black entertainment profession from both the business side and the performing end. His strong work ethic, knowledge of what audiences wanted and flexibility served him well. Yet, a black journalist, even one of Jackson's stature, was not able to make a living writing feature articles in race papers. After the demise of "The Page," there were no indications that white publications sought Jackson's services. It is not surprising, therefore, that Jackson left show business and theatrical writing to become the first black to serve as a business specialist with the Department of Commerce in Washington, D. C., from 1927-33. Claude Barnett, the Director of the *Associated Negro Press*, recommended Jackson for the position. For several years, Jackson served as executive correspondent in New York for ANP, during which time he and Barnett became close friends. Barnett later negotiated with Herbert Hoover, then Secretary of Commerce, about placing Jackson in the Commerce Department to work with the press through the ANP to promote Negro business. "Jackson wrote a regular business column for ANP and in a discreet way served Barnett and other news fronts in the nation's capital."[38] With the election of Democrat Franklin Delano Roosevelt in 1933, Jackson, a Republican, lost his job.

From 1933 to 1954, Jackson worked in private industry for the Standard Oil Company (ESSO). He traveled more than a quarter of a million miles and gave thousands of speeches on behalf of the company's products. He was instrumental in getting black entrepreneurs started as managers of their own service stations. Even though Jackson retired in 1941 at age 65, he served as a special representative of ESSO's public relations department for an additional thirteen years. For many years he played a prominent role in a dozen or more black religious, fraternal, and business organizations. His religious affiliation was with the Grace Congregationalist Church in New York.[39] Among the many associations in which he claimed membership was the New York branch of the Prince Hall Masons. He was a 33rd-degree active Mason, of Scottish rite consistory—an honorary degree of the highest order for exemplary work as a grand lodge member or for outstanding community service. The Masons commended Jackson for both. Jackson also held an extra degree of Honorary Past Master.

Jackson's ability to transcend racial barriers at a time when most blacks were fighting "Jim Crowism"[40] is significant. He was a bright, confident, self-motivated, and indefatigable journeyman who left home at an early age to pursue his destiny. His creditability among whites had already been proven as a railroad detective, military staff officer, bank clerk, and writer. Another consideration might have been the color-caste system of the time.

Given that he was light complexioned, tall, articulate, and educated, he may have had opportunities to advance in ways almost nonexistent for darker-skinned blacks. Nonetheless, given the social and political milieu of the time, "Billboard" Jackson's accomplishments were remarkable. He not only advanced himself but his fellow performers and ultimately, the status of African-Americans. Seldom were black performers viewed with the same callousness, indifference, and ridicule as they had been before the 1920s in New York.

Notes

[1] A cultural construct based on the superiority of one culture over another.

[2] One who posts notices, posters, or advertisements. They also call them "billstickers."

[3] Joseph and June Bundy Csisda, *American Entertainment: A Unique History of Popular Show Business* (New York: Watson-Guiptill Publications, 1978) 14.

[4] Csisda, 15.

[5] William H. Donaldson, ed. "Announcing a New Department," *Billboard* (Cincinnati: *Billboard Publication*, October 30, 1920) 4.

[6] Csisda, 14.

[7] Ibid.

[8] Ibid.

[9] Boris J. Johnson, ed. *Who's Who in Colored America 1928-1929.* 2nd ed. (New York: Who's Who, 1930) 202.

[10] Henry Sampson, *Blacks in Blackface* (Metuchen, New Jersey, Scarecrow Press, 1980) viii.

[11] "Jubilee" groups, associated with minstrelsy, were the general public's major interpreter of the plantation and of slave lore.

[12] Tom Fletcher, *100 Years of the Negro in Show Business* (New York: Burdge and Company, 1954) 31.

[13] Magill, 5.

[14] Charles T. Magill, "Jackson Joins the Staff of the *Billboard*," Chicago *Defender* (22 Jan. 1921) 5.

[15] Fletcher, 31.

[16] Ibid., 30.

[17] Ibid.

[18] Ibid., 31.

[19] Magill, 5.

[20] Fletcher, 31.

[21] Magill, 5.

[22] Fletcher, 33.

[23] Ibid., 31.

[24] Magill, 5.

[25] Ibid.

[26] Ibid.

[27] Roland E. Wolseley, *The Black Press, U. S. A.* (Iowa: Iowa State University Press, 1978) 24.

[28] Helen Armstead-Johnson, *Review of Annual Research and Recognition* Vol 1.1 (Baltimore, Maryland, NCAAT 1995) 47.

[29] Armstead-Johnson, 47.

[30] Sampson, viii.

[31] Sam Hay, *African American Theatre: An Historical and Critical Analysis* (Cambridge, Cambridge University Press, 1994) 3.

[32] Hay, 3.

[33] Ibid.

[34] Theophilus Lewis, "Survey of the Negro Theatre—III," The *Messenger* Vol. VIII, N 10 (October 1926) 302.

[35] Richard Schechner, "One View of Performance Studies," in *Performance Studies, A Newsletter of the Department of Performance Studies*, Vol 3.1 (Fall 1982) 4.

[36] Armstead-Johnson, 47.

[37] Havelock Nelson, "J. A. Jackson's Page," *Billboard* (1 Nov. 1994) 75.

[38] Lawrence D. Hogan, *A Black National News Service: The Associated Negro Press and Claude Barnett 1919-1945* (Rutherford, N. J.: Fairleigh Dickinson University Press, 1984) 104.

[39] Both J. A. Jackson and his wife Gabrielle were active members of The Grace Congregationalist Church in Harlem. The church attracted show business people not welcomed at many orthodox churches because of their profession—performing then was not considered an honorable profession, unless it was for the church. Funerals for both Jackson's were also held at this church (James, 1960, Gabrielle, 1961).

[40] Segregated treatment of public and private facilities that began in the South after the Civil War.

Top, 307 E. High Street today—where J. A. Jackson grew up, circa 1878—1895; William A. Mills (grandfather of the Mill's Brothers) and his family also lived in this three-unit complex; below, 216-18 E. High Street—Former "Colored School" where Jackson and John Hutchinson Mills would have attended school. According to Daniel R. Clemson, the Mills brothers' biographer, the "structure once served as the community's school for black children, beginning in 1870. It remained in operation until 1885, when the Bellefonte School system integrated. . . . Black children attended the town's first integrated classes. Bellefonte became one of the first school systems in the nation to achieve integration. Nearly 70 years later, the U. S. Supreme Court ruled segregation was unconstitutional. . . . A group of black parents, among them Abraham V. Jackson and William A. Mills, convinced the School in 1885 to desegregate the system."

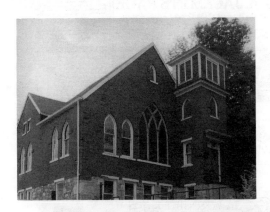

Left, St. Paul's A. M. E. Churches 1909 – present. J. A. Jackson attended during his early childhood. His father, Abraham V. Jackson and William A. Mills, were church officials; below, interor view of A. M. E. today.

Mastheads in "The Page" between 1920-25.

II

"J. A. Jackson's Page"
in Billboard
A Chronicle of Performance

To characterize the nature of "J. A. Jackson's Page," this chapter will divide the column into two sections: the early phase, 1920-22, and the later phase, 1923-25. It outlines the column's overall development—its general layout, content, style, theme, personnel and development, and it evaluates how the profession received it.

The Early Phase: 1920-22
    The appearance of the new column was on page 15 in the November 6, 1920 issue of *Billboard*. "Jackson's Page" included five items: "Salutation," "Our Interest in the Movies," "Interest Yourself in Demanding Railroad Rate Adjustments," "Pittsburgh to Have a Theater Owned By Negroes," and "Notes." Jackson greeted his reading public, explaining that "the department . . . instituted as *Billboard's* expression of appreciation for the success that has been achieved by artists of my race. Also it is an assurance that the publication wished to encourage and assist them toward further success."[1] He then outlined "The Page's" objectives:

- to supplement news with a sympathetic presentation of both professional
  and personal items of special interest to Negroes;
- to provide a forum for the discussion of problems; to provide a medium for
  an exchange of views;
- to better understand the Negro artist and his problems;
- to make possible the marketing of their service.[2]

For two months after its inauguration, the column received commendations from managers, agents, musical organizations, artists, professional black organizations, the general public, and the black press. During the holiday season, Jackson received numerous Christmas cards and remembrances—letters of encouragement from performers, managers, and agents; two sets of resolutions by professional organizations; and more than 200 letters from individuals who called to wish the new department well. Professional clubs and organizations also acknowledged "The Page": The Clef Club, the largest and most widely known black musical organization, and The Dressing Room Club, a prestigious club with a membership of over 250 leading black actors, performers, composers, musicians, authors, and artists. Also, the column received more than a dozen favorable newspaper comments from the black press. In addition, acknowledgment came from the *Negro Year Book* and the *Crisis* magazine edited by W. E. B. Du Bois. Many of these race publications maintained theatrical columns written by creditable journalists. "Jackson's Page," however, covered all aspects of black performance, and *Billboard* was the most widely circulated entertainment trade paper.

The initial response to the new column from the white community was also encouraging. Within the first year, the most significant display of approval may have come from the Theatre Owners and Booking Association (TOBA). At the annual meeting, the Board of Directors adopted a resolution thanking the management of *Billboard* and J. A. Jackson for their kindness and display of interest in the TOBA and for what they had done toward advancing the organization.

To establish the column's identity, Jackson changed its masthead frequently during the early phases of "The Page." The first masthead read: "The Negro Actor, Actress, Artist and Musician: Conducted by J. A. Jackson." with the "The Page's" address listed below the rectangular border. For the second edition the heading changed to: "J. A. Jackson's Column: In The Interest of The Actor, Actress and Musician of America." By the third edition, "Column" gave way to "Page," and "Colored" was included in the subtitle but was dropped within a month then reinstated. By January 1921, the name of the column appeared in bold block print: "J. A. Jackson's Page in the interest of the Colored Actor, Showman, & Musician of America." For the next few months, the masthead was unchanged save for the editor's name that became more elongated with block-print lettering. Before the end of the second year, only the heading "J. A. Jackson's Page" remained in the modified rectangle with the other information placed below it. By then, the column became known as "J. A. Jackson's Page" and its editor as "The Page," or "Billboard" Jackson

Advertising was the lifeline of the column. Donaldson informed the readers that he would try "The Page" on an experimental basis. He encouraged agents, managers, artists, theater owners, and record companies to send their ads in on small, simple cards. The ads were to be ethical in content and limited to five lines. In the second edition, Joseph C. Herbert submitted the first ad, soliciting minstrels for his company. Jackson placed it at the bottom of "The Page," where subsequently he located the other ads. The most frequent advertisements were requests for specialty acts and minstrel shows performers; film makers promoting their latest photo plays; and booking agents and theater owners listing their latest shows. By the seventh issue of "The Page," on December 18, 1920, Jackson began what became one of his more effective ploys to attract attention to black performance—the display of photos of blacks in the profession. The first was a picture of Charles Gilpin costumed as Brutus Jones, sitting on a throne in the New York production of *Emperor Jones* by the Provincetown Players. Future editions of "The Page" averaged about one photo every other week.

A unique idea "The Page" offered was its services for those in the profession: a letter, address, and routing file and a hotel and directory listing. Jackson appealed to race performers and friends to use the column as a repository for personal and professional information. He encouraged the use of this ongoing service to better facilitate interaction among show business folks. He printed periodic notices on: "Where Can You be Found?"; "Have You Looked Through the Letter List?" or "There May Be a Letter Advertising for You." Artists on tour seldom left forwarding addresses, and after shows ended, frequently found themselves stranded in remote sections of the country with little or no money and out of touch with the show business world. But for "Jackson's Page," their whereabouts would sometimes be unknown for several weeks, keeping them out of touch with the industry and limiting their job opportunities. Jackson encouraged managers and artists to be personally responsible for themselves or to appoint someone to fill out their permanent address, routing, or forwarding cards, and to report on hotels in "The Page." He also requested that they leave forwarding cards with every post office before they left that town.

The response was astonishing. Information poured into the column about accommodations, routing, updates on shows, unscrupulous managers and agents, vulgarity, the whereabouts and activities of artists; and how a particular theater or town treated them. Jackson analyzed the information and placed it in appropriate categories, depending on its nature and significance. On occasion, Jackson reproduced a detailed letter in its entirety, or excerpts under its own topical heading. He preceded or concluded it with a brief editorial.

Accommodations were of major concern to black performers traveling to unfamiliar places or to areas where the racial climate was uncertain or hostile. Since there were few hotels for black artists, Jackson provided a list of "Stopping Places" throughout the country that were mostly private homes in which blacks could rent rooms; many of the places provided home cooked meals. Jackson's father, Abe, even encouraged performers to stay at his home in Bellefonte. These quaint settings gave itinerant actors a chance to share their vast experiences with the locals about the exotic and exciting places they had traveled throughout the country and abroad as well as an opportunity to sway the impressionable young women their way. Jackson compiled the list from recommendations submitted by respected members of the industry and from show people who frequented these boarding houses. Jackson encouraged the show folks to keep "The Page" updated on the condition of the facilities. The Hotel List and Letter File were free. The Address and Routing File, however, cost $2 and $1, respectively, but the fee guaranteed subscribers a listing. Jackson printed information for the other services at his discretion depending on availability of space. Otherwise, he left the material on file to be available to those who inquired.

The "Here and There Among the Folks" column contained notes, brief comments or updates on activities in the industry, human interest stories, social affairs, one-line reviews, and anecdotes about performers. Jackson obtained the news from members of the profession or from his observations. He gave topical headings to more detailed news of particular interest to the industry, ranging from the professional to the general or from the political to the social. The subjects included featured performers, theater houses, groups, acts, and cities; activities of performers and show openings; updates on blacks on Broadway, in motion pictures, or giving concerts; coming attractions; women in the industry; novelty acts; business interests, clubs, and organizations; reprinted letters; reviews by the black press; censuses; editorials on the industry; responses to issues; and performers known, unknown, or just becoming known.

An important factor in the column's early growth was Jackson's ability to "sell" the black performer to the public at large and to create a climate whereby the white and black public might empathize with the plight of the black performer. Jackson believed that tolerance and harmony between the races would only come through a better understanding of the colored performer. He tried to explain in early editorials why the public should be patient with the black performer since he was new in that profession, and why his dilemma was unique. Jackson reported on the progress of the race for 1920, and looked at the prospects for the coming season in vaudeville, musical comedy, music, drama, burlesque, motion pictures, minstrelsy, and the out-of-doors. Enlightened by the findings in his first study, he commented that proportionately, "The colored performer is now receiving a more reasonable measure of opportunity than ever before [which contributes] to the high morale in the colored entertainment business after the war."[3]

On August 6, 1921, Jackson printed what may have been the first list of black theaters and attractions. According to "The Page's" survey of 1921, *Shuffle Along* was the most significant achievement in black performance. It was, however, Jackson's editorials in "The Page" promoting *Shuffle Along* that were greatly responsible for attracting interest in the show and getting it produced on Broadway. Jackson received a letter from Lew Henry suggesting that it was time to produce another big "Colored" musical on Broadway since there had not been one for more than ten years. Jackson knew just the team that had the talent to put together this kind of show— Noble Sissle, Eubie Blake, Flournoy Miller, and Aubrey Lyles. Not since the days of the famed Bert Williams and George Walker a decade earlier, had there been a black musical comedy to play Broadway—the zenith of the actors' desires. Williams, the only black performer on Broadway between 1910-1917, was still there, however, appearing in *Broadway Brevities* at the Garden Theater. Before the 1920s, organized shows, musicals, vaudeville acts, burlesque, dramas, and out-of-doors activities presented entertainment primarily to black audiences. When these acts were not playing vaudeville houses, they appeared as an added attraction with road shows.[4]

Jackson heard the great piano player Eubie Blake's innovative jazz style in Blake's hometown of Baltimore. He had met Miller and Lyles at the famous Pekin Theater in Chicago, where they were part of a stock company. They wrote the books (story line) for the different shows mounted each week. Henry's letter was just the catalyst Jackson needed. In the next edition of "The Page," entitled "Is not the Time Ripe for a Big Colored Show,"[5] Jackson underscored the need for black theatricals. He reminded theater goers of how delightful musical comedy groups were some twenty years earlier when groups like Bert Williams and George Walker and Bob Cole and J. Rosamond Johnson were the rage of Broadway. He pointed to the success of the special shows for white people only at the Lyric Theater in New Orleans, Louisiana. He talked about the popularity of the numerous colored acts appearing in clubs, with burlesque companies as well as the arrival of the colored dramatic actor. When Broadway producers Al Mayer and John Scholl read the editorial and contracted actor-lyricists Miller and Lyles and composers Sissle and Blake, *Shuffle Along* was born. Meyer outlined a proposal for the show, but negotiations were delayed—both teams had twenty or more weeks of vaudeville work contracted ahead before they could work on the new production.[6]

Mayer and Scholl assembled the company in New York City in February of 1921. "They opened in Trenton, New Jersey," Jackson recalled,

> I went down to see the opening and helped the reporter of the local newspaper review the show. This was the local reporters' first try at reviewing any show, and after I had shown him my card, he told me he would put anything I wrote for him under his byline. I wrote the story and waited for the paper to come out the next morning so I could take it back to my own paper.[7]

Shuffle Along opened at the Howard Theater in Washington, D.C. in late March for two weeks. It finally settled at the Sixty-Third Street Theater in New York. "At first, [promoters were skeptical] as to whether white audiences would accept the colored show. But their . . . ability to dance with feverish precision and abandon made them instant hits. The sepia torso-wielders were latent bundles of energy and their vivaciousness gave birth to the speed show that was to characterize black shows during the next twenty years."[8]

All the while, "The Page" reported on the progress of the show. In Jackson's 1922 survey of the black entertainment industry, he talked about why the company of more than sixty singers and dancers of the race was the season's sensation:

> The big musical melange won the unique distinction of becoming an "actor's" show during its over two-hundred performances at the Sixty-Third Street

Theater, New York. Recording companies have marketed every one of the
eighteen songs . . . of the piece. Lottie Gee and her "Love will Find a Way"
song gave the public something to talk about for days.[9]

Other songs in public favor were "I'm Just Wild About Harry," "Gypsy
Blues," "I'm Cravin' for That Kind of Love," and "Shuffle Along." The
show fared even better in Jackson's 1923 survey. It showed that the piece
was the most accomplished musical comedy within the last two years. Its
record run was unprecedented. It ran for fourteen months at the Sixty-
Third Street Theater in New York, followed by three months in Boston
and the Olympic Theater in Chicago. Request for previewing the show
extended across the ocean from both London and Berlin. George Wintz
even mounted a "creditable version" of the *Shuffle Along* that played the
smaller cities. The show broke down racial barriers by playing to white
audiences in the better houses in the South. Traveling from coast to coast, it
had eighty-three weeks of uniform success. Jackson reminded readers that
"The responsibility for the success of the show should be equally divided
between the composers, the actors, and the personal deportment of
diplomatic managers."[10] Modesty aside, Jackson was greatly responsible for
the success of the show and the advancement of the black musical comedy
genre.

Shuffle Along was the most significant achievement in black theater to
date. The landmark production renewed interest in black theatricals by the
public and marked a decided turning point in the history of black
entertainment in America. It introduced to the Broadway stage a black
chorus of partially garbed "girls" in the style of the white "Follies."
Because of the popularity of *Shuffle Along* the entertainment profession
witnessed the return of musical comedies to Broadway on a regular basis.
It was this type of personal involvement with the companies and artists that
enabled Jackson to accumulate the wealth of information on black
performers that appeared in his column.

A key issue in "The Page" was ethics. Early editorials made it clear that
Jackson had a broad sense of ethics that was in keeping with the policy of
Billboard. One issue was standards of conduct. Along with developing a
better understanding of the black artist, Jackson felt that in order for
audiences of color and those on the "big time" circuits to accept black
artists, the profession had to "clean up its act." Theater houses catering to
white patrons discontinued the practice of allowing vulgarity and profanity

early in the century, but there was no such regulation in the black entertainment industry. Jackson made scathing attacks against "filth" and unfair practices by members of the profession, men as well as women, and in his first editorial on standards of conduct headed "Facts Pleasant and Otherwise," in January 22, 1921, Jackson vowed to attack unethical practices by members of the profession.

Jackson's views were consistent with Booker T. Washington's philosophy of self-restraint, but today the more radical sector of the black community might consider them "conciliatory." Hence, I must evaluate Jackson's beliefs in relation to the social atmosphere of the 1920s. In the South, lynching blacks was still prevalent. Although blacks experienced a different kind of freedom in the North, they found themselves thrust into ghettos and discriminated against in the areas of housing and employment. Because of the personnel shortage during World War I, black men and women were able to work in manufacturing plants. However, they lost their jobs after the war. Black soldiers who fought to help keep America "safe for democracy" returned home to find that most racial attitudes toward African-Americans had not changed. Violence erupted throughout the country during the "red summer" of 1919.

The more "militant" writers of that period such as W. E. B. Du Bois and George Schuyler could not get published in white publications. Regardless, when Jackson wrote commentaries that were critical of artists in the profession, as an expression of his sincerity of purpose, he would often close the column with an extract that a comedian friend gave him:

> When you are right, I am your friend, and I am with you;
> But when you are wrong, I am still your friend, but I am not with you.[11]

After Jackson's initial efforts to "sell" the black performer to the general public and to "clean up" the industry, the next step was to improve conditions on the black circuits to attract the better acts and boost attendance among black audiences.

Yet another key issue in "The Page" was organization among black theatricals. In response to the many complaints by business interests and performers, Jackson shifted emphasis from his concern with conditions on the circuits toward the need to organize black theatricals in general—which in itself would be one way to improve conditions. He encouraged all those involved in black show business to join a union such as Actors' Equity Association or organize with some large body for protection. Before the summer of 1921, in response to performer discontent with Actors' Equity, Jackson helped to formulate and nurture the Colored Actors' Union. Jackson toured the black entertainment circuit again that summer, this time to Georgia and North Carolina to take a look at outdoor entertainment. Being the astute businessman that he was, it was not surprising that shortly after his trip, he began writing editorials urging black fairs to organize a national body and align themselves with a financial concern such as the Negro Business League. In the November 19, 1921 issue, Jackson compiled a partial list of the many fairs that blacks in the country promoted and patronized—the first such list to appear in a major entertainment trade paper. Further, Jackson outlined a prospectus for a national fair association that came to fruition a year later.

Reprinted editorials from "The Page" frequently appeared in Tony Langston's theatrical column the Chicago *Defender* as well as in other black weeklies. These reprints did not generate additional revenue for "The Page." *Billboard's* policy was not to charge fees for reprinting articles. Jackson believed that it provided free publicity. His only stipulation, as a matter of professional ethics, was that the papers had to give recognition to "The Page" when they ran the articles. Meanwhile, "The Page" began to gain national recognition. *The Negro Press in The United States* by Frederick G. Detweller, a 375-page survey of black entertainment released in August 1922, designated Jackson and "The Page" as the authority on theater.

Other black journalists and newspapers who espoused "The Page" and reprinted Jackson's articles in their own column included Romeo Dougherty of the New York *Amsterdam News* and the Western Writer's Association of Los Angeles. Performers also submitted reviews such as: Maharajah the Mystic, on black carnivals; Coy Herndon, the hoop roller, on out-of-doors activities; and Leigh Whipper the actor-filmmaker, on African-American films. On April 15, 1922, Whipper reviewed the Reol Motion Picture Company's production of *Easy Money* that starred S. H. Dudley,[12] the comedian, theater owner, and organizer of the first black theater circuit. It was Dudley's first motion picture role.

In addition, "The Page" received reviews from individuals in the profession throughout the country. Among them were: monologist Boots Hope; theater owner S. H. Dudley from Washington D. C.; filmmaker, actor and director Leigh Whipper from New York; Hi Tom Long from the Vendome Theater, Hot Springs, Arkansas; Gary Lewis' "Doings in Chicago"; Garfield L. Smith from the Douglass Theater, Macon Georgia;

Willie Walls from the Lafayette Theater in Winston-Salem, North Carolina; and William J. Farley, who gave a general account of Circus and Tent shows and vaudeville. By the final year, however, only Hi Tom Long remained as the lone field correspondent.

Over the next two years, there were a few changes in the general layout, content, and format of "The Page." Before the end of the early phase, women artists began to gain more than minimal attention in "The Page." Initially Jackson included them in the general discussion of performers; but after the first year, topical headings with titles such as "Women's Issues" and "To The Ladies," began to appear. In addition, there were numerous photos of women artists; however, women were not exempt from criticism when their conduct was unbecoming, especially if their actions reflected "smut" (vulgarity and profanity). During the summer of 1922, there was a general business depression in the black entertainment industry, but before the end of that year, it slowly lifted. "The Page's" survey indicated that 1922 had been the most activity-filled year in the history of the African-American in the amusement field. Various organizations, artists, and business interests applauded "The Page" and its editor for their efforts in helping to achieve this end and for the courtesies accorded the different organizations.

The Later Phase: 1923-25

If the number of well-wishers during the 1922 holiday season, numbering in the hundreds, is used as a barometer to measure the degree of approval, then "The Page" was a resounding success. By 1923, the column's major theme—the need to improve black performance—became well defined. Editorials indicated that during the second phase, black show business made progress in almost every field except in films, which had fallen off. There were many tangible improvements in vaudeville, burlesque, publishing houses, record manufacturers, tabloid[13] companies, musical comedy, minstrelsy, drama in the South, fairs and carnivals. Jackson noted, however, that as in any new venture, many of the problems still needed to be resolved.

The theme of improving standards of decency in the colored entertainment industry garnered support from theater owners and managers and from performers such as Bill "Bojangles" Robinson and Clarence Muse. A particular concern of Jackson's was ridding the industry of "smut." Besides "The Page's" disdain with "smut shooters," Jackson addressed other areas of conduct: contract jumpers, "boozers," mountebank managers, acts "splitting" (groups separating), proper street dress for performers, and exploitation by local promoters.

The format that within the early years of the column only changed slightly during the later phase. The one-page spread grew to two pages and occasionally expanded to three pages. The masthead that had gone through slight changes during the first two years to establish an identity took on three different looks in 1923, before Jackson settled on the final one. The first masthead for that year depicted a theater setting with a minstrel theme. In the front of a stage, a rectangle resembling a stage border hung by three ropes. The rectangle contained the familiar inscription: "J. A.Jackson's Page in the Interest of the Colored Actor, Showman and Musician of America"; tassels hung from the bottom. On each side was a male performer in black-face, dressed in minstrel costume. The one on the left, Mr. Interlocutor, stood with a cane in his right hand next to the curtain cord. The one on the right, Mr. Tambo, sat on a chair strumming the banjo next to the folds of the curtain. The next year, the theater theme gave way to writing and performing. The edges of the rectangle were rounded. Within this boundary, on the right side, a tragic female figure presided over a theater building fringed by an open curtain that revealed two actors on stage in dramatic poses. With her left hand she held an emblem. It read: "Service Leading to Achievement. On the left of the rectangle, a feather pen in an inkwell sat on a play script. The theme for the last masthead emphasized writing and composing. It was the most decorative with rounded ribbon-like folds on the bottom of the rectangle with the same inscription: "Service Leading to Achievement," A theatrical figure was on each side. On the left there was a feather in an inkwell next to a play script overshadowed by the grim profile of a male mask in the background. The head with a gaped mouth was adorned with a wreath of flowers. The figure on the right is similar but a violin and sheet music replaced the feather and inkwell. The wreathed mask was also the same except a violin suspended within the mask.

Reviews by journalists as well as artists on various aspects of the field became a regular feature in March 1923. For the 1923, fall season, Jackson added two new columns, "Minstrel and Tent Show Talk" and "Picked up by The Page." Both supplied general information on the prospective fields similar to the "Here and There Among the Folks column except that the former was a comprehensive coverage of minstrel affairs and the latter dealt with New York activities only. Jackson always confronted major issues head on, but his use of subtlety characterized his use of tact and diplomacy. During the later phase of the column, however, Jackson's attitude and philosophy appeared to change noticeably. He became more outspoken on racial matters and conduct that he thought was unbecoming to the black profession. He acknowledged that the black entertainment business had made progress but was quick to point out that segregation policies in most theater houses had not changed, particularly in the Southern ones, and that racism still permeated the industry. This concern became the third key issue in "The Page." Jackson began airing grievances by performers about the TOBA. He accused some members of the black press (Romeo Dougherty in particular) of receiving what he called "paid writeups" and publicly challenged Marcus Garvey's philosophy behind the United Negro Improvement Association.

"The Page's" 1924 survey showed that the progress made in black show business was remarkable. Jackson commented that:

> Negro performers had just reached the place where their presence in every phase of the business is taken. . . . Indeed, things look great, but it must be remembered these advantages, gained at the cost of struggle and privation, bring with them certain responsibilities. [14]

A letter from Henry Hartman, the manager of a Rockville, Maryland band, and publicity man for the Fairfax, Virginia fair, was typical of the kind of response the column received from the field and the general public: "I am now a regular subscriber of the *Billboard* and am wondering how I have managed to get along without it in the years gone by."[15] Another letter was from R. P. Penny, business manager of the *Bronze Bostonian's* musical comedy group: "It is with pleasure that I note you have opened a department for the Negro artists of the country, as there can be no denying the fact of the constantly growing field for the Negro entertainer."[16] No negative responses appeared in "The Page," but during its "honeymoon" period, it seems unlikely that there would be. Among the many respondents were the Chicago *Defender*, the *Manhattan Newspaper Men's Association*, the New York *Amsterdam News*, the New York *Dispatch*, the Pittsburgh *Courier*, the Kansas City *Call*, the Chicago *Star*, the Denver *Star*, the *Negro World*, and the Atlanta *Independent*.

Blacks began to appear in every phase of show business: current local and national attractions, artists on Broadway, dramatic discoveries, and novelty acts. "The Page" also featured those who made inroads in their respective fields or were involved in ventures that Jackson thought would help to make a change in black show business: important whites with black business interests, children of show business personages, relatives of famous performers, and behind-the-scenes personalities. Within the first six months, Jackson replied to over 1,000 letters. The services bridged the communication gap between performers and the industry at large.

Also, in "The Page," various kinds of news items appeared. There were the one-line reviews: "Harry Fidler with the Harvey Greater Minstrels is Performing a Chinese Impersonation Act with Special Setting in the Olio." Then there were the social ones: "Charles Gilpin becomes a Mason," as well as those of social significance: "Ethel Waters goes South, four members quit. . . . Waters defended her position stating that someone has to make sacrifices."[17] There were comments on artists and other entertainers in the news: "Jack Johnson the fighter, released from prison, considering proposals for the Continental Baseball League as an umpire at $1,500 per week." Also, there were the ones of human interest: "Tom Fletcher, the well-known singer, comedian is convalescing in Booker T. Washington Sanitarium in New York. . . . Ira Duncan of *Shuffle Along* had the pleasure of opening in her hometown in Trenton, New Jersey." In addition, there were humorous ones: "Coy Herndon, the hoop-roller, and Billy Tucker, actor, writer, want permission to woo Princess Wee Wee." Finally, there were human interest ones: "Leigh Whipper an unfortunate victim of a woman's wrath, emphasized with a pair of scissors that nearly reached his jugular vein, has been released from the hospital"; "M. B. Maxwell, the magician, marries a sixteen year old girl in Ypsilanti, Michigan. The father-in-law objected and an arrest followed. We are advised that all is now serene. Here's congratulations. Both Maxwells are now old married folks of about one month. That's one worry off our hands."[18] In a December 10, 1921, editorial entitled "The Present Situation of the Colored Performer: The Most Handicapped, Yet the Most Hopeful of Artists," Jackson wanted to "disclose a background of experience in fortitude that has sustained the colored performer in the present crisis and made it possible for him to extract such possible good there was from the situation."[19]

Jackson stated his position on conduct considered detrimental to the race, in a June 25, 1921, editorial. In Tulsa, Oklahoma, a race riot broke out after rumors circulated that a black had attacked a white orphan girl. Of the thirty-one people killed, twenty were black. At the time of the riot, the Cleo

Mitchell Jazz Repertoire Company was playing Mrs. Williams' Dreamland Theater in Tulsa. The fire totally destroyed the theater, along with ten blocks of the black business and residential area, leaving 3,000 African-Americans homeless. The company lost $6,000 worth of costumes, wardrobes, properties, and personal belongings. Although Jackson was aware that blacks did not cause the riot, he ran a headline that condemned the riot: "Tulsa Riot Ruins." He felt that blacks were only hurting themselves and the profession. He reminded black artists that the society-at-large will judge the entire race by their conduct, that they were at a disadvantage socially and in numbers, and that restraint, diplomacy, and tact had to be their motto. As a humane gesture, he encouraged readers to send financial assistance to aid the unfortunate victims of the riot. Jackson was the only major black voice in a white entertainment trade paper, therefore, he had to walk a tight line between the realities of the time in which he lived and how he could assure economic and professional survival for the black entertainment industry.

Since *Billboard* was the largest entertainment trade paper in the United States and the only major publication to offer a theatrical column devoted to black performance, it had to impact its growth. On June 20, 1925, "The Page" disappeared unexpectedly. *Billboard* stated that the lack of black advertising in the publication was the cause. Closing the column for this reason, raises many questions and brings to mind what Woody King, a prolific black New York promoter, once stated: "Show business is a business." Dick Campbell actor, singer, producer, director, founder of the Rose McClendon Players, and a theater veteran of more than 50 years, commented on ads in "The Page":

> Blacks never advertised. There were but only a few top black entertainers and agents and, there were two record companies (The Black Swan and The Okey) with colored clients who did the advertising for them to help sell their records and music. *Billboard* was strong in American music. They listed top records of the phonograph industry who were selling the music of Fletcher Henderson, Ethel Waters, Fats Waller and others.[20]

Lawrence Joseph Bailey, a concert promoter for over thirty years, thought that perhaps Jackson may have done his job too well. "By the time 'The Page' was closed, Jackson wasn't needed anymore. *Billboard* knew all that it needed to know about black show business, the scope of the industry, the kinds of acts, how much money they could make, but most important, by then they knew how to control it."[21] Close observation of

Jackson's attitude during the later phase indicates that his commentaries on conditions in the industry may have become too radical for *Billboard's* policies. On the other hand, *Billboard* might have initiated a less liberal policy after the untimely illness and subsequent death of Donaldson, only about a month after "The Page" closed. Perhaps shortly before Donaldson's death, he no longer controlled the publication. Until further documentation can be obtained, I can only conjecture the reasons that "The Page" closed. Still, the short-lived column tried to validate black performance and move it into the mainstream of the American entertainment industry. Once "The Page" gave voice to black performers, it was impossible to stifle the onslaught of talent that demanded proper recognition.

Notes

[1] James Albert Jackson, "J. A. Jackson's Page," *Billboard* 6 Nov. 1920: 15.

[2] Ibid.

[3] Jackson, "Why Cry; Bad Business?" *Billboard* 8 July 1922: 107.

[4] Tom Fletcher, *100 Years of the Negro in Show business* (New York: Burdge and Company, 1954) 33.

[5] Jackson, "Is not the Time Ripe for a Big Colored Show, *Billboard* " 8 Jan. 1921: 36.

[6] Ibid.

[7] Ibid.

[8] Ibid.

[9] Ibid.

[10] Ibid.

[11] Jackson, *Billboard* 22 Jan. 1921: 34.

[12] Ibid., (15 Apr. 1922) 47.

[13] Tabloid companies are shows that perform one hour or ninety-minute condensed versions of successful musical comedies.

[14] Jackson, "The Gifts of the Year in Amusement," *Billboard* 15 Dec. 1924: 100-106.

[15] Ibid., (30 Dec. 1922) 49.

[16] Ibid., (20 Nov. 1920) 45.

[17] Ibid., (11 Feb. 1922) 46.

[18] Ibid., (8 Oct. 1921) 95.

[19] Ibid., "The Present Situation of the Colored Performer: The Most Handicapped, Yet the Most Hopeful of Artists," *Billboard* 10 Dec. 1921: 16.

[20] Interview with Dick Campbell at the National Conference on African American Theater at the Days Inn Hotel in Baltimore, April 10, 1987.

[21] Interview with Lawrence J. Bailey at the Marriott Hotel in Woodland Hills, California, June 1995.

NOVEMBER 6, 1920 · The Billboard 15

The NEGRO
Actor, Actress Artist & Musician
Conducted By J.A. JACKSON.
COMMUNICATIONS TO OUR OFFICES, 1493 BROADWAY, NEW YORK.

The first edition of "The Page" (6 Nov. 1920).

HERE AND THERE AMONG THE FOLKS

CALL FOR INFORMATION ON OUTDOOR ATTRACTIONS

To have our group satisfactorily represented in the big Spring Number, the Page requests that those interested write in at once and advise us of their season's plans, lineup of companies, the carnivals to be joined, etc.

Parks will please send personnel and attractions, and fair associations are requested to send their dates and addresses of the secretaries and booking representatives.

Should you contemplate advertising, don't delay, but get your order and copy in at once, so as to insure its being placed as you desire.

Willie Hightower had the misfortune to lose his mother. She died in Chicago January 27.

Osgood's Orchestra, lately with the Hartman & Edmonson Amusement Co., is in Palatka, Fla.

Bert Williams was the honor guest at a stag given by the Appomattox Club in Chicago January 21.

Walker Thompson is at 3300 Rhodes avenue, Chicago, convalescing. He would like to hear from the bunch.

Charlie Stone's Orchestra, Detroit, is featuring "Annabel," published by H. D. Tripp, of Allegan, Mich.

Grace Green, pianist, formerly with Howell's Jazz Girls, is now at the Foraker Theater, Washington, D. C.

O. P. McClane, manager of the Lincoln Theater, Charleston, S. C., is in Philadelphia and New York for a time.

Oscar Jenkins writes from Greenville, S. C., that he will begin his season's activities by coming North in March.

After having made personal appearances with a number of Lincoln pictures in different cities of the East, Clarence Brooks, leading man of

the company, has returned to the Coast to work in another picture.

John H. Wade, motion picture agent, of Philadelphia, lost his wife February 2. The funeral was in Baltimore.

Essie Whitman has a chorus and band at Raymond's Garden of Joy, 130th street and Seventh avenue, New York.

H. K. Leigh announces that he expects to take out the minstrel show on the Mighty Doris and Col. Francis Ferari Shows.

See the list of houses in the hotel department recommended by Marshall and Conner, who write from the Northwest.

The Gus Smith Trio—Gus and Virginia Smith and Maud De Forest—are with the Ethel Waters Black Swan Troubadours.

Dustball and Cook are doing nicely on the Southeastern end of the T. O. B. A. Circuit. Week of January 30 they were in Greenville, S. C., at the Liberty.

Simms and Warfield will be in Detroit the week of February 20; Toledo, February 27; Cleveland, March 6, and Indianapolis, March 13, playing the Sun Circuit.

The Tabor and Green act was obliged to lay off of their Loew Time tour for two weeks, due to Mr. Tabor having contracted laryngitis during the New York engagement.

Dan Michaels, president of the Mutual Amusement Company, owner of Happyland Park, New York, spent the winter at May-Pen, Jamaica, B. W. I. He is now in New York.

Fitz Small, Henry Johnson, Herman Bayard, Blanche Dixon, Geraldine Lloyd and Mabel Lancaster comprise the miniature minstrel that gives merriment to the program at the Harlem Museum, New York.

Leigh Whipper's "Reel Negro News" has been selected, after a personal showing to officials, for presentation at Tuskeegee Institute. The first exhibition was February 11, and the showing resulted in an order for a continuous service of these films at the big

(Continued on page 45)

A unique feature in "The Page" was the "Here and There Among the Folks" column. It contained brief comments or updates on activities in the Colored Entertainment Industry, human interest stories, social affairs, one-line reviews, and anecdotes about perfoumers.

The first survey of black show business listed in "The Page" (18 Dec. 1920).

A typical format in "The Page": a play review, topical headings, one-line reviews, anecdotes about performers, social affairs, illustrations, and advertisements.

"(1) Charles S. Gilpin, whose characterization of "The Emperor Jones" has made him a national figure. England wants him when he has finished touring America. (2) Helen E. Hagan, the first colored woman artist to appear at Aeolian Hall, New York, October 28. She is a pianist of merit. (3) Harper and Blanks; who have scored wonderfully in Shubert Vaudeville. (4) Clarence Brooks, leading man with several of the successful Lincoln Film Productions." (Jackson)

"Members of the Lafayette Players: left to right: Sidney Kirkpatrick, character lead; Cleo Desmond, leading lady; Edna Lewis Thomas; Andrew Bishop, the high salaried leading man." (Jackson)

"Members of the Lafayette Players, cont.:   Laurence Criner; Mrs. Charles Anderson, emotional leads; Charles Moore pioneer Lafayette character actor and president of the C. T. & P. clubs." (Jackson)

A TRIO OF FAMED ACTORS

"Charles S. Gilpin, creator of the "Emperor Jones" character; Solomon Bruce, whose "Jokannon" in the Ethiopian Art Company presentation of "Salome" marked an epoic in Negro art, and Paul Robeson, co-star with Mary Blair in "All God's Chillun", first presented at the Provincetown Playhouse, New York, but slated for a run in a commercial house this season. The picturing of these three in one group, to say nothing of one of them journeying from Chicago for the purpose, tells more forcibly than could anything else, the pride each Negro artist takes in the achievement of another of his group. They are all interested in their people's progress more than in self. Yet each is ambitious to do great things." (Jackson)

"The Principal People in the Ethiopian Art Theater group, now presenting a series of dramatic offerings at the Frazee Theater, New York. The pictures show characters in Oscar Wilde's "Salome." From left to right they are: Evelyn Preer, in the title role of "Salome"; Sidney Kirkpatrick as Harod and Laura Bowman as Herodias." (Jackson)

AUGUST 6, 1921   The Billboard   63

FOREWORD TO THE LIST OF COLORED THEATERS AND ATTRACTIONS

The first list of colored theaters and attractions ("The Page," 6 Aug. 1921).

LIST OF COLORED THEATERS AND ATTRACTIONS
(Continued from page 63)

City, Negro Population, Theater Type.	Owner or Manager.	Address	Remarks.

SOUTH CAROLINA—NEGRO POPULATION, 864,719; WHITE, 818,596

City	Theater	Owner/Manager	Address	Remarks
Anderson	Grand—V	R. Sloan Driscoll		W.O.&M.
Bennettsville	Picture—S	King & Covington		C.O.&M.
Camden	I—P			C.O.&M.
Charleston 52,793	Columbia—S			W.O.&M.
Charleston 52,793	Lincoln—V	J. C. V. Cannon, V.P.; C. P. McClane, Mgr.		C.O.&M.
Charleston 52,793	Milo—V			C.O.&M.
Charleston 52,793	Lincoln—V	C. P. McClane		C.O.&M.
Columbia	Lincoln—V	W. H. Tolbott		W.O.&M.
Columbia	Royal—P	L. T. Lester		W.O.&M.
Florence	Princess—V	G. Brown		C.O.&M.
Greenwood 8,729	Rijou—P	Mr. Adams		
Greenville	Liberty—S	Wilson & Kurts		W.O.&M.
Orangeburg 8,000	Palmetto—P	Mr. Brown		W.O.&M.
Rock Hill	Broadway—P	W. E. Alston		C.O.&M.
Sumter	I—S			C.O.&M.

TENNESSEE—NEGRO POPULATION, 451,758; WHITE, 1,885,993

City	Theater	Owner/Manager	Address	Remarks
Chattanooga 57,943	Grand—P	M. H. Silverman, Ninth St.		W.O.&OP.
Chattanooga 57,943	Liberty—V	Sam Reevin, Prop., Ninth St.		W.O.&M.
Knoxville 77,638	Gem—P	W. C. Kennedy		
Knoxville 77,638	Dixie—P	Chas. Roth		
Memphis 52,441	Daisy—P	Joe Maceira, 329 Beale Av.		
Memphis 52,441	Palace—V	A. Barrasso, 324 Beale Av.		W.O.&M.
Memphis 52,441	Venus—V	Paul Zerilla		
Memphis 52,441	Grand—P	Paul Zerilla		
Nashville 36,523	Lincoln—P			C.O.&M.
Nashville 36,523	Bijou V	Milton D. Starr		C.O.&M.
Nashville 36,523	Star—P			C.O.&M.

TEXAS—NEGRO POPULATION, 741,729; WHITE, 3,918,186

City	Theater	Owner/Manager	Address	Remarks
Austin	Dixie-Dale—P			
Beaumont	Verdun—P	A. N. Adams		C.O.&M.
Beaumont	Lincoln—P			W.O.&M.
Beaumont	Pastime—P			W.O.&M.
Beaumont	Lee's Tent—V	Ed Lee		C.O.&M.
Benham	Star—P	Chas. Jordan		C.O.&M.
Bryant	Star—P	Queen & Baylor		
Clarksville	Princess—P	J. R. Thornton		
Dallas 24,023	Aironeath—P			W.O.&M.
Dallas 24,023	Park—V	Chintz Moore, Owner		C.O.&M.
Dallas 24,023	Grand Central—P	Jack Harris		
Denison	Dreamland—P	P. Woods		
Ennis	I—P			
Ft. Worth 15,896	Douglas—V	S. Lewis		
Ft. Worth 15,896	Washington—P			C.O.&M.
Galveston	Lincoln—V			W.O.&M.
Galveston	Dixie 3—P			W.O.&M.
Galveston	Princess—P	A. R. Mendell		W.O.&M.
Galveston	Star—P			W.O.&M.

City, Negro Population, Theater Type.	Owner or Manager.	Address	Remarks.
Greenville	Pastime—V		C.O.&M.
Hillsboro	Palace—P	H. D. Jackson	
Houston 53,843	Odin—P		W.O.&M.
Houston 53,843	Lincoln—P	O. F. DeWalt	C.O.&M.
Houston 53,843	Washington—P		W.O.&M.
Houston 53,843	American—V	O. A. Coffey	C.O.&M.
Martin	I—P		
Morehead	Cozy—S	W. A. Hogge	
Orange	I		
Paris	Alhambra—V		C.O.&M.
Rusk	Queen—P	Ed. Conley	C.O.&M.
Port Arthur	Dream—P		W.O.&M.
San Antonio 14,856	American—S	Chas. Coffey, San Felipe St.	
San Antonio 14,856	Dreamland—V	A. N. Rock	W.O.&M.
Sherman	Andrews—P		C.O.&M.
Taylor	I—V	W. Lewis	
Temple	Rink—P	J. J. Dawson	C.O.&M.
Tyler	Longs—P		C.O.&M.
Wichita Falls	Victory—P	R. C. Lewis	
Waco	Majestic—P	M. L. Gardner	
Waco	Gayety—P	W. H. Leonard	

VIRGINIA—NEGRO POPULATION, 690,017; WHITE, 1,617,909

City	Theater	Owner/Manager	Remarks
Alexandria	Virginia—P	R. Shapiro	
Alexandria	Lincoln—P	H. A. Bramlow	
Berkley	Liberty—P	M. C. Harkson	
Danville	Hippodrome—V	W. A. Donlevy	
Hampton	Lincoln—V	Mr. Barchon	W.O.&M.
Hampton	Lyric—V	George C. Barchon	
Lynchburg 8,586	Empire—P	O. K. Smith	
Martinsville	Dubois—P	H. Ball	
Newport News	Lincoln—V	W. L. Mouly, 20th and Jefferson	
Norfolk 25,038	Attucks—V.&D.	Rob't Cross, Mgr., 1006 Church St.	C.O.&M.
Norfolk 25,038	Palace—V	Hoffheimer Corp.	W.O.&M.
Petersburg	Rialto—P	O. H. Johnson	
Petersburg	R. H. Dudley—V	R. H. Dudley	C.O.&M.
Portsmouth 11,931	Lincoln—P	John Mills	
Roanoke 9,504	Hampton—P	P. F. Tolliver	
Richmond	Hippodrome—V	Chas. Somma	W.O.&M.
Richmond 54,047	Rayo—V	George Hollenger	
Richmond 54,047	Globe—P	Ray Hollenger	W.O.&M.

WEST VIRGINIA—NEGRO POPULATION, 86,345; WHITE, 1,377,850

City	Theater	Owner/Manager	Remarks
Charleston	Armory (Plays Colored companies)		
Clarksburg	Kelly Miller School (Plays race films)		
Norfolk	Clark—V	P. H. Alexander	C.O.&M.

Picture houses, 156; houses (laying vaudeville, drama or road show, 107; houses running pictures, equipped for road show or vaudeville, 22. Total, 285.

Owned and managed by Negroes, 88; owned and managed by Whites, 114; owned by mixed corporation, 1; owned by Whites, managed by Negroes, 9; ownership and management undetermined, 73.

Additions to August 6, 1921, list of Colored Theatres and Attractions
("The Page," 31 Dec. 1921).

ADDITIONAL J. A. JACKSON'S PAGE NEWS

ADDITIONS

To Theater List Since Original Compilation of July 1 Was Published in The Billboard August 6

ARKANSAS
Hot Springs—Majestic—V.—B. C. Troeman, O.
O.&M.
Hot Springs—Airdome—P.—Lucien Wilson,
Guelph st., O.O.&M.
Pine Bluf—M.—Enterprise Amusement Co., O.
O.&M.

DELAWARE
Greenwood—Greenwood—P.
Dist. of Columbia—Airdome—P.—Mr. Coleman,
O.O.&M.

FLORIDA
Daytona—Midway—E.—J. H. Cuthbert, O.O.
&M.

GEORGIA
Savannah—Dreamland—P. & V.—W.O.&M.
Cordele—Picture—P.

ILLINOIS
Jacksonville—Empress—E.—R. Chase, O.O.&M.
Chicago—Elba—P.—Fred Rosenthal, W.O.&M.

LOUISIANA
New Orleans—Othello—P.

MARYLAND
Annapolis—Star—P.—J. M. L. Amusement Co.

MISSOURI
Kansas City—Gem—P.—Gem Amusement Co.

NEW YORK
Buffalo—McKvoy—V.—Robert B. Joplin, O.O.&
M.

NORTH CAROLINA
Roxboro—Picture—E.—James Bolden, O.O.&M.
Reidsville—Gem—E.—J. M. McGeehee, O.O.&M.

SOUTH CAROLINA
Spartasburg—Star—E.—O.O.&M.

TENNESSEE
Knoxville—Gem—P.—W. O. Kennedy, O.O.&M.

VIRGINIA
Alexandria—S. H. Dudley—E.—S. H. Dudley,
O.O.&M.
Portsmouth—Capitol—M.—H. S. Reed, O.O.&M.

WEST VIRGINIA
Bluefields—Empire—E.—C. C. Cole, 293 Bland
st., O.O.&M.
Huntington—Benton—E.—J. B. Henton, O.O.&
M.
Huntington—Dreamland—E.—Dr. Adams, prop.
Montgomery—Empire—E.—H. S. Shields W.O.
&M.

Key—W means white; O means ownership;
O means colored; M means management; V means
plays vaudeville or road shows; E means
equipped for shows, but operated at present
with pictures only; P means pictures only; D
means drama.

HOTEL LIST

The following list of hotels, boarding and lodging houses has been compiled for the benefit of the colored performer. Some have been submitted by performers with their recommendations and others the Page has visited in person.

An indexed card file is being established by the Page for your service. We invite the profession to assist in enlarging and correcting this list by advising us of stopping places, the treatment accorded the profession and the prices prevailing where you stop. (*) indicates those catering especially to the profession.

Any hotel desiring to remain listed in the column as a permanent advertisement may do so for $3 per month, payable in advance.

CALIFORNIA
Los Angeles—*Elite Hotel, 1217 Central ave.
Los Angeles—Cathron, 743 Oeler st.
Los Angeles—The Lincoln (Japanese owner)
Los Angeles—The Waldorf, Fourth and Stanford.
San Francisco—Olympus Hotel, 617 Jackson st.
San Francisco—Gem Apartments, 848 Stockton
st.
San Diego—Oakland House (Mrs. Borland)

COLORADO
Denver—Hotel Barnes, 2716 Welton st.

CONNECTICUT
New Haven—Mrs. Anthony, 44 and 46 Foote st.
Bridgeport—Mrs. Jordan, 828 Broad st.
New London—Mrs. Sampson, 43 Shapely st.

DELAWARE
Wilmington—Mrs. Jenkins, 911 French st.

FLORIDA
Jacksonville—*Stevens Rooming House, West
Ashley st.
Jacksonville—*Eggmont Hotel, Opposite Strand
Theater.
Jacksonville—Richmond Hotel, 412 West Broad.
Jacksonville—Sanders Hotel, 636 West Ashley.

GEORGIA
Atlanta—*Del Monte, 143 Auburn ave.
Atlanta—*Reid House, 94½ Decatur ave.
Atlanta—*Howells, Decatur st.
Atlanta—Craig House, 154 Redmont.
Macon—*Douglas Hotel, opp. Douglas Theater.
Savannah—Mrs. Ewing, 521 Broad st.

ILLINOIS
Chicago—Hotel Vincennes, 36th and Vincennes.
Chicago—Mrs. Lee, 3626 Belmont ave.
Peoria—Mrs. Wauce, 400 N. adams.
Peoria—Givens Hotel, 203 N. Washington.
Springfield—Brown's Hotel.

INDIANA
West Baden—Hotel Waddy.
Vincennes—Mrs. Hattie White, 9th and Berry.

IOWA
Sioux City—Mrs. Pemberton, 208 Seventh st.
Davenport—Mrs. Green, 516 Fifth st.
Des Moines—Mrs. Lee, 909 W. 13th st.
Iowa City—Mrs. Moore, 219 E. College st.
Burlington—Mrs. Wilson, 136 S. Sixth st.

KENTUCKY
Louisville—*Hotel Bonne downtown, Sixth st.
Glasgow Junction—Princeton Hotel.

LOUISIANA
New Orleans—*Lyric Hotel, 1015 Ibenville.
New Orleans—Elite Hotel, 1321 Ibenville.
New Orleans—*Astoria Hotel, 225 S. Lampert.
New Orleans—Chicago, Belleville st.

MARYLAND
Annapolis—Riverside Hotel.
Baltimore—*Smith Hotel, 435 David Hill ave.
Baltimore—Mrs. Dorsey, 611 N. Paca.
Baltimore—Mrs. Florine Murray, 2003 McCullough st.
Baltimore—*Chas. Anderson, 1142 Penn. ave.
Cumberland—Mrs. Trent, 32 Glenn st.
Hagerstown—Hotel Harmon, 226 Jonathan st.

MASSACHUSETTS
Boston—Hotel Melbourne, 815 Tremont st.
Boston—*Hotel Bostonia, 45-A Howard.
Springfield—Mrs. Herk, 65 Vernon st.

MICHIGAN
Detroit—*Hotel Biltmore, 1918 St. Antoine.
Detroit—*Hotel Tancre, 2474 St. Antoine.
Detroit—*Hotel Pierce, 280 St. Auburtac.
Detroit—*Mrs. Bessie Whitman, 240 Gratiot ave.

MINNESOTA
Minneapolis—Twin City Stag, 246 Fourth ave.

MISSOURI
Kansas City—*Sofroais Hotel, 1211 Highland
ave.
Kansas City—Billy McClan, 1316 Garfield ave.
Kansas City—Mrs. Todd, 1806 M. 14th st.
Kansas City—Atlas Hotel, 915 Oak st.
Kansas City—Hotel Tam-way, 907 East 18th st.
St. Louis—Grand Central Hotel, Jefferson and
Penn st.
St. Louis—Hotel Newport, 2323 Market st.
St. Louis—*Dunbar Hotel, 20th and Market.
Moberly—Irvin Hotel.

NEBRASKA
Omaha—Midget Hotel, 24th & Pabrick st.
Omaha—Hotel Fulton, 1014 N. Eleventh st.

NEW JERSEY
Atlantic City—Dauber, 204 N. Conn. ave.
Atlantic City—Bay State Hotel, 334 N. Linnen
st.
Trenton—*Higgens Hotel, 25 Barns st.
Cape May—Hotel Dale.
Burlington—Mrs. Robinson, York st.

NEW YORK
Auburn—Mrs. Braxton, 18 Cornell st.
Binghamton—Matt Austin, Prospect ave.
Buffalo—*Hotel Francis, Exchange st.
Buffalo—George Boutte, 4 Vine st.
Cortlandt—*Hotel De Wyant (White)
Howell—Mrs. Lee, 82 Erie st.
Hudson—Mrs. Mary Brown, 503 Diamond st.
Ithaca—The Cayuga House, 501 West State.
Middletown—Wm. Harriston, S. King st.
Rochester—Mrs. McDonald, 44 Smith st.
New Rochelle—Grand Lodge, 33 White Oak st.
New York City—The Olga Hotel, 603 Lenox
ave.
New York City—De Van Hotel, 205 W. 132d st.
New York City—Mrs. Anna Jennings, 135 W.
130th st.
New York City—Mme. Robinson, 223 West 140th
st.
New York City—The Bradford, 73 W. 134th st.
New York City—*Mrs. Trent, 236 West 131st
st.
New York City—*Mrs. Harris, 247 West 37th st.
Rochester—Hotel Gibson, 187 Caledonia.
Troy—Al Martin, 77 River st.

NORTH CAROLINA
Durham—Jones Hotel.
Raleigh—Arcade Hotel, Hargett st.
Rocky Mount—Hotel Lawrence, 230 Albemarle
ave.
Winston-Salem—Pratt's Palace, 739 Depot st.

OHIO
Akron—Dr. Strawbridge, 456 Livingston st.
Akron—*H. H. Hearing, 113 Lincoln st.
Athens—Berry Horne, renters to general public).
Canton—W. H. Gregory, 862 Cherry st.
Canton—Fred Singer, 801 Lafayette st.
Cincinnati—*Mary Mack, 520 Carlisle st.
Cincinnati—*Hotel Sterling, 6th and Mound sts.
Cincinnati—The Palmetto, 512 W. Fifth st.
Cleveland—Mrs. Webb, 2221 East 37th st.
Cleveland, Mrs. Blanche Key, 3638 Central ave.
Cleveland—*Bellevue Hotel, 2578 E. 40th st.
Cleveland—Royal Inn, 2286 55th st.
Cleveland—Central Ave. Hotel, 2307 Central ave.
Columbus—Litchfield Hotel, 96 N. Fourth st.
Dayton—*St. Regis Hotel, opp. B. R. station.
Dayton—Palace Hotel, opp. R. R. station.
Defiance—Mrs. Goins, 688 Harrison st.
Lima—Mrs. John King, 123 W. Spring st.
Lima—Mrs. Simmons, 1233 W. Spring st.
Lima—Southern Hotel, 133 Wayne st.
Lorain—Mrs. Winfrey, 203 East 22d st.
Marietta—Mrs. Curtis, 108 Saire ave.
Newark—Re. Cooper, 263 E. Fair Ground st.
Newark, Mrs. Johnson, 607 Evans st.
Newark—Mrs. Frank Ransom, 78 Hoover st.
Portsmouth—Mrs. Branch, 1128 Eleventh st.
Springfield—Mrs. Mary Armstead, 36 W. Clark
st.
Toledo—*Hotel Pleasant, 11 North Erie.
Youngstown—Mrs. Clark, 723 Erie st.
Youngstown—*Rideout Hotel, Federal st.
Zanesville—Mrs. Lulu Gry, 114 Main st.

OREGON
Pendleton—Hotel Flu, 560 Cottonwood ave.
Portland—*Hotel Golden West.

OKLAHOMA
Muskogee—Hotel Givens, 728 Elgin st.

PENNSYLVANIA
Allentown—Mrs. Benjamin, 247 Fifth st.
Allentown—Mrs. Clark, 243 S. Fifth st.
Bellefonte—A. V. Alango, 105 E. Elgin st.
Coatesville—Subway Hotel.
Connellsville—Mrs. Stanton, 133 North Alley.
Harrisburg—*Wilson Apartments, foot of 3d st.
Lancaster—*Elite Hotel, 30 So. Green st.
Lancaster—Roy Wilson, 345 North st.
Newcastle—Mrs. Dillard, 131 Elm st.
Philadelphia—*Attucks Hotel, 18th st. and
Christian.
Philadelphia—Dale Hotel, Broad and Catherine.
Philadelphia—Rondside Hotel, 514 S. 15th st.
Philadelphia—Baltimore Hotel, near Dunbar
Theater.
Philadelphia—*Moss McQuitty, 1622 South st.
Philadelphia—*Mrs. Moore, 1310 South st.
Philadelphia—*Capt. Ina Wayne, 1417 Wylie ave.
Pittsburg—Fulton Hotel, 67 Fullerton.
Pittsburg—Bailey Hotel, 1306 Wylie ave.
Pittsburg—Metropole Hotel, 7th & Chestnut.
Reading—Hotel Mason, 7th & Chestnut.
Scranton—Mrs. Meyers, 601 Lackawanna st.

SOUTH CAROLINA
Charleston—Jobnson Restaurant, 619 Long st.
Greenville—M. Miller, 493 East Curch st.

TENNESSEE
Nashville—Delmonico Restaurant, 407 Cedar st.
Nashville—Duncan Hotel (Y. M. C. A.), Cedar
st.

TEXAS
Dallas—*Frazier Hotel, 837 No. Central ave.
Dallas—*Del Monico Hotel, 302 No. Central ave.
Dallas—*Waukesha Hotel, 2503 Elm st.
Dallas—*Lincoln Hotel, 901 Good st.
Houston—*Oriental Hotel, 421 San Felipe st.
Houston—*French Cafe, 503 San Felipe st.

VIRGINIA
Danville—*Manhattan Cafe, 207 Craighead st.
Danville—Mrs. Pearl Logan, Union st.
Lexington—Rowlands Hotel, 18 Nelson st.
Richmond—*Miller's Hotel, Second and Leigh.
Richmond—*Union Music Studio, 516 N. 3d st.
Richmond—Morris Hotel, North Second.
Lynchburg—Hotel Pleasant, 816 Fifth st.
Norfolk—Mt. Vernon Hotel, Queen & Church
st.
Norfolk—Douglas Hotel, 716 South st.
Norfolk—Palace Hotel, Church st.

WASHINGTON
Spokane—Robert Connup, 212 S. Bernard st.
Seattle—N. P. Hotel, 305 Sixth ave., So.

WEST VIRGINIA
Clarksburg—Mrs. Ross, 436 Water st.
Fairmont—Cobbs Hotel, 226 Jackson st.
Huntington—Howe's Hotel.
Martinsburg—Clarence Roman, Charles st.
Morgantown—G. Scott, 123 Walnut st.
Parkersburg—Mr. Smith, 816 Clay st.
Wheeling—Peter Green, 31 Alley 8.

CANADA
London, Ont.—Richmond Hotel.
Guelph, Ont.—Mrs. Phillip Smith.

Left, additions to August 6 List of Theatre, Census Figures; Right, The first list of hotels for colored performers ("The Page," 31 Dec. 1921).

PARTIAL LIST OF COLORED FAIRS

The following is the first attempt ever made to compile a list of the many fairs promoted and patronized by the colored people of the country.

It is far from complete, and is published at this time to awaken the interest of those concerned to the value of listing their organization and its dates with The Billboard.

Such publicity attracts to your fair the manufacturer who is routing his exhibits; the amusement enterprises which play such dates and the concessioner who pays for the privilege of operating.

Your name and dates in The Billboard lists relieve your officials of considerable anxiety as to where to obtain certain necessary elements of a successful fair. They are offered to you.

Then too, the Page is interested in promoting an effective organization among colored fair officials that will function as does a similar body among the whites.

Their International Association of Fairs and Expositions has recently closed its annual meeting in Chicago, and with it many of the cares and anxieties concerning the next fair—anxieties that will burden the unorganized colored official for many months to come.

Let's get together, organize an association, work in harmony, co-operate with one another and with the National Negro Business Men's League and thereby add dignity and prestige to our fairs; increase the income, reduce the expenses, better the program of events, better the exhibits, improve methods and keep more of the profits within the race.

It is all possible if you organize. Colored showmen will get a better chance. With definite knowledge as to dates, better attractions may be commanded, and your visitors who pay at the gate will be more interested because you can offer a wider variety of race accomplishments. Get together. Write us your views. Address J. A. Jackson, The Billboard, 1493 Broadway, New York City.

ALABAMA
Athens—Limestone Co. Negro Fair, W. H. Cox, secy.
Birmingham—Colored State Fair.
Bessemer—Colored Fair.

GEORGIA
Dublin—Oconee Negro Fair, H. H. Dudley, secy.
Statesboro—Colored Agrl. & Ind. Fair, Wm. James, secy.
Swainsboro—Seven County Fair, H. W. Wadley, secy.
Savannah—Auto Races (write The Savannah Tribune).
Augusta—Colored Fair.
Moton Chapel—Clarke Co. Community Fair, Mr. Moten, promoter.

KENTUCKY
Lexington—Lexington Colored Fair, John H. Scruggs, secy.
Covington—K. of P. Indoor Bazaar, W. A. Creevey, mgr.
Mt. Sterling—Montgomery County Colored Fair, James Mitchell, secy.
Hickman—Fulton Fair Assn.
Owensboro—Fair and Chautauqua.
Paducah—Colored Fair.

LOUISIANA
Franklin—Washington Parish Fair.

MARYLAND
Pocomoke—Pocomoke Colored Fair, Stephen H. Long, secy., Pocomoke, Md.
Salisbury—Colored Fair.
Cullington—Colored Fair.

MISSOURI
Bunceton—Cooper County Colored Agrl. Fair, B. W. Morris, secy.

NORTH CAROLINA
Raleigh—Negro State Fair, Dr. John Love, secy., Blount st.
Winston-Salem—Colored Piedmont Fair, H. M. Edmonson, secy.
Asheville—Deatrice Col. Agriculture Fair, R. W. Pearson, secy., P. O. Box 261.
Wilson—Colored County Fair.
Smithfield—Colored County Fair, H. R. Goodson, secy., Clayton, N. C.
Jamestown—Colored Community Fair.
Norway—Colored County Fair.
Goldsboro—Wayne Fair and Park.

PENNSYLVANIA
Philadelphia—Autumn Fair Association, Beresford Gale, pres., 432 South Broad st.
Bristol—Harvest Home Fair.

SOUTH CAROLINA
Columbia—Colored State Fair, Rev. A. W. Hill, secy., Aiken, S. C.
Orange—Colored Day at White Fair (Negro attendance about 40,000).
Dillon—Colored Fair.
Princeton—Colored Fair.
Sumter—Colored Fair.
Chester—Colored Fair.
Mt. Carmel—Colored Fair, Saxon Bros., mgrs.
Mt. Carmel, S. C.
Greenville—Colored Fair, E. W. Biggs, secy.
Bishopville—Colored Fair, W. A. Covington, secy.

TENNESSEE
Memphis—Tri-State Fair, Dr. L. G. Patterson, secy., 364 Beale ave.
Pulaski—Colored Fair.
Hartsville—Colored Fair, Lee Hall, secy.

TEXAS
Houston—Annual Fall Festival.

VIRGINIA
Suffolk—Fairfax Colored Fair.

WEST VIRGINIA
Charlestown—Charleston Colored Horse Show.

Corrections and additions will be appreciated, as the list is admittedly incomplete. It is a beginning.

A LIST OF COLORED COMPANIES

(* Indicates Known Ownership White)

Anita Bush Stock Co.
Austin Dramatic Players.
Barringer's "Dixie Girls."
Billy Mack's "Merry Makers."
"Broadway Rastus," Irvin Miller, prop.
"Bombay Girls," Drake & Walker.
Billy King, King & Weingarden, prop.
"Bandanna Girls," Poise De Legge.
Bob Russel Co.
Billy Young, "Shoulder Shakers."
Cleo Mitchell Co.
*Colored Comedy Co., Phillips & Hawthorne, prop.
"Chocolate Brown," Irvin Miller, prop.
Cooper & Lamar Co.
"Cotton Blossoms," Billy Bowman.
"Cotton Blossoms," Prof. Taylor.
"Dainty Maids, Drake & Walker.
"Darktown Swells" with Stella White.
"Dixon's Jazz Girls," Henry Dixon, prop.
"Delegates from Dixie," Arthur Boykin.
Ed Lee, "Creole Belles."
"Florida Blossoms," Oscar Rogers, manager.
Fisher's "Fun Festival."
Gus Smith Co.
"Georgia Troubadurs," William McCabe, prop.
Hardtack Jackson Co.
Henderson's Lyric Road Show.
Hightower's "All-Star Review."
Hayes King, "Posey Girls."
"Hello Rufus," Leon Long, prop.
James Crescent Players.
Jesse Brown Co.
Joe Byrd Co.
Kid Thomas Co.
Lafayette Players, Cleo Desmond & Andrew Bishop Co., Quality Amusement Co.
Lafayette Players, Evelyn Ellis & Simmons Co., Quality Amusement Co.
Lafayette Players, Mrs. Anderson Co., Quality Amusement Co.
Lafayette Players, Unit No. 4, Quality Amusement Co.
Lincoln Stock Co., Kansas City, Lincoln Amusement Co., prop.
Mills & Frisby Co.
Masten's "Happy Days in Dixie."
Mason's "Dixie Beach Girls," John Mason, prop.
McGarr's "Ragtime Steppers."
Martin's "Joyland Girls," Edgar Martin.
Montgomery's "Hello 1921," featuring McClain and Montgomery.
Madam Rainey's "Gold Beauties."
Ollie Burgoyne "Dancing Girls.
Pat Williams' "Dixie Belle" Co.
Ridley & Ridley Co.
Sam H. Grey Co.
Smith & Butlers Co.
Silas Green Co., Eph Williams, prop.
"Sun-kist Southerners," Gus Smith, prop.
"Shuffle Along," Nicco Producing Co., New York (Indefinite Engagement).
"Smarter Set," Whitney & Tutt.
Sandy Burns Co.
Sid Perrin Co.
"Sunny South," J. S. Rockwell, prop.
Watts & Wills Co.
Weaver's "Green River" Co.
"Willie Too Sweet" Co.
Wooden's "Bon Tons."
White's "Stylish Steppers.

CENSUS FIGURES OF INTEREST TO US

The census bureau has released the following figures for our race in several cities. We hope to furnish a complete list at an early date. So far we can only report

Chicago	109,954
Baltimore	108,390
Louisville	40,118
Cincinnati	30,636
Atlantic City	10,696
Mobile	23,893

MINSTRELS

Allen's Minstrels, A. G. Allen.
Campbell's Minstrels.
"Dixie Moon Minstrels," Robert King.
"Down in Dixie Minstrels," Robert Wing.
Mixon's Minstrels.
Harvey's Minstrels, R. M. Harvey, prop.
Herbert's Minstrels, Joseph Herbert, prop.
Harry K. Main "Georgia Minstrels."
Jack Shaefer's "Georgia Minstrels."
J. B. Davis "Dixieland Minstrels."
J. B. Cullen "Superior Minstrels."
Jackson's "Jazland Minstrels."
*New York Minstrels."
O'Brien's "Georgia Minstrels," J. C. O'Brien, prop.
"Old Kentucky Minstrels."
Rusco & Hockwald's "Georgia Minstrels."
Smith's "Georgia Minstrels."
"Southern Exposition Minstrels."
Scott's "All-Star Minstrels."
Thomas & Fields' "Dixieland Minstrels."
Washington & Adams' Minstrels.
Young's "Greater Minstrels."

A list of vaudeville acts and concert artists is in process of preparation. It will be published in a future issue.

For this purpose we yet must obtain the names of acts, their personnels, their permanent addresses or agents, preferably both.

A later list will give the hotels and boarding houses catering to the profession and recommended by performers.

A LIST OF COLORED FILM PRODUCING COMPANIES

Lincoln Motion Pictures Co., 1121 Central ave., Los Angeles, Cal.
Micheaux Film Corp., 538 South Dearborn st., Chicago, Ill.
Real Production Corp., Robt. Levy, pres., 12 West 46th st., N. Y. C.
Rockettes Film Co., 1718 West Jefferson st., Los Angeles, Cal.
Democracy Film Co., 1718 West Jefferson st., Los Angeles, Cal.
North State Film Co., Ben Strasser, mgr., Winston-Salem, N. C.
Norman Film Co., 1614 Laura st., Jacksonville, Fla.
Ardslaur Productions Co., Ozark Bldg., Kansas City, Mo.
Gate City Feature Films, 1701 East Twelfth st., Kansas City, Mo.
Afro-American Film Exhibitors, 1120 Vine st., Kansas City, Mo.
Monumental Pictures Corp., 1816 Twelfth st., N. W., Washington, D. C.
Maurice Film Co., High and Antoine sts., Detroit, Mich.
West Motion Picture Co., Boston, Mass.
Delight Film Cd., 2139 S. Wabash ave., Chicago, Ill.
Mount Olympus Dist. Co., 110 West 40th st., New York City.
The Del Sarte Film Co., Clarence Muse, director, 1919 Broadway, New York.
Royal Garden Film Co., 459 East 31st st., Chicago, Ill.

EXCHANGES OFFERING NEGRO PRODUCTIONS

Comet Film Exchange, 1331 Vine st., Phila., Pa.
Savini Film Exchange, 83 Walton st., Atlanta, Ga.
Cummings Film Exchange, 107 No. Bayles st., Jacksonville, Fla.
Southern Distributing Co., 192 Aubrun ave., Atlanta, Ga.
Star Theater, Supply Exch., 301 Realty Bldg., Jacksonville, Fla.
Florentine Film Mfg. Co., 1905 "U" st., N. W., Washington, D. C.
Mount Olympus Distributing Co., 110 West 40th st., New York City.
Pathe Exchange, West 46th st., New York City.
National Exchange, 398 Fifth ave., New York City.

The foregoing is published in the interest of the many exhibitors who are constantly inquiring for the address of producers to the Page.

The managers of houses exhibiting this type of pictures all seem to know just where to inquire for the needed information. As ad giving the address of the concerns having films for this market would greatly reduce the amount of time and correspondence necessary for an exhibitor seeking their product.

Partial lists of Colored Companies ("The Page," 19 Nov. 1921).

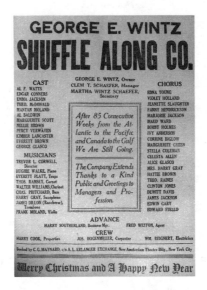

Above, typical Christmas ad for "Shuffle Along"; below, Messrs, Aubrey Lyles, Eubie Blake, Noble Sissle and Flournoy Miller, co-stars and authors of "Shuffle Along."

"Above, George McLennon. Two views of a most remarkable comedian now with the Whitney & Tutt "North Ain't South" Company; below, two types of New York musicians: Mildred Franklin, director of the mixed male and female orchestra at the Lafayette Theater, New York. She was trained at the New England Conservatory and at the Institute of Musical Art, New York. Herbert H. Leonard, winner of second prize in the recent city wide harmonica contest in New York. He and the winner are features in Keith vaudeville." (Jackson)

"Mr. and Mrs. Eugene Hooten, whose characterizations of the old-time preacher and the country girl have made the Hooten and Hooten act a favorite wherever it has been seen. It is a TOBA. favorite." (Jackson)

"Easton and Stewart, with Tom Sullivan's "Monte Carlo Girls", one of the very few colored vaudeville acts in burlesque. They celebrated their first anniversary as partners in Buffalo N. Y." (Jackson)

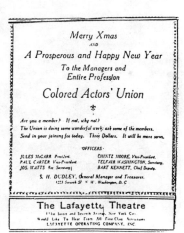

Ads in "The Page," circa 1922

PROMINENT IN MOTION PICTURE FIELD

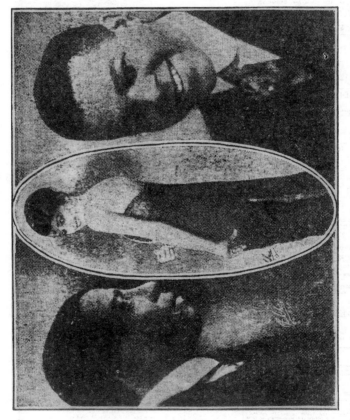

"Left to right: (1) Clarence E. Muse, director of the Del Sarte Film Co., and a former member of the Lafayette Players. Mr. Muse has had fifteen years's experience in Negro amusements. (2) Elizabeth Boyer, the clever little leading lady in Reol Production Company's release of Paul Lawrence Dunbar's 'The Sport of the Gods.' (3) Sydney P. Dones, the lead in the Bookertee Film Company's 'Loyal Hearts,' 'The Reformation' and 'My First Love.'" (Jackson)

"FROM DIXIE TO BROADWAY"

WM. VODERY
MUSICAL DIRECTOR

DANNY SMALL
JUVENILE LEAD

.FLORENCE MILLS
STAR

SHELTON BROOKS
COMEDIAN

KOVAN & THOMPSON
DANCERS

HAMTREE HARRINGTON
COMEDIAN

"Florence Mills, star of "From Dixie to Broadway", and some of the members of the company whose offering has been receiving the unanimous praise of the critics. It is the first colored attraction ever to command a $3 top price of admission. Now playing at the Broadhurst Theater, New York ("The Page," 13 Dec. 1924)." (Jackson)

The Billboard

J.A. JACKSON'S PAGE

IN THE INTEREST OF THE COLORED ACTOR, ACTRESS AND MUSICIAN OF AMERICA

COY HERNDON

FAIRFAX COLORED FAIR

NEGRO EXPOSITION IN 1922

WESLEY VARNELL'S REVIEW

LINCOLN PARK IMPROVED

COLORED FAIR IMPROVEMENTS

The Views of a Practical Showman Expressed

By OSCAR JENKINS

COY HERNDON

OSCAR JENKINS

"Left, The Ridley Trio, a Southern act that made a recent appearance in New York and made good; right, John W. Cooper, old-time ventriloquist, who has been doing lyceum work in recent years, has returned to vaudeville." (Jackson)

"Hatch and Hatch, Joe and Lillian, one of the clever and busy colored vaudeville teams that is regarded as a standard act on the bigger circuits; right, Long and Jackson in their act. 'The South-Bound Train', now in vaudeville in the East." (Jackson)

PROFANITY MUST GO

Vaudeville houses and musical comedy shows catering to the general public have long since placed a ban upon profanity and the broader forms of vulgarity. The time has arrived for the practice of the same policy in houses dependent upon Negro patronage. A number of managers are quite outspoken in their opinion against the practice. Others have expressed themselves as being willing to help eradicate the evil. The days of the comedian who depends upon "cuss words" for a laugh are numbered. He must get clean or get out. The mere fact that a few ignorant, loud-mouthed, feet-stamping ones in the audience greet profanity and vulgarity with approval is no reason for insulting the intelligence of the many decent people who have paid for entertainment rather than for an exhibition of depravity.

Public sentiment is rapidly crystallizing against such performers, and the managers of houses and companies will, of course, protect their business by dispensing with comedians who are not funny enough to get a legitimate laugh. These fellows will have to go back to the livery stables and the levees from which they came. The handwriting is on the wall. Take heed!

SMUTSHOOTERS, READ THIS AND WEEP

DECENCY VINDICATED

"Producers of modern musical comedies, revues, vaudeville, or just 'girl shows', might learn a lesson from their dark-skinned brothers.

"Duluth witnessed a musical revue last week which was entirely the work of Negroes. It was composed by Negroes, staged by Negroes, and every member of the company and of the orchestra was a Negro.

"The lesson which these Negro entertainers had to teach was not just the value of spontaneity, altho they demonstrated that most effectively.

"It was not that a modern, popular musical entertainment should have life, color, rhythm, 'class' and 'pep', altho they demonstrated that also.

"But they did prove to producers whose skins don't happen to be black that it is possible to present the liveliest and most entertaining of revues without the faintest hint of vulgarity.

"Many a producer with a white skin will tell you that the public wants smut. We might thank our dark-skinned entertainers for proving that is a lie, and that good taste and decency can compete with vulgarity and indecency on better than an equal footing."

The editorial reprinted above is from a Duluth daily paper, the name of which was not provided to the editor of this page when it was sent in; and it is one of the most wonderfully encouraging expressions of editorial opinion that has been passed to the Negro professional entertainer. It was prompted by the appearance in that city of one of our better shows.

Some of our stink-talk stars will not earn that much real praise in the whole history of their careers. Imagine the sort of editorial some tabloid shows we know would have inspired in the same paper, and the chance ANY colored show would have to play the town after them.

MANAGERS

Who Respect Neither Audience Nor Artists and Comedians Who Need Disinfecting, Read This

Under the caption, "Toning up the Negro Theater," The New York Age, issue of November 12, said, in part:

"With the development of the Negro theater there has been much to encourage the workers for racial progress, while at the same time there have also cropped out certain manifestations that need to be corrected. An impartial observer of the growth of the Negro theater recently made the criticism, in good faith, that it needed 'toning up.' The deduction to be drawn from this remark was that there appeared to be a perceptible lowering of the tone of the entertainments afforded, with a tendency to showing 'too much rough stuff.'

"Such pandering to the taste of the vulgar and prurient minded may seem to the managerial judgment good policy, but for the smaller number who seek performances of that nature, a larger number are repelled in disgust. Toning

A Word to the Smut Shooter

It is reported that the Columbia Circuit, the guiding power of burlesque, has delivered an order directing the owners of attractions on that circuit to refrain from employing two certain artists.

The reason assigned is that the work of the two performers is below the standard of decency required by the Columbia Amusement Company.

Neither the man nor the woman involved is a Negro, but the undying principal applies with as much force to members of our race as to any other group of artists. The audience of tooday wants clean amusement and will have it. Even if some managers and performers must be retired from the business to accomplish the desired result.

MUST ALL SUFFER FOR THE SINS OF THE FEW

Two teams of colored fellows on two burlesque shows have by their conduct placed in jeopardy the hard won places now held by many of our sex in burlesque. Unless the managers are willing to make exhibits of these fellows with promptness, the axe now poised may fall on the necks of every Negro act on the Columbia Circuit; and a number of really worthy performers would suffer for the mental and moral weakness of a few evil-minded fellows who let their animal instincts dominate them. Again, all would suffer for the few.

Insulting women, fighting managers and attempting to cultivate girls is no way to succeed. In justice to the men complained of, it is only fair to state that the source of provocation did not, in one instance, originate with them. However, it must be remembered that because of a certain always present general antagonism, it is all the more important that patience and diplomacy of the highest degree be exercised.

PUBLIC WON'T STAND FOR STAGE FILTH

Rapid Rise of Theatricals Means That Players Must ."Come Clean" or Be Left Home

WOMEN AT FAULT TOO

Swear and Make Up Vulgar Sex Jokes Like Male Performers

By WM. E. READY

This is the era of the colored actors' "Day" in the theatrical profession in this country. Last season witnessed the undreamed of spectacle of a Negro actor rising in a single night from the obscurity of cheap vaudeville houses to the very front ranks of the nation's most celebrated mimes, in the case of Charles Gilpin in the "Emperor Jones," which was recently presented in this city.

The present season, tho scarcely under way, has seen two musical shows. "Shuffle Along" and "Put and Take," both of whose cast is composed entirely of colored players, launched in New York, with no little trepidation by their producers to become over night the talk of

"Smut," a key issue in "The Page."

III

Setting Standards of Conduct

"Can artists of color embody the same standards of
decency as those found in other professions?"

E arly in "The Page," J. A. Jackson posed the above question to black
artists. During the developmental stage of the column, Jackson began
attacking what he considered to be improper or unethical behavior. He
believed that conduct unbecoming to the profession was retarding the
advancement of blacks in the industry. Among his targets were vulgarity,
contract jumping, exploitation of performers, "splitting," inappropriate
conduct for small towns, irresponsible planning, lack of neatness, and
slovenly appearance. Stand-up comics such as "Pigmeat" Markhum,
"Moms" Mabley, Richard Pryor Eddie Murphy, Martin Lawrence, and
others, may be indebted to the performers of the 1920s; but during
Jackson's time, the industry labeled such comedians as "smut shooters"
because they depended on vulgarity and profanity to elicit laughs. Many of
these performers were popular, but they presented what Jackson felt was
the wrong image for African-Americans, that is, if they wanted to attract
families and a broader audience. More than twenty years earlier, houses
catering to the general public banned profanity and the broader forms of
vulgarity in vaudeville and musical comedy shows. Douglas Gilbert in
American Vaudeville: Its Life and Times contends that the person
responsible for "cleansing" the New England legitimate vaudeville theater
was Mrs. Mary Catherine Albee, wife of Edward Franklin Albee of the
Keith-Albee Vaudeville Chain of theaters. According to Gilbert some theater
owners nailed verboten signs on the bulletin board back stage. The signs

read: "Don't say . . . 'slop' or 'son-of-a-gun' or 'hully gee' on this stage unless you want to be canceled peremptorily. Do not address anyone in the audience in any manner . . . if you are guilty of uttering anything sacrilegious or even suggestive you will be immediately closed and will never again be allowed in a theater where Mr. Keith is in authority."[1]

This kind of censorship could be frustrating to actors. Despite the unusually strict guidelines for performers' conduct, by the 1920s the Keith-Albee chain of theaters numbered more than 400 houses throughout the East and Midwest—perhaps more a reflection of audience desires than backstage morality. There was no such policy similar to that of the Keith-Albee chain in houses dependent upon black patronage; but because of social condemnation, the *Billboard* policy against vulgarity and Jackson's declaration of principles, the black entertainment industry did not always accept performers of this kind. The practice of allowing "Smut" in theaters for black patrons outraged Jackson. They were, he felt, unfit for the very audience they wanted to attract—women and children. He wanted to know whether black artists could at least have the same respect for the women and children of their race as they showed to others. Jackson urged managers of houses and companies to protect their business by dispensing with the smut of comedians. "These fellows," he declared, "will have to get back to the livery stables and the levees from which they came. The handwriting is on the wall. Take heed!"[2] On October 22, 1921, in an article, "Public Won't Stand for Stage Filth," Jackson struck again: "Many black comedians, not funny enough to get a legitimate laugh, resort to loud mouthed swearing and double entendres with filthy sexual expressions."[3] "What made matters worse," Jackson asserted, "was that they [were] encouraged by certain managers and . . . a few ignorant, loud-mouthed, feet-stomping ones in the audience [who] greet them with approval . . . insulting the intelligence of the many decent people who have paid for entertainment rather than for an exhibition of depravity."[4]

Jackson seldom printed the names of performers in "The Page" that used abusive language and exhibited unacceptable behavior unless they ignored his warnings. A glance at other columns in *Billboard* leads me to believe that its policy was not to identify performers by name when it reprimanded them. Since the offenders seemed indifferent to Jackson's campaign, he often threatened to reveal their names in print to respectable theater-going patrons—in other words their audiences.[5] Many promised "The Page" that they would clean-up their acts, but seldom did. Although Jackson verified reports on violators through correspondents in the field, occasionally he received misinformation. In these instances, he was quick to issue a public apology.

Harrison Blackburn complained about a review of his act at the Frolic Theater in Birmingham, Alabama, by "The Page" correspondent Billy Chambers. It appeared in the October 14, 1922, edition of *Billboard*. Two weeks later, in the October 28 issue, Jackson explained: "If such is the case we shall be the most pleased persons to tell the world of that fact. Jackson has no desire to injure any act or performer. Mr. Blackburn knows whether he 'came clean' on the performance mentioned or whether he did not. If he did, we owe him an apology; and here it is, cheerfully rendered."[6] The apology was probably not as whole-hearted as Mr. Blackburn may have wished, but Jackson's retraction was prompt and clearly stated. Jackson warned that public indignation against indecency often takes the form of prejudice against all black acts. He cited an example of a Broadway "angel" who had such painful experiences with black artists that it prevented him from making any further contributions toward helping Broadway to take on a darker hue. As another illustration, in the December 15, 1923, survey, "The Gifts of the Year in Colored Amusement," he reported that a group of cities in two adjoining states not far from New York City, considered for years a good territory for Negro attractions, decided not to book black shows.

Jackson and other black journals constantly agitated for a higher standard of theatrical entertainment. To make things more difficult, the black theater-going public did not always support the "clean" acts—profit as always being the final determining factor in the matter. The "pertinent question," Jackson said, was whether black audiences really wanted a cleaner stage. His query was a reaction to the lack of attendance for the Chappelle and Stinnette Act at the Douglas Theater in New York. These artists, whom he considered "two of the classiest stage artists in the country, white or black . . . intelligent, refined, with an act that is staged with no little elegance and, above all—more than willing to give their audience a run for their money. . . . They were 'hard workers' as stage parlance has it, . . . but they played to a practically empty house all week."[7] He then compared how the Shubert Vaudeville Circuit house for whites received the same group at the Academy in the same city three weeks before their appearance at the Douglas: "They were pronounced by critics of the daily papers as the headliners of the bill which, besides their act, was composed of all-white acts. Their jazz band was called by one critic the best that had appeared in this city this year."[8] Jackson then noted that colored patrons had supported a white jazz singer headlining at one of the local vaudeville houses during the same week that Chappelle and Stinnette played at the Douglas. This artist, in Jackson's opinion, was "for class, talent and artistry . . . no more to be compared with Miss Stinnette than a 'Tin Lizzie' compares with a Stuts,[9] and yet the gallery of this white house was packed to suffocation every night by colored theater goers."[10] Why did black patrons not support their own theaters and lend encouragement to the players of their own race? Jackson felt that the theater goers in question had an ever-ready stock answer: "They would if colored houses cut out trash and played first-class acts."[11] Considering the "facts" reported by Jackson that all black acts were not vulgar, it would appear that some black spectators preferred white acts to smut; yet, many of the white vaudeville acts were also vulgar. Therefore, one might conclude that some blacks simply wanted to attend white theaters. Hence, we have a classy black act confined to empty houses and the inevitable choice of becoming smutty or going into permanent retirement. Jackson had the stock answer, but did he have the right one?

Lew Henry, a black manager at the Lincoln Theater in Cincinnati, could not believe that his patrons did not want good, clean, wholesome acts. His contention was that the acts mentioned in the "Pertinent Question" article would pack any house and please any audience if only the manager knew how to sell it. He based his argument on his experience in Cincinnati, one of the hardest "sell" towns in America. "Any patron, white or colored," he stated, "will tell you that Cincinnati people know what they want and he means to please. If they don't get the goods the theater loses."[12] "The Page" did not indicate whether any other theater managers took up Henry's proposal, but the lack of response from Jackson might indicate his support of this idea. These suggestions and many others printed in "The Page" did not rid the industry of vulgarity. Obviously there was a segment of the black audience that wanted it. Theater owners who were eager to accommodate gave venue to many of the stand-up comics who became popular at theaters such as the Apollo in New York. Artists may have felt that Jackson was infringing upon their artistic freedom and their livelihood by condeming "smut shooters"; after all, many of them were very good at it. Many agents, artists, promoters, theater owners, black papers, and the CAU joined Jackson's fight against indecency. His opinions undoubtedly influenced attendance among black audiences concerned with good entertainment as well as ethics.

Next to the "smut shooter" according to Jackson, "probably the heaviest brake against the progress for the colored artist is the "contract jumper." the fellow who has no regard for his word, or for the written contract."[13] In an editorial "A Word With Contract Jumpers" on September 23, 1922, he enumerated the many reasons why some artists don't honor their contracts: "Salary too low," "Contract unreasonable," "that guy don't count," "He don't notify anybody," "Got a better offer." Jackson's credo was that a person's word was his bond, that a contract was a sacred and legal document, and that all will suffer from doubts and suspicions from those stung by the irresponsible among them.[14] However, a closer look at why an artist might break a contract is revealing. One reason was that competing theater owners offered higher wages to performers. Clarence Muse and David Arlen, in *Way Down South*, told a humorous tale of how one theater owner dealt with Stringbeans, a comedian, when he tried to break a contract. Stringbeans, next to Bert Williams, was perhaps the most famous black comedian in America among black theatergoers. A tall, gangling comic sporting a diamond tooth that he was able to unscrew and remove from his mouth, this peculiar fellow could sit on a tiny stool in the center of a stage, clad in skin-tight pants and, with one long leg flung over the top of the grand piano, inspire more hilarity in an audience than a whole revue of average comedians. According to Hawkins, Stringbeans signed a contract with Mr. Wiley Bailey, the owner of the 81 Theater in Atlanta. When Stringbeans accepted an offer to work down the street at the Famous Theatre for more money, Bailey, kept on advertising Stringbeans—so did the Famous Theater. Hawkins then described the unusual aftermath of the performer's action:

> The first matinee at the Famous, Mister Bailey went down to the theater with a patrol wagon and a gang of cops and hauled Stringbeans off to the hoosegow. He was good to him . . . gave him anything he wanted to eat and drink, had his clothes pressed for him and everything. But he kept him in jail. In the evening, the patrol wagon brought Stringbeans here to the theater to give a show. As soon as the performance was over they carried him back and locked him up again. They kept repeating this every matinee and evening during the entire week. . . . Then at the end of the week, he paid him the same money the Famous had offered him to jump his contract. 15

The remedy for this contract breaker was an exception. Jackson, however, directed his attention to what he called horrible examples and atrocities: "Vaudeville acts [that] received contracts and failed to report for work at the appointed time; . . . novelty acts that had their chance at last only to disappoint the agent and the attraction when time came for the delivery of their goods; . . . minstrel and musical comedy artists who begged advances, and sometimes rehearsed for a week [and] 'blew.'"[16] Women were also cautioned—they were the worst offenders, say some members of the profession.

"The Page" was astounded by the amount of money lost to the treasury of black circuits because of acts that obtain railroad tickets from a theater owner, only to commit larceny by not showing up. When Jackson recommended one performer to a booking agent and he failed to show, Jackson stated that his credibility as editor of "The Page" would be in jeopardy if his reputation had not already been established.

The problem of contract jumping was not just confined to poorer theaters. An artistic and financially successful show was not always a guarantee that the problem of contract jumpers would not occur. Salem Tutt Whitney, a writer, actor, and one of the most prolific producers of the 1920s, reported to "The Page" that the enormously popular *Shuffle Along* company had the misfortune of having irresponsible artists who left without notice. It was surprising to Tutt in that the paydays were regular without holdouts and the company made advances for upwards of $1, 250. He noted that "in spite of the liberal treatment, one [was] a girl owing $24 and the gratitude due for help advanced because of family illness."[17]

Promoters did not always live up to their contractual obligations either. Jackson's editorial in the October 7, 1922 issue on "Mountebank Managers" is one of the rare occasions where Jackson cited the name of the accused. "The Page" cautioned performers against "callous-hearted mountebank promoters preying upon the confidence of colored performers with a lot of nerve, very little cash, less knowledge of show business, and a total lack of moral responsibility."[18]

The column chastised publicly Mr. Rosen, as a "lying scoundrel." He took out a New England company of more than 90 talented people to New York. Rosen wanted to open the *Dumb Luck* show for a "few weeks" tryout performance, hoping to sell it to an "angel" on the strength of the reviews. Rosen found an "angel" to finance the show for several days, but there was not enough money to pay the actors. Regardless, the supporting actors played their parts out of loyalty to the principals, whom Rosen made the "goats" since the show was not successful at the box office. When the actors asked for food money, the so-called show owner reportedly said: "There's too many, send 'em back."[19] Jackson asked artists to "quit wasting long weeks of weary rehearsal with mountebanks, speculators, and cheap hustlers. . . . Deal only with the recognized business people of the show world."[20]

The TOBA Black Vaudeville Circuit also complained of irresponsible managers and "contract jumpers"; however, Clarence Muse contends that the real victims during the early and middle 1920s were the show managers and the performers. In an August 18, 1928 article that appeared in the Pittsburgh *Courier*, Jackson talked about why performers mistrusted managers and the "iron clad" TOBA contracts that bound them both. "Before taking a show out on the TOBA, the show manager had to sign a contract, the terms of which were clearly in favor of the Theater manager. . . . At the beginning of the season, on or about Labor Day, six-or-seven week contracts [would] be issued to well-known producers and managers of shows. The terms of the contracts [were] carefully worded, unlike any other theatrical contract in the world. But if the show [failed] to appear, they [payed and payed] dearly even more than the contract will [earned]."[21]

Another conduct issue that was costly to vaudeville teams was the "foolish" habit of "falling out" and "splitting." Jackson explained at length how this practice accomplished nothing and how acts would lose the prestige that gave value to the team. He referred to two incidents. The first was of a black music writer who "split" from his partner: The former partners each went their separate ways. Each took a new partner and tested the waters. "With new partners, each tried to place songs with the publishers who had taken the compositions of the team. They were unsuccessful. The public wouldn't have anything to do with the unknown partnerships."[22] Jackson explained that the old team reunited, resolved their differences, and that the theater goers are accepting their songs. The second example was the team of Black and White. "They were a known act that separated—each taking a new partner."[23] He then explained that, "Now we have a team of Black and Blue and the team of White and Brown. Neither has a reputation, nor can either take into itself the value of the old Black and White team, so both lose. Fortunately, the composers [referred to in the earlier part of this article] were able to get together. We urge vaudeville to take the lesson seriously whenever they feel inclined to say: 'After this week you go for yourself, I can make it without you.' It's bad business to throw away reputation. It is your biggest and best asset."[24] "Splitting" was, in Jackson's consideration, a definite negative; however, rampant discrimination was another problem in black entertainment.

For many entertainers, one of the more appealing aspects of the black entertainment business is the opportunity to travel. However, as Tom Fletcher points out in *100 Years of the Negro in Show Business*, only a few decades earlier, artists "exposed themselves to discrimination more often by traveling into areas where they were not wanted and were more likely to be 'reminded' of their places because they were in positions to 'be somebody.' "[25] W. C. Handy recalled an incident in which one of the black minstrels in his troupe contracted smallpox in the 1890s. The local authorities held the entire company outside of the nearest Texas town. They threatened to lynch them if they left the compound. The locals denied the company treatment even when the disease spread throughout the group. County officers came a short while later to inform the company that the appearance of only one more case of smallpox would be the signal for them to burn the car and carry out the doctor's lynching threat. Denied food, water and sanitation facilities, they survived only because their train carried water and food reserves in case of just such "emergencies." Finally, under cover of a diversionary show, the troupe smuggled the fourteen sick men out in women's clothing so they could escape from Texas to some place "where the benefits of a hospital might be enjoyed."[26]

"Defiant blacks were not always that lucky,"[27] says Robert C. Toll, in *Blacking Up*. He relates the story of how whites in Missouri attacked a fiercely proud black minstrel, Louis Wright, and his lady friend. Wright retaliated by cursing at them. With only this "provocation," an angry crowd, threatening to lynch him, invaded the theater. Although they dispersed when Wright fired his gun at them, they returned later that night, surrounded the minstrel railroad car and demanded Wright to give himself up. When he refused, authorities arrested the entire company and beat several members to force them to identify Wright. None did, but a member of the crowd recognized Wright, and they took him into custody. In the middle of the night, the sheriff "released" Wright to the crowd, who lynched him, cut out his tongue, and shipped his mutilated body to his mother in Chicago.[28]

Douglas Gilbert in *American Vaudeville: Its Life and Times* speaks of a time when even the great Bert Williams "was subjected to racial affronts, at one time by, of all people, the cast of the *Follies of 1910*. Ziegfeld ordered that a substantial part be written in for Williams. When the cast learned that a Negro was to act with them they threatened to strike this forced Ziegfeld to eliminate the part and substitute Williams' vaudeville specialty. Williams' artistry dissolved the difficulty. He stopped the show—he was such a hit that [Ziegfeld revised] the rejected material and restored [Williams'] part."[29] These conditions that black entertainers faced a decade or so earlier were just as prevalent during Jackson's time.

In the period from 1910 to 1920, the total black population of New York, Chicago, Philadelphia, and Detroit increased by nearly three-quarters of a million. Crammed into ghettos, blacks who migrated from the South to the North faced a different kind of discrimination that extended into housing, employment, education, and civil liberties. Conditions in the big cities worsened and the racial climate became more tense.

W. E. B. Du Bois predicted a race war. Organizations such as the NAACP, The Urban League and the black press, including the *Crisis*, *Messenger*, and the New York *Age*, protested lynchings and other civil rights violations. Meanwhile, black America raised an important question: How to react to racism? There was no easy answer given the different philosophies by the two most dominant civil rights leaders, Marcus Garvey and W. E. B. Du Bois. Garvey was a separatist. He believed that blacks should return to Africa to create their own resources and to escape the many evils of racism in America. Du Bois was a radical, but also an integrationist who wanted entry for blacks into all aspects of the greater American society as equals. Conservative blacks tended to embrace Du Bois' philosophy, but radical blacks labeled them "Uncle Toms" for valuing the white culture more than their own. The question remained twofold: whether to practice restraint as a survival technique when confronted with racism and possibly be called a "Tom"; or maintain your pride, be defiant, but run the risk of losing your life? This was a decision that entertainers had to make when forced into unpleasant situations in show business while traveling throughout the country to major cities and small towns.

Jackson took the conservative approach. The debate continues today just as it did during Jackson's time as to which direction blacks should take when confronted with racism. Given this schism, some artists might think Jackson's advice was educational and informational, and others might view it as "Uncle Tom" concessionism. An artist bases his beliefs on personal convictions and how strongly he feels the need to strike back or deal with racism in other ways.

There is no indication in black journals such as the *Crisis*, the *Messenger*, and the Chicago *Tribune* how artists felt about Jackson's advice on how to react to racism. However, the recurrence of confrontational incidents would indicate that there were some who did not believe that silence was the best recourse. The black publications were just as divided in their philosophy on how to deal with racism as black actors must have been. Considering the social climate of the 1920s, Jackson's advice represented an alternative that was part of a package to "sell" African-Americans to the general public and increase attendance for black performance. It wasn't for everyone.

Jackson also advised performers about neatness and appearance, important standards sometimes overlooked on stage. One theater patron wrote to "The Page" complaining about how "shabbily" attired performers distracted from an otherwise fine performance. The report was as follows: "There appeared on the scene a well-meant dressed dude, [who] pranced delightfully, but the soiled linen and the grease spots on his trousers completely covered up the enthusiasm which was rightfully due him for his excellent dancing."[30] "The Page" was concerned with neatness and appearance off stage as well. "Their dress and cleanliness off the stage was their stock in trade and that it would do well for some of them who had been there to boost their stock."[31]

Actors dying broke and leaving a financial responsibility to loved ones and friends was another subject on which "The Page" took a stance. An actor died in a western city. A former partner solicited in the local paper for assistance to provide a decent burial for the deceased. Jackson thought that this was a humane gesture but felt that performers should avoid this kind of humiliation to wives, mothers, and other relatives. He suggested that they make proper provisions before they "descend to the great beyond" by starting a savings account with even a dime a week, or joining a union or fraternity that cared for its members in distress.[32] Jackson's tone at times seemed a bit preachy but that may have been due to the educational level of his reading public. Reportedly, of the estimated 10 million blacks living in the United States in the early 1920s, 26 percent of those who had migrated from the South were illiterate.[33] Therefore, Jackson might overstate his point at times to attract a broader black audience—many who had little or no education.

Of all the standards of conduct Jackson espoused, the one that seemed to be the most important was ridding the black entertainment industry of vulgarity. Unfortunately, without the full support of theater owners and artists who gave the audiences what they wanted, Jackson did not reach a certain segment of the black community, which denied them the opportunity to enjoy the rich and enormous talents of the black performer. Nonetheless, throughout the life of "The Page," its insistence upon clean entertainment helped to rid the black entertainment industry of many of the undesirable elements that were retarding its growth. Given that many artists were new to the entertainment profession or uninformed as to the proper conduct for showmen, the column gave them direction and provided guidelines that enabled them to increase their drawing power and to interact in the profession with dignity and self-respect.

Notes

[1] Douglas Gilbert, *American Vaudeville: its Life and Times* (New York: Atheneum, 1975) 74.
[2] James Albert Jackson, "Facts Pleasant or Otherwise," 22 Jan. 1921: 43.
[3] Ibid., "Public Won't Stand for Stage Filth," *Billboard* 22 Oct. 1921: 45.
[4] Ibid.
[5] Ibid., "Warning," *Billboard* 5 Nov. 1922: 47.
[6] Ibid.
[7] Ibid., "A Pertinent Question," *Billboard* 9 Dec. 1922: 48.
[8] Ibid.
[9] Jackson compares these artists to an older used car ("Tin Lizzie"), a top-of the-line luxury model automobile (Stuts Bearcat).
[10] Jackson, "A Pertinent Question," *Billboard* 9 Dec. 1922: 48.
[11] Ibid.
[12] Ibid., "An Answer to A Pertinent Question," *Billboard* 23 Dec. 1922: 49.
[13] Ibid., "A Word With Contract Jumpers," *Billboard* 23 Sept. 1922: 48.
[14] Ibid.
[15] Ibid.
[16] Ibid.
[17] Ibid., "Whitney Writes on Contract Jumpers," *Billboard* 5 May 1923: 50.
[18] Ibid., "Mountebank Managers," *Billboard* 7 Oct. 1922: 48.
[19] Ibid.
[20] Ibid.
[21] Clarence Muse, Pittsburgh *Courier* 18 Aug.1928: 4.
[22] Jackson, "Splitting Up," *Billboard* 25 June 1921: 46.
[23] Ibid.
[24] Ibid.
[25] Tom Fletcher, *100 Years of the Negro in Show Business* (New York: Burdge and Company, 1954) xvii.
[26] Fletcher, 50-52.
[27] Robert C. Toll, *Blacking Up* (New York: Oxford University Press, 1974) 222.
[28] Ibid.
[29] Gilbert, 284.
[30] Jackson, 56.

[31] James D. Williams, writing under the nom de plume of "Specks," "Street Dress for the Performer," *National Herald* 30 June 1923: 49.

[32] Jackson, "Performer Died Broke," *Billboard* 13 Dec. 1924: 95.

[33] Peter M. Bergman, *The Chronicle History of the Negro in America* (New York: The New American Library, 1969) 395.

IV

Improving Conditions on the
TOBA
Black Vaudeville Circuit

P oor working conditions on the black vaudeville circuits was the second major issue Jackson felt was retarding the advancement of the black entertainment industry. Around the turn of the century black performers excelled in musical comedy and variety shows on the Keith, Orpheum, Loew, and other "big time" white vaudeville circuits—that is, when they were allowed to perform. Racial division in American theatre ran deep. When a theatre manager did book a black act it was for only one act per show; and he confined colored audiences to the "peanut gallery" in segregated theatres;[1] however, between 1912 and 1927, with the advent of the S. H. Dudley, Southern Consolidated, Theatre Owners and Booking Association (TOBA), and Managers' and Performers' (M. & P.) theatre chains, black artists made vast strides in vaudeville circuits catering to black patrons. For the first time, theatre audiences, both black and white, were offered a wide range of talent. It was not unusual for a black theatre to present minstrel acts, comedians, acrobats, contortionists, magicians, roller skaters, violinists, concert singers, animal acts, clowns, jugglers, classically trained dancers, and jazz musicians all in the same evening.[2] On these circuits, many of the leading black acts and artists of the day gained experience and fame in the show business industry. Among the more notable names were: S. H. Dudley, Andrew Tribble, Jeannie Pearl, Laurence Chenault, Ethel Waters, the Whitman Sisters, Butterbeans and Susie, Ida Cox, Bessie Smith, "Sunshine" Sammy, and Ma Rainey.

Top left, S. H. Dudley; top right, ad for *His Honor the Barber*, circa 1909; bottom left, Dudley and his famous mule in *The Smart Set*, a musical comedy that played practically every vaudeville and combination house in America; bottom right, one of Dudley's Mid-City Theaters in Washington D. C.

The largest employer of black entertainment was the TOBA or "Toby Time" as it was called, but it gained a reputation for being "Tough on Black Actors" reportedly because of unfair treatment by theatre managers. Black artists frequently complained about the endless series of one-night stands, cheap hotels, take-out meals, crowded "Jim Crow" trains,[3] excessive transportation costs, salary discrepancies, and long jumps.[4] "Unless you were a headliner, the pay was dreadful," says Jim Haskins in *Black Theatre in America*, "You traveled 'second-class' train, playing small towns as well as cities. Costumes and sets were minimal, and performers had to depend on the resident band of each theater for back-up or background music."[5] Did TOBA provide the solution for the black entertainer's deplorable condition? Or did it merely serve its own best interest economicaly? This issue was a much-debated topic, but not easy to remedy. Actors wanted better working conditions, visibility, and steady work; theater owners wanted attractions that would draw; producers wanted to find theaters to book their acts; and inattentive black audiences wanted better shows for their theaters.

"J. A. Jackson's Page" provided a forum to discuss these issues surrounding the black entertainment industry. The crucial question then is: What impact did "The Page" have on improving conditions of the black vaudeville circuit? To address the question, this chapter will firsts provide an historiography of early black vaudeville circuits between 1907 and 1925 with an eye on the "feud" among the circuits to gain control of the industry; then it will address three key issues in "The Page" that Jackson felt retarded the industry: poor routing, segregated theatres, and salary discrepancies; and then it will assess Jackson's efforts to improve conditions on the circuits, in particular the TOBA.

The S. H. Dudley / Southern Consolidated Circuits
The idea of establishing a chain of black theaters originated in 1912 with S. H. Dudley owner of several theaters in Washington, D. C. and Virginia. As the first known booking agent for black talent, Dudley developed a chain because he believed that white theaters did not want to hire black performers even though they were capable of playing anything from low comedy to Shakespearean drama. He wanted black artists to play in high-class houses, not honky-tonk halls, and to stop worrying about who and what he could get next week for his show.[6] The honky-tonks were gambling and prostitution houses, "where paid and volunteer entertainers . .

. . . , men and women met to drink, dance and have a good time,"[7] says James Weldon Johnson in *Black Manhattan*. They were the prototypes of the modern night-clubs. Douglas Gilbert in *American Vaudeville: Its Life and Times* describes the kinds of honky tonk halls that Dudley wanted to avoid:

> Throughout the country every barn and shooting gallery that had a roof over it with room for a bar and a hall in which 150 folding chairs could be assembled bid for 'specialties' and advertised in the trade journals. . . . The rough-hewn 'palaces' where the shows were presented were makeshifts, as across the continent churches, barns, warehouses, dye works, livery stables, markets, and other abandoned buildings were converted into variety halls.[8]

Between 1911 and 1913, Dudley bought several theaters in Washington, D. C.: the Mid-City, S. H. Dudley, Fairyland, Foraker, and the Blue Mouse. His first purchase outside the city of Washington was in Newport News, Virginia. Dudley hired Leigh Whipper as Manager and they persuaded other theater managers to join the circuit. Eight original theater houses were on the circuit (see Map I). By 1916, after Dudley merged with two other houses catering to black patronage to form the Southern Consolidated Circuit (see Table 1, Map II), there were over twenty-eight theaters covering the South, East, and Midwest. President, E. L. Cummings, a white, of Pensacola, Florida, handled the Southern end of things; the Vice-President, S. H. Dudley did much of the Eastern booking; and the Secretary, Martin Klein, also white, the Chicago agent and manager, looked after the Chicago booking. The circuit claimed that for the first time they made it possible for black acts to get contracts for eight months out of one office.

The TOBA Circuit

On January 1920, the TOBA, a black vaudeville circuit, controlled mostly by whites, reorganized. As the first order of business, Milton Starr, the newly elected president, accused the Southern Consolidated Circuit of gross mismanagement. Starr stated in a letter to Jackson, why he restructured the TOBA "It was to save the colored theatrical industry . . . to offer better booking for black performers [and] to protect [his] own considerable investment. The whole profession, including performers and theater operators, were practically at the mercy of one man who made himself more or less obligated to performers and managers alike by his unreasonable and unjust demands"[9] (prabably referring to S. H. Dudley). If

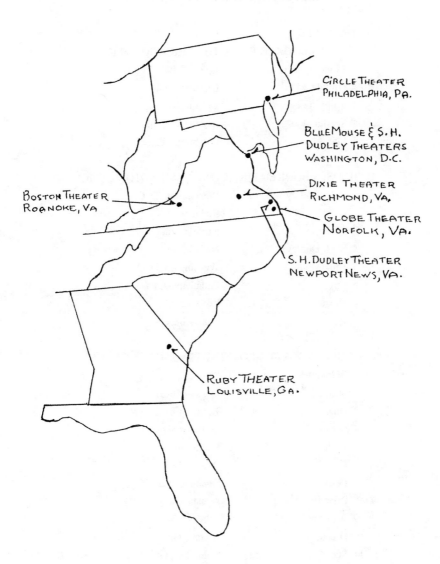

CIRCLE THEATER
PHILADELPHIA, PA.

BLUE MOUSE & S.H.
DUDLEY THEATERS
WASHINGTON, D.C.

BOSTON THEATER
ROANOKE, VA

DIXIE THEATER
RICHMOND, VA.

GLOBE THEATER
NORFOLK, VA.

S.H. DUDLEY THEATER
NEWPORT NEWS, VA.

RUBY THEATER
LOUISVILLE, GA.

Map I
S. H. Dudley's Theatrical Enterprise, circa 1911.

Table 1: (see Map II)
SOUTHERN CONSOLIDATED CIRCUIT, circa 1916

THEATERS   CITY
A. HOUSES BOOKED FROM THE CHICAGO OFFICE
1. Monogram   Chicago, Il.
2. Grand Central   Cleveland, Oh.
3. Koppin   Detroit, Mi.
4. Washington   Indianapolis, In.
5. Star   Pittsburgh, Pa.

B. HOUSES BOOKED FROM THE WASHINGTON OFFICE
1. S. H. Dudley   Washington, D. C.
2. Dixie   Richmond, Va.
3. Globe   Norfolk, Va.
4. S. H. Dudley   Norfolk, Va.
5. Blue Mouse   Washington, D. C.
6. Circle   Philadelphia, Pa.
7. Boston   Roanoke, Va.
8. Ruby   Louisville, Ga.

C. HOUSES BOOKED FROM THE PENSACOLA OFFICE
1. Belmont   Pensacola, Fl.
2. Strand   Jacksonville, Fl.
3. Palace   Tampa, Fl.
4. Dream   St. Petersburg, Fl.
5. Lyric   Miami, Fl.
6. Lyric   Ocalo, Fl.
7. Pekin   Savannah, Ga.
8. Palace   Agusta, Ga.
9. Morton   Athens, Ga.
10. Dream   Athens, Ga.
11. Star   Columbus, Ga.
12. Pike   Mobile, Al.
13. American   Houston, Al.
14. Dreamland   Texarkana, Ak.
15. Liberty   Greensville, Ak.

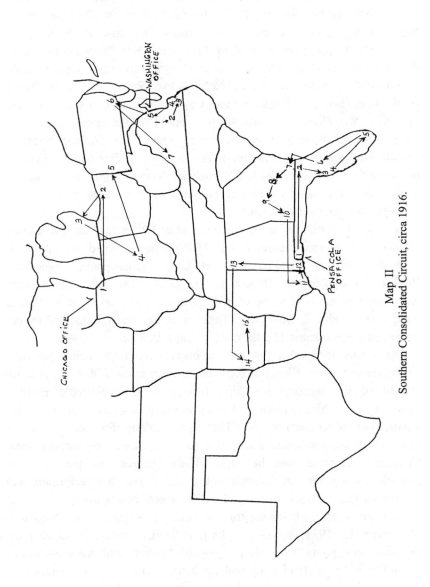

Map II
Southern Consolidated Circuit, circa 1916.

one glances at the TOBA's prior history, one might also question its conduct.

"As early as 1907, F. A. Barrasso of Memphis organized a small number of Southern theaters for Negroes," says Paul Oliver in *The Story of the Blues*. Owing to the success of this venture, his brother, A. Barrasso, founded the Theatre Owners Booking Agency in 1909. "Sam Zerilla opened the Pastime Theater on Beale Avenue in Memphis and some while later the Pacini Brothers followed with the Beale Avenue Palace the largest Negro theater in the South."[10] Unfair treatment by theatre managers was a concern even then. Recollections of artists who worked on the circuit were about the notorious Charles P. Bailey at the 81 Theater on Decatur Street in Atlanta. He required acts to obtain passes to stay out after dark."[11] (This is the same theatre owner who had Stringbeans kept in jail when he was not performing.) The actor's contract that was clearly in favor of the theatre manager, was another concern.[12]

Reportedly, TOBA ran more efficiently after Milton Star and his partner Charles Turpin reconfigurated the TOBA. Starr owned the Bijou in Nashville, Tennessee, and Turpin, a St. Louis ragtime pianist, owned the Booker T. Washington Theater in St. Louis. The new stockholders mandated that the circuit be owned, controlled, and operated by theater owners (see Table 2, Map III). "These were the most influential theater owners in the South and Middle West,"[13] says Jackson.

The TOBA attracted a few theater owners from the larger Southern Consolidated Circuit. Klein lost some of its theaters to TOBA but retained control of the booking for thirty houses in Consolidated's Eastern, Southern, and Chicago circuits. Dudley trying to maintain control of his artists, put advertisements in "The Page" calling for acts to report immediately and announced that he was going to release a big surprise soon. Cummings reported that he replaced the houses on the Southern Consolidated Circuit that defected to the TOBA, and that performers and companies had contracts for several weeks of continuous work.

The Chicago *Star*, a black theatrical journal, ran an editorial in "The Page" of January 15, 1921 objecting to the new TOBA Circuit. It accused the organization of being "a lily white syndicate of houses and managers whose patronage is Negro [and that] without black owners in the organization, whites could continue to control the booking of black shows."[14] Jackson directed attention to two blacks: first to T. S. Finley, an associate of TOBA who owned the Lincoln Theater in Cincinnati; and then to John T. Gibson,

Table 2 (see Map III)
THEATRE OWNERS WHO WERE ORIGINAL MEMBERS OF TOBA IN 1920
("The Page," *Billboard*, 1920)

OWNERS	THEATRES	CITY / STATE
1. H. J. Hury	Gay	Birmingham, Al.
2. Milton Starr	Bijou	Nashville, Tn.
3. E. B. Dudley	Vaudette	Detroit, Mi.
4. E. C. Foster	Brooklyn	Wilmington, NC.
5. C. H. Turpin	Booker T. Washington	St. Louis, Mo.
6. N. C. Scales	Lafayette	Winston-Salem, NY.
7. M. A. Eightman	Plaza	Little Rock, Ak.
8. A. Barrasou	Place	Mimphis, Tn.
9. Charles F. Gordon	Star	Shreveport, La.
10. J. J. Miller	Milo	Charleston, SC.
11. T. S. Tinley	Lyceum	Cincinnati, Oh.
12. C. H. Douglass	Douglass	Macon, Ga.
13. Sam E. Reevin	Liberty	Chattanooga, Tn.
14. William Warley	Lincoln	Louisville, Ky.
15. Bordeaux and Bennett	Lyric	New Orleans, La.
16. Clemmons Brow	Lincoln	Beaumount Tx.
17. F. C. Holden	Liberty	Chattanooga, Tn.
18. C. C. Schreiner	Pike	Mobile, Al.
19. Chintz Moore	Park	Dallas, Tx.
20. W. H. Leonard	Gayety	Waco, Tx.
21. Lee and Moore	Lincoln	Galveston, Tx.
22. C. H. Cattey	American	Houston Tx.
23. W. J. Stiles	Strand	Jacksonville, Fl.
24. K. W. Talbutt	New Royal	Columbia, SC.
25. Bordeaux, Bennett & Gordon	Majestic	Montgomery, Al.
26. W. J. Stiles	Pekin	Savannah, Ga.
27. O. J. Harris	Grand Central	Cleveland, O.
28. E. S. Stone	Washington	Indianapolis, In.
29. Lawrence Goldman	Lincoln	Kansas City, Mo.
30. Breaux and Whitlow	Aldridge	Oklahoma City, Ok.
31. L. T. Brown	Dreamland	Tulsa, Ok.

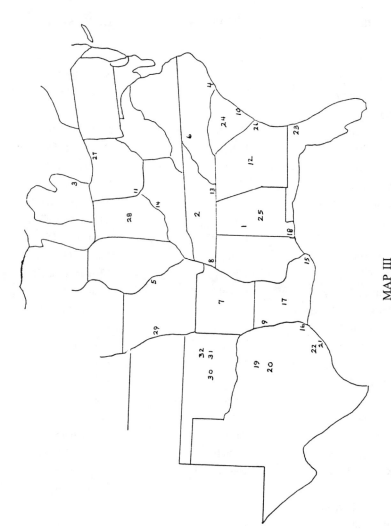

MAP III

Theatre owners who were original members of TOBA in 1920 ("The Page," *Billboard*, 1920).

whom Starr selected as Special Eastern Representative of the TOBA in late September of that year. Gibson, an astute showman and all-around businessman, was a pioneer producer who owned the Standard and Dunbar Theaters in Philadelphia, which Jackson considered "one of the finest theaters playing road shows and dramas to black audiences in the country."[15]

Jackson maintained that the "feud" could only benefit the performers and that it would mean more shows with larger costs. Given that initially Jackson supported the TOBA it might appear that he was serving the best interests of that organization; or that he recognized that it had the potential of being the largest employer of black talent in the country.

"The Page" remained entrenched in the "feud," publishing advertisements and commentaries from all sides to keep readers informed about the latest developments on the circuit. To keep the issues in the public's eye, "The Page" solicited first-hand reports from personalities within the circuits. The more bitter and frequent complaints from the field dealt with poor routing, segregated audiences, and salary disputes. Jackson felt that these issues retarded the advancement of black vaudeville in general and limited economic opportunities in particular.

The Poor Routing Issue

In the February 2, 1921 issue "As 'The Page' Predicted," Jackson spoke of a three-cornered struggle between the independent houses, TOBA, and the Southern Consolidated Circuit over the control of theatricals supported by black patronage. The "feud" was primarily between the latter two. Since both circuits were in good shape financially, Jackson speculated that the circuits could offer more big colored shows to the public for the next season. Although Consolidated claimed thirty houses and TOBA listed twenty, Jackson wanted to know if the circuits would alleviate the routing problem.[16]

Jackson cited a typical route that saps the life out of circuits: "An act was offered St. Louis to follow Philadelphia. The act gets around $400 for ten people. The fare is $34.60 each. Another act was jumped from Cincinnati to Shreveport, Louisiana. The fare is only about $30."[17] Taking into consideration the prevailing prices, Jackson questioned how much profit a team could make when it has to jump from San Antonio to Shreveport, just a bit more than 400 miles on a salary of fifty dollars a week? To Jackson, it seemed possible to route an act in such a way as not to spend all the salary on travel; but there seemed to be no way of including the routing in the contracts (see Map IV).

By May 28, 1921 "The Page" revealed that the number of theatre houses represented by the TOBA and the Southern Consolidated Circuit had grown from 50 to 80 or more; but, what affected the houses was competitive bidding for the better attractions, and the inability of circuits to control houses at points necessary to break long and expensive jumps. Martin Klein, S. H. Dudley and E. L. Cummings met with TOBA officials to discuss these concerns. The representatives accepted TOBA's proposal to absorb the Southern Consolidated circuit, but they did not resolve the pertinent issue of poor routing that resulted in long jumps.[18]

Theater houses that could help bridge this gap wavered between joining one of the circuits or remaining independent. Some, wanting certain attractions, were going to the circuit that could produce the desired act at the required time. Jackson reported that there were about 100 houses in the eleven states involved; that the "feud" directly affected over 2,000 black performers who desired continuous employment; and that there were at least sixty large vaudeville companies, forty "tabloid" companies, 140 teams, and over eighty single acts affected by the struggle over who would control the circuit.

Meanwhile, summer of 1921 was very hot, forcing many theaters to close until the opening of the fall season. At the end of the summer, the TOBA reopened with twenty-five vaudeville theaters and adopted a new policy of offering smaller companies for the new 1921-22 season. The intention was to furnish bookings for the better acts. Since the public favored vaudeville acts that required fewer people, the companies reduced the size of the acts from eight to ten people. One advantage of this move that benefited the actor and theater owners was that for the first time, acts and companies were routed throughout the Eastern half of the United States from one central booking point which reduced transportation cost.[19]

With the formation of the Managers' and Performers' Circuit in March 1922, under the direction of E. L. Cummings (see Map V), Jackson felt the new circuit had the potential to alleviate the routing problem. The M. & P Circuit reported to "The Page" new additions to its list of houses in the West and Texas that made it purportedly the largest black circuit in existence; but it came into conflict with the TOBA. In the March 25, 1922 edition of "The Page," a headline captioned "Battle on Between Managers' and Performers' and TOBA" signaled the start of the "feud." At the first M.

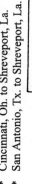

TOBA ROUTES:

1. Chicago, IL - Home Office
2. St. Louis, Mo - Booker T. Washington Theater
3. Nashville, Tn. - The Bijou Theater
4. Chattanooga, Tn. - Liberty Theater
5. Birmingham, Al. - Frolic Theater
6. Atlanta, Ga. - 81 Theater
7. Memphis, Tn - Palace Theater
8. New Orleans, La. - Lyric Theater
9. Durham, N. C. - Durham Civic Aud.
10. Norfolk. Va. - Palace Theater
11. Baltimore, Mo - Royal Theater

* Philadelphia, Pa. to St. Louis, Mo.
* Cincinnati, Oh. to Shreveport, La.
* San Antonio, Tx. to Shreveport, La.

Map IV
Vaudeville Routes, Circa Early 1920s.

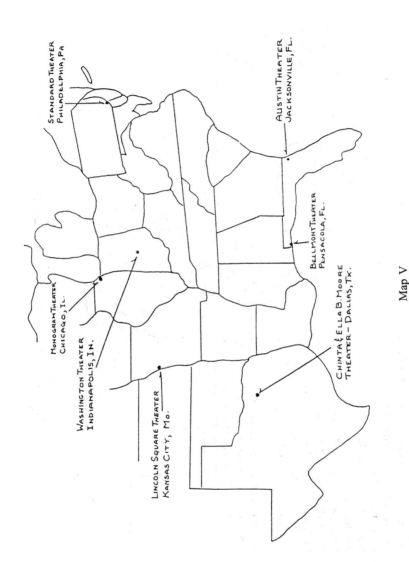

Map V

Managers' and Performers' Circuit ("The Page," 24 July 1922).

& P, July 24, 1922, stockholders were most enthusiastic over the fast growth of the new circuit. They elected E. L. Cummings as head of the organization, owner of the Belmont Theater in Pensacola, Florida, and former president of the Southern Consolidated Circuit that TOBA absorbed about a year earlier. Jackson mentioned the wealth of experience the newly elected officers brought to the new body: Vice-President John T. Gibson, a former Eastern Representative of the TOBA was the wealthiest black man in the amusement world. The Chairman of the Board of Directors, Martin Klein, formerly with the Southern Consolidated, owned the Monogram, a small house in Chicago and one in the suburb, was a vaudeville agent who had long specialized in headlining black acts. The Secretary, S. A. Austin, better known as "Buddy" Austin, owned a theater in Jacksonville, Florida. He too was black. Mrs. E. L. Cummings was Treasurer. Other owners on the circuit were E. S. Stone of the Washington Theater in Indianapolis, Indiana; Lawrence Goldman of the Lincoln Square Theater in Kansas City, Missouri; and Park in Texas. Chintz Moore and his wife Ella B., both blacks, were instrumental in the development of black entertainment in that state.[20]

Jackson watched the fight for the control of black theatricals, or more specifically, for the control of the conditions, but he found it difficult to predict who was winning. Many of the closed houses were either uncommitted or being claimed by both offices. Jackson also received conflicting reports on the quality of the acts and the theaters committed to the circuits. As an advisable check on some of the wild self-press agenting forwarded to the column, Jackson assigned correspondents unknown to actors, managers, or agents to report on the acts. "The Page" verified the information through similar reports in three other cities. Jackson's contention was that "only merit could command such uniform approbation."[21] By the summer's end in 1922, two authorized personnel representing "The Page" reviewed TOBA acts at The Star 1 Theater, in Shreveport, Louisiana and the Frolic and Star in Birmingham and Bessemer, Alabama—Wesley Vernell reported on the former and Billy Chambers on the latter. Before the new 1923-24 season opened, there was no indication of a compromise between the circuits. Jackson felt that if something did not change soon, the black actor would find himself in an awkward position. Neither circuit could offer a full season's work, nor offer a route that did not require the greater part of the actor's transportation.

Peace came between the TOBA and M. & P black circuits before the end of the year (1922). "The Page" was not privy to how this came about, but was informed that the organizations adjusted difficulties by establishing four regional offices with divided authority. This move eliminated much of the traveling. After a half year of "warfare," they reached a compromise agreement that gave regional offices virtual control its his territory. It is not clear what Jackson's influence was in the amalgamation of the two circuits; but, considering his editorials pushed for steady employment and the elimination of long jumps, his ideas may have affected their decisions. In the December 16, 1922 annual survey, "The Year With the Colored Performer," Jackson endorsed the idea of adding new houses and arranging booking that promised continuous work for the performers. He stated: "Since the TOBA is pretty well divided into four distinct groups of theaters . . . with a minimum of over forty houses and a maximum possibility of more than a hundred in the association. . . . It gives the acts a route over each of these sections, with the minimum of 'layoffs ' between the groups."[22]

Under the new arrangement, S. H. Dudley of Washington, D. C. would handle the booking of acts in the territory from Pittsburgh, East and as far South as the North Carolina border. E. L. Cummings at Pensacola, Florida, would care for the 15 houses in the extreme Southeastern States and along the Gulf Coast. Martin Klein of Chicago would route the acts over five houses in Ohio, Michigan, Illinois, and Indianapolis. The office of the general manager of the association, Sam Reevin in Chattanooga, would handle The Middle South and the Southwest. This consisted of nearly thirty houses (see Table 3, Map VI).

The arrangement had the potential for much improved routing, but would the circuit keep the performer busy? Jackson asked this question after receiving a letter from an act that complained while working at two independent houses, the Temple Theater in Cleveland and the Lincoln Theater in Kansas City. The letter stated that the newly organized circuit intimidated acts for working at another theater while on their circuit. Jackson explained: "that these houses do not have circuit franchises is a matter between the houses and the circuit, and it's unfair for the latter to be against acts for playing them . . . since they are at liberty and have the time to do so is proof positive that the circuit is not keeping the acts busy."[23] He modified his statement, however, saying that an act cannot expect to play an opposition house and a circuit house in the same town, but felt that threatening an act was unacceptable. He also reminded the TOBA that the court took action against other circuits for similar actions.

Table 3: (see Map VI)
UNITS OF THE COMBINED T.O.B.A. AND M. & P. CIRCUIT
("The Page," *Billboard*, December 16, 1922)

THEATER	CITY	MANAGER

A). HOUSES BOOKED FROM THE CHATTANOOGA OFFICE

1. Bijou	Nashville, Tn.	Martin Starr
2. Liberty	Chattanooga, Tn.	Sam E. Reevis
3. Palace	Memphis, Tn.	A. Barrasso
4. Star	Shreveport, La.	J. A. Welsh
5. Lyric	New Orleans, La.	M. Bourdreaux
6. Dreamland	Tulsa, Ok.	Zella N. Breaux
7. Aldridge	Oklahoma City, Ok.	L. T. Williams
8. Majestic	Montgomery, Al.	I. Berger
9. Frolc	Birmingham, Al.	H. J. Hury
10. "81"	Atlanta Ga.	Charles. P. Bailey
11. Douglas	Macon, Ga.	C. H. Douglass
12. Bellinger	San Antonio, Tx.	Luke A. Scott
13. LaFayette	Winston-Salem, N. C.	W. S. Scales
14. Rex	Charlotte, N. C.	S. W. Craver
15. Lincoln	Cincinnati, Oh.	Lew W. Henry
16. New Queen	Anniston, Al.	S. J. Reave
17. Booker T. Wash.	St. Louis, Mo.	C. H. Turpin
18. Lincoln	Louisville, Ky.	F. C. Dillon
19. Truman	Hot Springs, Ak.	M. Lightman
20. Plaza	Little Rock, Ak.	M. Lightman
21. Liberty	Galveston, Tx.	Jim Brown
23. Royal	Columbia, S. C.	L. T. Lester, Jr.
24. Rink	Port Arthur, Tx.	Jim Brown
25. Glove	Cleveland, Oh.	Bob Dravis
26. Lincoln	Charelston, S. C.	Sam Bonov
27. Venus	Memphis, Tn.	A. Barrasso
28. Star	Meridian, Ms.	R. C. Catcher

B) HOUSES BOOKED FROM THE CHICAGO OFFICE

1. Monogram	Chicago, Il.	H. B. Miller
2. Grand Central	Cleveland, Oh.	O. J. Harris
3. Koppin	Detroit, Mi.	E. B. Dudley
4. Wahington	Indianapolis, In.	E. S. Stone
5. Star	Pittsburgh, Pa.	H. Tennenbaum

C) HOUSES BOOKED FROM THE WASHINGTON OFFICE

1. Mid City	Washington, D. C.	S. H. Dudley
2. Foraker	"	"
3. Dudley	"	"
4. Blue Mouse	"	"
5. Palace	Norfolk, Va.	?
6. Hippodrome	Danville, Va.	?
7. Colonial	Newport News, Va.	?
8. Lincoln	Baltimore, Md.	?
9. Star	"	?
10. Hippodrome	Richmond, Va.	?
11. Dudley	Petersburgh, Va.	?

D) HOUSES BOOKED FROM THE PENSACOLA OFFICE

1. Belmont	Pensacola, Fl.	E. L. Cummings
2. Strand	Jacksonville, Fl.	Buddy Austin
3. Palace	Tampa, Fl.	?
4. Dream	St. Petersburg, Fl.	?
5. Lyric	Miami, Fl.	?
6. Lyric	Ocala, Fl.	?
7. Pekin	Savannah, Ga.	J. W. Jennings
8. Palace	Agusta, Ga	James Patterson
9. Morton	Athens, Ga.	?
10. Dream	Columbus, Ga.	G. S. Love
11. Star	Gulfport, Mi.	?
12. Pike	Mobile, Al.	?
13. American	Houston, Al.	?
14. Dreamland	Texarkana, Ak.	J. N. Jones
15. Liberty	Greenville, Ak.	Robert Wilson

*?: manager unknown

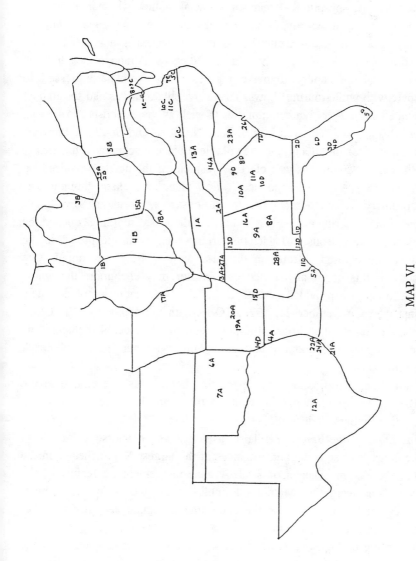

MAP VI

Units of the Combined TOBA and M & P Circuit ("The Page," *Billboard*, 16 Dec. 1922).

The Issue of Segregated Theatres

Along with poor routing, segregated theatres was another key issue that Jackson felt was retarding the growth of black vaudeville. The American stage since its inception maintained a racial policy whether it was in minstrelsy, musical comedy, or in the established American stage. Shut out of playing to the major legitimate theatre audiences, black artists were limited to performing for largely colored audiences. Although they had the skills, it was not enough to make a profit. They were hard pressed to compete with white touring shows. To survive, black artists had to build an audience within their own communities as well as the established American stage. Despite racial conventions in both Northern and Southern theatres, "The Page" brought attention to the volatile subject of segregated theatres.

When E. L. Cummings was elected President of the newly organized M. & P. August 1, 1922, he announced a new plan that Jackson thought was extraordinary. At his Belmont Theatre in Pensacola, Florida, a "key" house on the circuit catering exclusively to black audiences, Cummings opened the doors to white patrons.[24] Under this arrangement white people sit in the balcony and colored patrons on the first floor. "The Page" noted, "the success of this policy at the Belmont Theater may encourage the whole circuit to adopt it provided of course that local sentiment is not definitely against it."[25] On October 25, 1922, TOBA with the addition of the Globe Theater in Cleveland on Fifty-Fifth and Woodland Avenue, also changed its policy by opening its doors to patrons of both races and using both black and white acts.

With slight modifications, however, this policy was not unique to the TOBA. The idea of admitting white patrons at black theatres was an innovation by Sam Zerilla, in 1909, on the original TOBA, says Paul *Oliver in The Story of the Blues.* "Zerilla set aside shows on Thursday for whites and coloureds at separate performances at the largest Negro theater in the South, the Pastime Theater on Beale Avenue in Memphis, a feature of the presentations were the 'Midnight Rambles'—late shows in which blues were especially popular, and these became a regular feature of TOBA theaters throughout the South."[26]

According to Jackson, however, it was Jerry Thomas, manager of the Lyric Theater in New Orleans, who renewed interest in this policy on November 11, 1920 when Perrin & Anderson returned the Lyric Road Show to the Lyric Theater after a year's absence in the East. The company of talented artists included: Slim Henderson, Iris Hall, George Wiltshire, Ines

Dender, Helen Daily, Rosa Henderson, Ida Wilson, Willie Eldridge, Mattie Spencer, and Isabel Johnson. They opened the Lyric's season of "Midnight Revues" twice a month for whites only.

Jackson provided a fuller account of these "revues" under the subject heading "New Orleans Theater Establishes Unique Policy" in the 20 November edition of "The Page": "The Theater would close after the regular performance and again reopen at 11:30 p. m. to white patrons only. Invitations [were] issued to the newspapers and hotels, which [gave] them out to their friends. Standing room only is the rule at these shows." He went on to say: "The Lyric Theater, with a seating capacity of eighteen hundred, was opened two years ago as a black house and today is the leading black theater in the South."[27] Within months the Gayety in St. Louis, and the Renaissance in Harlem picked up on the idea.

Irrespective of the success of the "Midnight Revues," the Attucks Theater in Norfolk, Virginia prohibited midnight performances because of racial codes. As of November 16, 1922, the Norfolk City Council passed an ordinance forbidding the Attucks Theater and any other theater in that city to give shows after midnight—this being the only theater in the city where these shows prevailed. Robert Levy had bought the house from a black syndicate based in New York. The City Council did not specify the names of the former owners but rejected the notion of "Midnight Revues" as an "unwholesome mingling of the races." Jackson, in a headline entitled "Forbids Midnight Shows," reported: "The Friday midnight shows at this house have been a source of income and at the same time have provided opportunity for such white people as were interested in colored shows to visit the theater. Its audience, regularly a colored one, was on these occasions augmented by a sprinkling of whites. . . . There may be some significance . . . that Mr. Levy is a New Yorker, since no notice was taken of the practice during the two years the theater was operated by local management."[28] On this point, Jackson's observations are noteworthy. Is he suggesting that Levy is unwelcome because he is a "Yankee" or because he is not one of the "good old boys"?

Ten months earlier at the TOBA's first annual meeting, the newly elected President, Clarence Bennett addressed this issue in the keynote speech on "tolerance." He took the position that maintaining a policy of segregated theatres on the circuit was in the best interests of the white and the colored man; that the black actor must be taught to respect his own color and race in his own theatres before colored audiences; and that he should not infringe upon the whites. "By doing this he will surely gain the respect of his white brother who has broken the way for him to civilization."[29] He asked every manager not to be led astray for the moment by the prospect of quick profits.

As expected, some voices from the black press and black theatre owners took exception to Bennett's paternalistic tone and endorsement of segregated theaters. Jackson clarified his position and the *Billboard*'s on the subject in a February 25, 1922 article under the heading of "Reaction of the Group on the Clarence Bennett Letter": "The opinions contained in the article . . . published by Mr. Bennett did not reflect the policy of the *Billboard* and . . . it did not believe in setting limitations on the colored performer."[30] Possibly because of social norms in the South and partly in deference to the TOBA. Jackson conceded: "The President of a theatrical circuit, of course, must view the business from many angles—its business possibilities, the people concerned in its management, what it has to offer to the public and the character of such entertainments."[31]

The clergy also took objection to the "Midnight Rambles," on moral grounds. The Reverend L. H. King, in a front-page editorial in the January 22 issue of *The Southwestern Christian Advocate*, opposed midnight performances that he considered indecent "riotous exhibitions of vulgarity and obscenity."[32] In addition, he advised Negro actors to dignify their profession by developing art that reflects the temperament of the times.

Jackson suggested that, "an excellent way to avoid such accusations is to do precisely as the white theaters do—set aside a section of the house for white patrons in Southern cities, encourage their attendance to the regular daily performances, and avoid such criticisms. Better still, permit both races to attend the midnight shows and there will be no occasion for any to doubt the propriety of what occurs at these midnight rambles."[33]

After a year-and-a-half of debating the issue of segregated theatres, however, Jackson seemed ambivalent with the idea in a January 31, 1925 article, in which he told of a Birmingham, Alabama city commissioner who prohibited the Frolic Theater management from presenting midnight performances to exclusively white audiences. The Frolic was one of a number of TOBA theaters to follow that practice. Jackson didn't know whether to hail the Birmingham commissioner's order as a blessing or not, since the box-office value of these midnight rambles were unquestioned; but he again raised the question: "Why don't the white people of Birmingham who like colored shows do as the folks in Macon, Georgia—

attend the regular performances. They would see the same attractions and not lose so much sleep. The Southern proprieties could be preserved in the usual manner, vis a` vis reserved section of seats."[34]

Along with the issue of segregated audiences at the "Midnight Rambles," Jackson received anonymous reports that neither TOBA nor M. & P. were paying artists for the additional midnight shows. The only allusion to this practice was in a May 30, 1925 article in "The Page" entitled "Being Fair to Everybody." It was an extract from the annual proclamation of I. H. Herk, President of the Mutual Burlesque Association (MBA), embodying the regulations for the operation of shows and theaters that comprise the circuit. Jackson prefaced the article by saying, "The extract is submitted here as a guide and suggestion to those interested in midnight productions in theaters playing exclusively colored attractions. The lesson in equitable treatment to show owners and performers is obvious. It represents that absolute fairness to which there can be no legitimate objection. Nothing but ignorance, selfishness and autocratic abuse of power could prompt any other arrangement."[35] The proclamation declared that theater owners will pay artists for each midnight show; and that TOBA will pay the theater owners one-twelfth or fourteenth of his show's guaranteed weekly salary. Whether the acts were paid or not, the practice of offering midnight shows in a few TOBA and M. & P. houses continued wherever theatre owners thought white audiences would support them and where the city ordinances would not restrict the circuits.

The Salary Discrepancy Issue

Inextricably bound within the subject of poor routing and segregated theatres is salary discrepancies—the third major issue that Jackson felt retarded the growth of the black vaudeville circuits. Black artists not only wanted to establish themselves on the American stage to increase marketability, but also to show that it was possible to make a living as an entertainer. Not paying acts for additional performances as was the case with the "Midnight Rambles" or paying low salaries, points to the numerous obstacles black performers had to overcome regarding salary disputes. One report that came to "The Page" complained about a policy on the new M. & P. Collington Hayes, owner of the High Steppers Show in Tampa, advised the profession to stay away from Florida, in that house managers were not giving black companies a fair deal. They fined his company $75 because two chorus "girls" went to a dance while playing a house on the circuit.

Hayes alleges that appeals to the heads of the organization failed to obtain an adjustment.[36] Another report was by a tab company owner playing the TOBA, who talked about a salary dispute involving a theater owner who withheld $50 from a chorus "girl's" salary for being absent from the cast. The prevailing price for the chorus members was $20 a week. The "fifty" was more than double the missing "girls" salary.[37] Yet another report described how a theater owner deducted money from a sick cast member. The proprietor also charged $9 more for transportation than had been advanced, and withdrew transportation costs from the week's pay of the show owner. Then there was a report that had to do with a sick woman who missed two performances and the theater owner obliged her to take a cut of $9 when she earned only $3.33 for two shows.[38] Finally, a report told of a manager who canceled a show, a standard one late in the week, so he might place an independent attraction that had taken his fancy.[39] Theatre owners as well as performers complained about fluctuating prices that the TOBA applied to franchises, ranging from no fee to thousands of dollars. Before we leave the subject of salary discrepancies, it is important to note, that for some artists the competition among agents and managers meant better salaries and better management. For example, Davis and Stafford, owners of the Wiff Wiff Warblers Company reported that they were receiving better treatment and finding the policy of the circuit satisfactory.[40]

Jackson's Proposal to Improve Conditions

Throughout the lifetime of "The Page," Jackson tried to find ways to improve conditions of black vaudeville circuits. In the matter of integrating theatre audiences, it did not appear that Jackson resolved this issue; but because of his persistence, theatre owners began to reconsider or change this policy long before the landmark desegregation decision was handed down by the United States Supreme Court in 1954.

In the matter of better salaries, Jackson felt that salaries were up to the acts: "If they accept them and sign to work for the sum specified, it is no longer the affair of any one but contracting parties."[41] Taking into consideration the high cost of living, Jackson thought it was unfair to engage acts at salaries that provide only a mere living, especially when the circuit re-routed the act and forced them to spend virtually all of their earnings on transportation costs.[42]

As one means of increasing a performer's salary, Jackson recommended that theatre managers reduce the number of acts on the bill. In 1922, when the TOBA and M. & P. divided the circuit into units, S. H. Dudley wanted to know what new ideas the black vaudeville acts and "tab" shows had to offer and what managers of colored theaters had in mind to influence acts and "tab" shows to get new material. Jackson suggested cutting down on quantity and providing more quality. Rather than play four acts and give them $60.00, he suggested that they play three and pay them the same amount. The bill would cost the same but the theatre would get a better class of act. It forces the acts to get better material, costume, and scenery for the bigger houses that expect larger things. He encouraged Actors and managers to get their heads together, call a meeting of managers, and have the actors select five delegates in the most convenient city and thrash things out; have the managers select a man from each section; then tax the manager a certain amount to provide expense money for both men and actors, since the acts could not afford to lose time and then pay their own expenses.[43]

Another means of increasing a performer's salary had to do with Jackson and Dudley's suggestion to classify acts at a tryout-house on the circuit, whereby an appointed official could inspect and censor all acts.[44] The circuits would invest this person with full authority as an adjuster or "super stage manager," a kind of overlord to the business at the demonstration theatre. He would "view each act, suggest changes, expurgations, make any alteration which in his mature judgment will improve the act, compel rehearsals and prevent too frequent repetition of song numbers. . . . This stage manager would classify acts as either 'A,' 'B,' or 'C,' and the established salaries will vary in accord with this classification."[45]

Reevin responding to the recommendation of a try-out house in Washington, D. C. issued a statement to "The Page" explaining why the TOBA would lose money on such a venture: "We [would] have to face the cold theaters of $200 a day expense, and this would include a salary for a critic to censor review and classify the acts, and we certainly do not expect to do $1,400 per week in a tryout house."[46] He also wanted to know who was going to put up the advance money and cover the weekly deficits at the Washington Theater to get refurbished? As to the suggestion by a performer to install four try-out houses one in Washington, Chattanooga, Chicago and Texas, Reevin retorted, "he failed to indicate any source or channel from where to derive the revenue to keep these houses going."[47] Starr shared Reevin's views on the classification of acts, stating that this would probably be one of the hardest tasks any agent had undertaken, since every actor considers himself the best and expects the highest salary.[48] From his observation, it seemed that neither side exactly understood the classification of acts and better salaries. Starr went on to say: "The managers seem to believe that the salaries they now pay are sufficient for the good act and the inferior get more than they deserve, and as some express it, 'are getting away with murder,' and on the other hand the better acts think that the salaries the managers pay now are not sufficient for the inferior acts, especially for their act, and both sides hope that the classification will help them."[49] He then noted that "after giving the matter some study and thought, the only logical solution seemed to be to pay better salaries to those who deserve it."[50] In closing, Starr emphasized that "patrons [would] much rather patronize a theater where they [were] welcome and where the front door was wide open for them, and when they find there is a good show worth their money, they will certainly patronize it, and once this is accomplished the managers will be able to pay better salaries and add an act or two on the weekly program. This will make more work and better salaries."[51]

Dudley's idea, however, was the most practical for Jackson. It was a modification of the proposal that the two outlined at the 28 March, 1923 meeting between the actors and managers. Dudley wanted to stabilize the black show business industry by having the acts exhibit their wares before starting over the circuit for the season; and to classify them according to entertainment merit and the value of the act as a box-office "draw." Jackson, however, objected to the use of the term "try-out houses," preferring that it be called a "demonstrating house," in that the former connotation implies abusive practices toward performers. Briefly, he outlined Dudley's proposal: "The house would be operated at a comparatively low scale of prices . . . and underwritten by all the managers on the TOBA circuit who profit by its results. A weekly donation of five dollars each is asked from them; any part of the fund thus created that may be unused [is] to be returned, as would any dividends that might accrue."[52] After that, Dudley talked about what happens to an act when it leaves the demonstration house: "They would not work for [peanuts], as they had often done for agents before, but for a salary sufficient to allow for the week's maintenance, plus enough to provide for the first jump."[53]

The TOBA officials approved the idea of a supervising stage manager and selected committee members to be in charge of the matter. They were:

"Dad" James, a performing producer of much experience; Joseph Watts, of the Watts brother's novelty team, and Telfair Washington, a performer who was also Secretary of the CAU. They were to work in conjunction with Messieurs Dudley and Reevin, who would select the theater, the city, the house staff, and handle the financing of the enterprise. Names placed in nomination for the position of "super" stage manager were: Robert Slater, an ex-performer and the present Secretary of the Colored Vaudeville Benefit Association (CVBA); Telfair Washington, Secretary of the CAU, and Cress Simmons, Manager of the National Theater of Baltimore. The committee sought other nominations as well.[54]

TOBA took no action on the "demonstration house" idea. A month after the meeting, however, Jackson received a letter from Milton Starr requesting space in its "valued publication." The letter touched on all the subjects inferred in the March 31 article. In part, Starr thanked Jackson and the *Billboard,* he expressed satisfaction over the interest in the Washington meeting stating that he agreed somewhat with the facts laid out; and he reminded the industry that "white circuits have gone through the same sort of period, and considering the improvements wrought in the past four or five years, one could only be very optimistic. Allow us a few more years and all the innovations suggested by yourself and Mr. Dudley will be in actual operation."[55]

About the "demonstration house" Star agreed with Mr. Reevin that it was not feasible at that time. He quickly brought to mind that over the past several months, he used his own theater, the Bijou at Nashville, as a sort of a try-out house to bring in the better and larger attractions. He said that if acts were successful, then they would book them on the rest of the time. By way of illustration, he points out that he recently brought the Lafayette Players for their opening arrangement on the circuit and that their appearance was "successful beyond [his] fondest hopes. . . And now they . . . have set full sail for a tour of practically all the larger TOBA houses."[56] To substantiate this statement, he explained, "I had to take quite a gamble bringing the company all the way from Philadelphia and playing them on a guarantee. I have started many other attractions out on the circuit on the same set up, among them being Sarah Milton, Josie and others." He vowed that "In the future, I shall always . . . play acts that have merit and will bring them to Nashville from any point in the country."[57] He then deferred the idea of a try-out house to a later date that might be more practical for the organization.

Regarding the proposal to classify acts, Starr stated, "Mr. Reevin [is] working out a system that will be in operation and which I am certain will be universally satisfactory."[58] On the subject of "big time salaries," he declared, after citing his years of experience and observations, that "the actor is worth just as much as he is able to draw at the box office. . . . Mediocre acts never earn their salary, while the latter class act more than earns his. The trend of public favor is apparently to the better class act, and the act of mediocre caliber is being crowded out. . . . The agent is wary in this matter. If he raises salaries that means the closing of houses."[59] In closing, he tried to make it clear that "The matter of setting salaries [was] a very delicate matter and one that requires an intimate knowledge of all conditions."[60] The opening of the New Roosevelt Theater in New York was a sign that better salaries were forthcoming and that business was picking up on the TOBA. "The Page" reported one of the largest crowds ever that attended an opening of a theater. The first two shows sold out months in advance. The opening bill consisted of The Woodens, a famous bicycle act, Claude Underwood (Whistling Pete), Harris and Harris, and Carter and Clark. Paul Carter, a producer who was at the opening, was optimistic about the results that will accrue with salaries. He speculated that there were acts on the circuit drawing from $130.00 to $450.00; and others were getting $1,000 or more for touring the circuit. He also revealed that he was going to put out a comedy sketch on the circuit called "Mariah," that he would book at a satisfactory salary.[61]

In the matter of routing, Jackson devised a plan to organize the black vaudeville circuit that might eliminate long jumps:

> We have theaters that equal any in the country, talent that ranks with the best, producers willing to spend real money on shows, and a public that is amusement hungry. All that is necessary is to co-ordinate these elements. . . . The first necessity . . . is to separate the smaller houses from the larger ones. Each is essential, but each has a field distinctly its own. They function differently and have different needs. Theaters of the two types on the same circuit . . . always means confusion.

> There are a number of theaters with sufficient seating capacity that have stage sizes and equipment for the handling of the bigger shows. Offering these houses for booking purposes with an office in N. Y. would encourage producers interested in this field to provide attractions of goodly size and quality. Dramatic companies, musical comedies, revues, spectaculars, and vaudeville combinations would at once be available in sufficient numbers and variety to create; and what's more important to a regular clientele for these houses.

Three weeks of musical comedy, a week of smut-clean vaudeville, two weeks of drama, two weeks of big revue, another week of vaudeville, then repeat. This would make a fair schedule that should hold patronage at a profitable scale of prices, provided that only the quality was maintained by proper supervision. Twenty big houses—even a dozen with the possibility of some additions and some occasional dates in white theaters would justify productions that would be real draws.

The smaller houses could then be organized in accord with the needs of their patronage with great ease. Let Keith's with its 'big time' and its family circuit, the Orpheum and Orpheum, Jr., or Loew's Circuit . . . , convey a message to you who own the houses catering to Negroes. If Klaw & Erlianger and the Shuberts with more experience, more capital and wealthier patronage at their command find this the intelligent thing to do, would it not be well for you to heed.[62]

Neither circuit responded to Jackson's proposals, but Milton Starr adapted Jackson's idea of offering a greater variety of entertainment for the patrons. Starr notified "The Page" that he was personally conducting a tour of the Andrew Bishop-Cleo Desmond Players through the biggest houses of the circuit. C. P. McClane, Manager of the Royal Theater in Philadelphia, was handling the business of the drama group. They opened at Starr's theater, the Bijou, April 2, with a route that included Memphis, Shreveport, New Orleans, Jacksonville, Charleston, and Savannah. Jackson emphasized that the whole show world will watch with considerable interest this experiment of sandwiching dramatic shows between the vaudeville weeks.[63]

A prominent theatrical man of the far West also requested detailed information on the present state of black vaudeville. Another, the Coleman Brothers, owners and managers of the Lafayette Theater in New York, were in accord with any project that sought to coordinate efforts of managers to secure a better and more dependable supply of entertainment for the houses.

But theater owners wanted to know: "who would be appointed to lead them out of the wilderness of uncertain bookings?" A pertinent question that Jackson sought to remedy. "The answer," Jackson replied, "will disclose a man capable of reorganizing three different types of owners broad-minded enough to see the immense possibilities of a stabilized and a systematized industry, and a command of sufficient confidence from the theater owners and managers to compel them thru the naturally trying preliminary states."[64] Jackson volunteered his services to be the agency through which those interested might assemble. Moreover, he suggested that managers get in touch with the Coleman Brothers as a start in the right direction.

At the second annual TOBA meeting in January, 1923, S. H. Dudley adopted the suggestion by Jackson to appoint an adjustor or super agent, with modifications. Dudley pointed out that "Will Hays had accomplished wonders in the motion picture business, and Judge Landis had done the same for the baseball game. . . . We need a man to act in similar capacity for the colored vaudeville actors and managers. . . . He must be a man familiar with the problems of both, one who knows the difficulties that beset the box office as well as back stage, with the ability to suggest reforms and the courage to enforce them . . . a man who commands the respect and confidence of both managers and artists, and whose dictums will be obeyed. At present if an act or artist is mistreated by a manager, he is without protection. The booking agent can afford him little assistance, for after all he is a member of the association of managers."[65] At that point Dudley, reemphasizing the importance of a person familiar with their field of endeavor, nominated "The Page's" J. A. Jackson of the *Billboard*. He is a sober, clean-thinking man, well acquainted with the theatrical situation in general and our field in particular."[66] Jackson, the "unofficial representative of the artists," was unable to attend the meeting, felt that this was highest compliment one could receive; but despite the commendation, he graciously declined the appointment. He thanked Dudley more for recognizing this need than for the recommendation; but he believed that it would be better for him to continue working in an area that he could serve well than to accept the position of immense responsibility and fail to measure up to his duty. He saw the post as being too important to the show folks to be directed by someone who might abandon it. He assured Dudley, however, that when the circuit selects a person, "The Page" would lend its assistance and support. He also expressed his gratitude for the organization's recognition of the *Billboard* as the recorder of the race artist's progress, and the unofficial counselor for their defense.[67] S. H. Dudley addressed the idea of a booking agent in more detail a few months later.

On March 28, 1923, black actors and managers met in Washington, D. C. in the office of S. H. Dudley to discuss ways to improve conditions on the vaudeville circuits. Jackson described the affair as "the greatest single advancement in the business since the opening of the colored theaters."[68] About forty artists, who played in the sixty-seven theaters composing the circuit, were present. Telfair Washington and J. S. Watts represented the performers; Dudley and Reevin, the TOBA Jackson chaired the meeting. Performers and acts read letters sanctioning the conference. The committees discussed better salaries, the sanctity of the contracts, the time limit on contracts and its variations, costumes and their attendance, deportment, the vaudeville unit, and the ideal tabloid company. No immediate solutions were forthcoming at this preliminary meeting. Only a limited number of managers were present and artists were unprepared and unauthorized to speak for the other performers—most of whom were there to perform in the Capital area.

By October of 1923, Jackson's report showed that a number of theaters in the combined TOBA and M. & P. units had grown to an imposing size and strength remedying many of the problems of salaries and long jumps. The TOBA was routing vaudeville through at least fifty houses; S. H. Dudley, the Washington magnet, was booking about nineteen houses in the Eastern territory, five of them his own; and Cummings' M. & P also showed signs of growth. But there were signs of a break. The first indication involved a group of theaters that were wavering between what circuit they wanted to side with. Some were considering the proposal for a routing of road shows into their Theaters by Messieurs Koppin and E. B. Dudley of the Koppin Theater in Detroit. Another sign had to do with Cummings, the head of M. & P. Apparently, he placed advertisements in black newspapers seeking talent for tabloids in large numbers.[69] Jackson felt that the defection would not greatly affect TOBA, since most of the theaters involved larger independent theaters, but thought it might have a direct bearing upon Cumming's circuit.

The TOBA resolved the threat of a break at a Nashville meeting, May 21, 1925. E. L. Cummings, president and general manager of M. & P. and Sam Reevin, general managers of the TOBA were present. Cummings announced that they had negotiated a cooperative contract that would ensure smoother operation of acts over the two circuits. Jackson stated, "this would probably obviate the congestion of acts that has often occurred in extreme Southern cities."[70] Eventually the circuit grew to include over eighty Theaters.

By July of 1924, the TOBA was almost three and a half years old. Milton Starr, President, noted: "With the co-operation brought on through this amalgamation process, it was easier to attract locals to invest in black theater. Theater owners were now permitted to use attractions that until recently only played to metropolitan audiences. By sending metropolitan attractions to the 'provinces' the TOBA enhanced the value of all local Negro theater investments and also encouraged the building of numerous theaters in towns that previously had no such place of amusement. . . . They were able to offer better routing and resolve many of the problems of long breaks."[71]

Starr also answered accusations by artists, of "being laid off so that they could be 'handled easier.'" He denied the charges in a letter to "The Page" stating, "it was a manifestation of the universal law of supply and demand."[72] He then explained the organization's policy toward theater houses that were "wobbly" and why TOBA permitted local managers considerable sway in the selection of the attractions they played: "The Negro theater, even with the assistance of the organization methods offered by the TOBA is still an uncertain venture outside the larger cities. According to the local managers, operaters as a rule operate . . . , on a frugal scale, if all of the theaters booked by the TOBA were certain and consistent money-makers, it would be a very simple matter of routing all attractions intact over the entire circuit. However, that is not the case. When a theater is in the TOBA, it does everything in its power to keep the house going until it is self operating. Through this period they cannot play all attractions. . . . Only the money-makers."[73] Turning his attention to the performer, Starr explained that "The policy of the TOBA to keep the 'weak' houses going was an advantage to [artists] and at the same time provided about twice as much work for [acts] than if we should let all of the weaker houses drop. . . . In taking care of the fifty percent cost deficit of weaker houses we cannot force them to take all shows in routing. The price of some of our shows would be prohibitive to them and the house would close or go into pictures."[74] In closing, Starr reemphasized TOBA's policy:

-that twice as many houses stay open;
-that the performer is provided with twice as many weeks' work;
-that the performer of recognized ability has a premium on his
 services. [75]

At the beginning of the 1924-25 season, TOBA informed "The Page" that better conditions would prevail the next season for meritorious acts or headliners. They promised fewer layoffs, more consecutive work and better routing to follow the shaking-out process that had been going on for two years. Their goal was to eliminate the undesirable and unprogressive acts. Stressing the point that "the fittest will survive," Jackson explained that more than four-hundred acts were available for a circuit that could keep steadily employed about half that number.[76] Infrequently, he published the routing of acts on the circuit. The last report in "The Page" on the TOBA circuit disclosed that the circuit was playing twenty-six tabloid companies and 100 vaudeville acts in fifty-three theaters to a daily seating capacity of slightly more than 40,000 patrons.[77]

The question remains: What impact did "The Page" have on improving conditions on the TOBA? Theater owners and performers did not resolve all the problems on the circuits; but taking into consideration that there was very little coverage of the TOBA in race papers other than paid publicity, Jackson's concern with conditions on the TOBA circuit kept the issues in the public eye and provided a platform for both the circuit and performer. Therefore, without columns such as "The Page" acting as a watchdog over the circuit, artists for one would not have had much representation. If the TOBA were interested in improving conditions to maximize their drawing power, then they too needed comments and direction from those close to the industry such as Jackson and readers of "The Page." The influence that the column had on the TOBA may not be measured through tangible examples; however, the changes within the circuit may have been influenced by suggestions brought forth by Jackson. More locals invested in theaters. Milton Starr tried-out Jackson and Dudley's idea of a try-out house at many of the Southern houses with the Lafayette Players. Salaries improved for the better acts. There was better routing once the TOBA merged with the M. & P. Circuit. Theaters paid classified acts according to their rating, thereby forcing acts to change their material to achieve a higher rating. This improved the quality of their act and offered more variety to the audiences.

The combined circuits did not formally adapt the idea of an adjuster or "super stage manager"; but on January 16, 1925, they appointed a white Press Agent, W. R. Arnold, as director of publicity to oversee activities on the circuit. Arnold was formerly a *Billboard* representative at Nashville where he did the publicity for various traveling amusement enterprises. By April of the same year, he edited a column in "The Page" under the title of "Arnold's News of the TOBA Circuit." By then, Billy Chambers and Wesley Vernell, two blacks, each had a regular column covering TOBA acts at the Frolic Theater, Birmingham, and the Star Theater, in Shreveport, respectively; but Arnold reported on the activity of performers on the circuit and on the officials in the organization. An example of his report read in part:

> President Milton Starr . . . in Louisville to lay out a route for Mame Smith. The blues singer and her company are dated to play a series of white theaters in Tennessee and Kentucky, going to the Palace in Memphis, March 30, and the Roosevelt in Cincinnati, April 6.
>
> Sandy Burns has a two-week engagement at the Strand, Jacksonville. Bob Russell has gone into the 81 Theater, Atlanta, for an indefinite stay.
>
> Ida Cox is in the Grand Theater, Chicago, and doing recordings between performances. Bessie Smith closed her tour at New Orleans to jump into New York to record.
>
> 'Sunshine' Sammy is in Louisville for the week of April 6. Quintard Miller spends the week in Indianapolis.
>
> Butterbeans and Susie have been set back for two weeks due to illness of Mrs. Edwards. Maggie Jones, a new blues singer, is having her route arranged.[78]

These artists represent the top-name entertainers who commanded large salaries in the mid-1920s. Taking into account that the TOBA was just four-and-a-half-years old when "The Page" closed, the improvements were crucial to the advancement of black performance. During Jackson's time for the next five years, before the circuit disbanded, TOBA was the largest employer of black talent. Although black performers were seldom seen by white audiences, the TOBA provided a training ground for performers and a place to hone their talent. Circuits paid high salaries to the top-notch entertainers. This opportunity to gain experience and acclaim was necessary for many artists to find employment during the difficult years of the Depression. By this time, top-name entertainers were appearing in night clubs, a few in white shows, and some in motion pictures. Until then, without the voice of a column like "The Page," the acronym for the organization had remained "Tough on Black Actors."

Notes

[1] Douglas Gilbert, *American Vaudeville: Its Life and Times* (New York: Dover Publications, Inc. 1940) 1.

[2] James Haskins, *Black Theater in America* (New York: Thomas Y. Crowell, 1982) 62, 63.

[3] Ibid.

[4] "Long jumps" were determined by the distances performers had to travel on a train from one city to the next and the time it took them. Some jumps took as many as one or

two days.

[5] Haskins, 63.
[6] Henry Sampson, *Blacks in Blackface* (Metuchen, New Jersey: Scarecrow Press, 1980) 43-44.
[7] James Weldon Johnson, *Black Manhattan* (New York: Atheneum, 1975) 74.
[8] Douglas Gilbert, *American Vaudeville: Its Life and Times* (New York: Dover Publications, Inc. 1940) 11.
[9] James Albert Jackson "Starr Candidly Discusses Circuit Conditions," *Billboard* 7 July 1924: 46.
[10] Paul Oliver, *The Story of the Blues* (Radnor, Pennsylvania: Chilton Book Company, 1982) 70.
[11] Ibid.
[12] Sampson, 16.
[13] J. A. Jackson, *Billboard* 12 Feb. 1922: 43.
[14] Ibid., 15 Jan. 1921: 17.
[15] Ibid.
[16] Ibid., 5 Feb. 1921: 42.
[17] Ibid., 14 July 1923: 50.
[18] Ibid., 28 May 1921: 45.
[19] Ibid., "Business Conditions," *Billboard* 6 Aug. 1921: 65.
[20] Ibid., "Battle on Between Managers and Performers and TOBA," *Billboard* 25 Mar. 1922: 45.
[21] Ibid., 15 July 1922: 42.
[22] Ibid., "The Year with the Colored Performer," *Billboard* 16 Dec. 1922: 87.
[23] Ibid.
[24] Ibid., 26 Aug. 1922: 42-43.
[25] Ibid.
[26] Oliver, 70.
[27] Jackson, "New Orleans Theater Establishes Unique Policy," *Billboard* 20 Nov. 1920: 45.
[28] Ibid., 25 Nov. 1922: 48.
[29] Ibid., "TOBA Elections," *Billboard* 4 Feb. 1922: 45.
[30] Ibid.
[31] Ibid.
[32] Ibid., 14 Feb. 1925: 52.
[33] Ibid.
[34] Ibid., "Picked up by the Page," *Billboard* 31 Jan. 1925: 50.
[35] Ibid., "Being Fair to Everybody," *Billboard* 30 May 1925: 48.
[36] Ibid., 7 Oct. 1922: 49.
[37] Ibid., "Things that Hurt," *Billboard* 14 July 1923: 50.
[38] Ibid.
[39] Ibid.
[40] Ibid., 19 Feb. 1921: 38.
[41] Ibid., "Things that Hurt," *Billboard* 14 July 1923: 50.
[42] Ibid.
[43] Ibid., "TOBA Elections," *Billboard* 20 Jan. 1923: 50.
[44] Ibid., 7 Apr. 1923: 48.
[45] Ibid.
[46] Ibid., 14 Apr. 1923: 50.

[47] Ibid.
[48] Ibid.
[49] Ibid.
[50] Ibid.
[51] Ibid.
[52] Ibid., 7 Apr. 1923: 48.
[53] Ibid.
[54] Ibid.
[55] Ibid., 12 May 1923: 52.
[56] Ibid., 20 Oct. 1923: 56.
[57] Ibid.
[58] Ibid.
[59] Ibid.
[60] Ibid.
[61] Ibid.
[62] Ibid., "Organizing Colored Theatricals," *Billboard* 9 Sept. 1922: 42.
[63] Ibid., 7 Apr. 1923: 48.
[64] Ibid., "Organizing Colored Theatricals," *Billboard* 9 Sept. 1922: 42.
[65] Ibid., "Dudley's Dope," *Billboard* 17 Feb. 1923: 50.
[66] Ibid.
[67] Ibid.
[68] Ibid., 7 Apr. 1923: 48.
[69] Ibid., 5 July 1924: 46.
[70] Ibid., 6 June 1925: 48.
[71] Ibid., 12 July 1924: 46.
[72] Ibid.
[73] Ibid.
[74] Ibid.
[75] Ibid.
[76] Ibid., 16 Aug. 1924: 71.
[77] Ibid., 28 Mar. 1925: 50.
[78] W. R. Arnold, "Arnold's News of the TOBA Circuit," *Billboard* Jan.-Apr.: 1925.

V

Organizing Outdoor Entertainment
The Colored Actors' Union
The National Association of Colored Fairs

Aside from tackling the issues of conduct and poor working conditions in the industry, Jackson also wanted to organize unions for protection. Within a few months after joining *Billboard*, Jackson traveled over 12,000 miles to fifty-two cities to get acquainted with black show business folks and those in other areas of the entertainment industry. He visited seven states, going as far south as Chattanooga, Tennessee, and as far west as Chicago, meeting over 377 black performers and 857 black musicians. He consulted with nearly 100 theater owners and interviewed over fifty owners and managers of traveling attractions. Jackson compiled a wealth of statistics that indicated more than anything else the immense economic possibilities in black show business. Yet, the industry had no mechanism to protect its interests from the abuses prevailing and to fight the exploitation endured by the black profession. Given his extensive involvement in unions and organizations, it is not surprising that Jackson's suggestion for black artists was to create their own union or join one for protection to be more effective; but they did not feel welcomed in the white unions—Actors' Equity being no exception. At an Actors' Equity meeting, the question was asked: What provisions are being made for black actors? Frank Gillmore pointed to several colored members in good standing with the organization and encouraged others to join. He insisted that there was "absolutely no bar of color; all that was necessary was for them to be bona

THE NEGRO OF THE OUTDOOR SHOW

Some Bands, Carnivals, Minstrels, Freak and Circus Acts

By J.A. Jackson

"MAMA, mama! Won't you please let's go to the show, just this time? They got colored men in the band, really!" With those words the writer gave expression to his first notice of the presence of his people in the realm of outdoor attraction.

That occurred nearly forty years ago. Mother's orthodox Methodist training prevented a more complete review of that day's entertainment; than was afforded by the parade, headed by a little band of probably eight colored men, attired in red coats with gilt trappings. As the years passed my opportunities for more intimate acquaintanceship with the circus bands, the minstrels, the old plantation and the medicine shows have greatly improved. And, I am glad to relate, so has the business.

Bonstabonts doing a black-face "turn" and nondescript canvasmen "doubling brass" have given way to well-organised groups of artists with professional training and pride. Many of this newer school are responsive to all of the ethics of the profession and are rapidly developing a set of traditions.

The ever-picturesque ballyhoo of the plantation show and the evening concert of the tented minstrel are today the productions of the directors who have studied their public, and whose directions are converted into amusement by performers who have studied the requirements of their work.

The talents of more than 4,000 Negroes are occupied in the entertainment of the American public when it seeks amusement in the open. Over a hundred bands of colored musicians interpret ragtime, jazz, or the traditional 6-8 music of the show world. These bands vary in size from eight to forty members each. The bands numbered are composed of bona-fide professionals, and the enumeration does not include the many "tinkers" scattered about the country, who, while they are entertaining, are of little credit to themselves or to those whom they serve.

If there is any phase of the amusement life of the country upon which Negro personality has been impressed, it is upon the outdoor enterprises. This fact is readily discernible in the many typically Negro words, practices and superstitions with which the business abounds. There is that about the constant change and the apparent freedom in the outdoor organisation, tinctured with just enough work and with its stern discipline, artlessly concealed, that is emphatic in its appeal to the naivete of the Negro mind.

Then, too, the colored brother responds readily to the sense of close personal relationship between master and man. The sense of inter-dependence show owner and the employee show him. In no other line is the spirit of loyalty so frequently exemplified as it is "under the tops."

Maha-Rajah
Ten years at Coney Island, New York

SOME FAMOUS BANDS

PROF. F. G. LOWERY and his band, for twenty-one years a feature of the bigger circuses, is probably known to more people than any other, in the long list of Negro musical organisations that have become established parts of the circus business. This band is one of the institutions of the big show. He is now with the Ringlings.

Its success is almost entirely due to the rigid discipline maintained by Mr. Lowery as being equally essential

(Continued on page 201)

Acrobats of Highest Type
Al and Luella Wells and Al and Alice Gaines
—Photo Courtesy Chicago Defender

P. G. Lowery
Most famous conductor of the race

Pioneer aviatrix. First black Woman to hold a U. S. and International pilots license. Rejected by U. S. aviation schools, she went to France for her training. Above left, French pilot license.

fide actors," but added: "If colored actors wanted to they could form their own branch and order their own charter with their own leaders."[1]

Jackson's investigation found two black Equity members, Leon Williams and Leigh Whipper, actors whom he considered to have "more than usual intelligence and men of extensive theatrical experience."[2] He noted, "In this day of political, industrial and social discrimination, it is a wonderful bit of news to hear of any organization that is sincerely fair and does not hesitate to say so."[3] Jackson urged other black entertainers to join the union. The designation of "bona fide actors" was at the discretion of Actors' Equity. Undaunted, a group of black artists met in Cincinnati, Ohio and organized the Colored Actors' Legion (CAL) on January 12, 1921. The temporary officers elected were H. Drake, President, R. Ross, Vice-President; I. C. Puggeley, Secretary; Lew Henry, recording secretary; and T. S. Finley, Treasurer. CAL solicited the cooperation of all professionals. Members appointed Salem Tutt Whitney to look after the matter of protecting managers against irresponsible actors whose conduct had done much to injure the entire group.

The Colored Actors' Union

Another association with similar goals, The Colored Actors' Union (CAU), organized in Washington, D. C. on March 6, 1921. In July of the same year, the CAU merged with the Colored Actors' Legion. The union stated its prime reason for the equity shop was to solicit the cooperation of all in the profession and to get everyone in the acting profession as well as managers into the organization to protect against irresponsible persons in the industry. Other goals outlined by Secretary Boots Hope included: putting actors on the right path; encouraging a variety of acts, songs, and jokes; guaranteeing timely and trustworthy contracts; insuring a respectful relationship between managers and actors; having song publishers send works quickly to enable acts to have new material every five weeks to avoid forced layoffs; and doing away with managers who use female performers for immoral purposes.[4] Also, as a means of protecting acts from getting their materials stolen, the union encouraged artists to file their material in their CAU office to prove that it belonged to them. The CAU also wanted to eliminate the practice of a manager not signing an act because he personally disliked one of the performers. The union asked "Why should he care what the act has done in the past if he has what the public wants? Play him," they insisted, "That's all the public wants. The public doesn't know what the trouble is between them." The association fee was two dollars.

Membership rose from 300 in May of 1921 to 621 in July; by September of the same year it reached 800. By then the CAU had twenty-seven stock companies and 500 vaudeville acts from which to draw talent. Their goal was to put the twenty-seven stock companies in twenty-seven houses to play twenty-seven weeks, then put 400 vaudeville acts in eighty houses—the other 100 targeted to play independent houses. This they felt would give actors thirty weeks' work without a layoff, which was unprecedented. In this way an agent could let a manager know who was going to play his house at least ten weeks at a time. "Never in the history of black show business has there been an organization as close to the managers as this one,"[5] says Jackson.

To secure a permanent Actors' Home and Headquarters in Washington, D. C., the union campaigned in "The Page" for donations. The column provided free publicity and advertised the National Colored Actors' Day. August 2, 1921. In addition, Jackson requested artists and theater owners to donate an entire day's receipt to the CAU fund. In a letter reprinted in the Page, Milton Starr President of the TOBA Circuit, personally pledged receipts of one day from his theater, the Bijou, in Nashville. Also thirty-seven theaters presenting vaudeville to black audiences donated receipts of the theaters for both performances that day; and many acts volunteered to present acts greatly augmented from their usual routines. Jackson encouraged other theater owners on the circuit to follow suit. For this cause, the CAU staged a "monster" midnight benefit show at the Howard Theater in Washington, July 22. Acts that gave their able support were The Gonzell White Six, Boots Hope, Edmonia Henderson, Washington and Samuels, Eddie Green, the Gibson Trio, the Too Sweet, Delly and Kelly, Nit' and Tuck, Eddie Burton, McLaurin and Thomas. As an expression of its gratitude CAU bestowed Jackson with an honorary lifetime membership in the union for his support in helping secure their home.[6] The Treasurer, S. H. Dudley advised "The Page" that in less than two years the CAU had rapidly disproved the traditional belief that blacks would not support a beneficial organization. The union provided protection for the managers as well as the actors. A few theaters such as The Lyric Theater in Fort Dodge, Iowa, became strictly union houses. Frequently, Jackson's editorials reinforced the importance of a union house: a theater owner told the act of Brown and Singleton that they could not play that house unless they were in the union. They showed their cards promptly and the theater hired them for a week and a half. Brown reported that it was an exceedingly pleasant engagement and a highly profitable one.[7]

If an artist or agent filed a complaint against a theatre, and the CAU felt it was warrented, the house was put on the unfair list. The Howard Theater was the first to be put on this list. Dudley pulled all union acts out of the theater and called for a boycott because the management of the house canceled Lonnie Fisher with only two days' notice. Dudley further explained that when the manager had canceled Jules McGarr on a one-day notice, they worked that out. Another issue that had to do with this theatre concerned a manager who cut the salary of Easton and Stewart on the second week, and still asked them to stay over—CAU negotiated a settlement; however, Dudley said that the real problem occurred when the performers asked him to come to the theater: He went to the House, found Mr. Tucker, the manager whom he said was in name only because of his color. Then he asked to return at 9:30 to meet the manager, but not Mr. Tucker. The real manager said that the show disappointed him, and it being Sunday night he wanted an attraction for Monday. Dudley was willing to give them a show, but they would have to sign a TOBA franchise. This, of course, would protect the acts in the future. They did not sign so Dudley refused to let any union act play the theater.[8] Dudley felt it was necessary to clarify what might appear as a conflict of interest, given that he was the manager of the CAU and Vice-President and Eastern booking agent for the TOBA. He explained that because of his "peculiar position" he was trying hard to do business with and protect both the actor and manager at the same time. To clarify his position, Dudley explained in "The Page" why the CAU was necessary:

> The CAU was not organized to fight the managers nor is it the intention to raise salaries, but simply to get the fair treatment. . . . When a theater can only pay a certain amount for its bill the union intends that it pay more money to the acts that deserve it and cut the acts that are not worth what they are getting and put that cut on the salary of the act that deserves it. By so doing the manager is not paying any more on his bill and at the same time he is encouraging every act to get a better act . . . to get a better salary instead of paying all the acts the same salary. . . . It is our intention to have every act in the business join the union.[9]

In a September 1924 press release to the column, the CAU President

McGarr announced the appointment of Bart Kennett chief deputy. His job was to travel throughout the country to secure accurate information on the profession. Kennett was also marketing a guide containing valuable tabulated information for the black performer and those interested in the element of the business (see appendices). In appreciation for the lifetime membership the column had with the union, Jackson offered the CAU the *Billboard*'s complete card index—the only one that existed that covered the black show world. Jackson maintained that "it was secured by more than 11,000 miles of travel, five years of correspondence, and many interviews. Much of it has been compiled and published from time to time. Yet by no means all of it, for it covers every phase of the business. We will cheerfully donate that to the union as the *Billboard*'s contribution to their cause."[10]

On February 17, 1924, the union and the TOBA Circuit took a major step towards developing a better working relationship. The two convened at the Hotel Summit in Washington, D. C. for a series of meetings. The headline in the March 28 edition of "The Page" read "Improved Conditions on TOBA Circuit: Spirit of Co-Operation Marks Joint Meeting of Theater Officials and CAU Leaders." The CAU held its first annual meeting in the morning. The three men charged with the responsibility of booking the TOBA theaters, S. H. Dudley, Martin Klein and Sam Reevin, met in the afternoon. Later these three met in joint conference with a committee representing the CAU. Comprising CAU's committee were: Jules McGarr, President of the union; Eugene Hooten, Walter Rector, Garret Warbington and J. Heri Bowman, Directors; with Dixie Kid, Bart Kennett, the traveling deputy; and Telfair Washington, the secretary. The committee presented a program for the improvement of circuit conditions. Among the requests set forth by the committee were demands for more consecutive bookings; a lengthening of the period that a manager may cancel a contract; more prompt responses to booking agents; elimination of salary cuts after an act is notified of acceptance; improved routing so that shorter railroad jumps are possible; recognition of the union, and a form of contribution to its support; better care of the lobby photographs of the acts; and more regularity in advance bookings. The circuits did not take immediate action, since only TOBA representatives were present; but they assured the committee that they would present the complaints to the board of directors at the semi-annual meeting in July.[11] Dudley reported, however, that the circuit favored the union and encouraged its activities. Another issue often debated in "The Page," was classifying acts to determine pay scales. Dudley supplied an update on this subject to "The Page;" that he read at the meeting.

The CAU and TOBA met a second time four months later in November 1924. Actors and agents often perceived the TOBA as a managers' association organized to oppress actors among other things, and to discriminate against union members. Milton Starr in his report on the meeting, stated that Sam R. Reevin made it clear that TOBA was never hostile toward any actor or group organized for their protection, never required a union card for acts, and never asked or questioned an act's affiliation. He added that they laid off acts without union cards as frequently as ones with; that the booking agent and the managers treat performers with the utmost courtesy; and that they grant many favors to reliable performers by both him, the managers, and the TOBA offices. He then called attention to the main TOBA office at Chattanooga, how it not only looked after bookings of acts, but also after their welfare by helping several companies secure suitable material for their shows. "In many cases" he said, "they loaned managers cash for shows that needed . . . improvements . . . and to enable them to organize their own shows; but a few betrayed their trust and failed to make good [forcing them] to discontinue the practice. We have quite a sum of outstanding money on the acts that were given in good faith to seemingly reliable performers and which we are still waiting to collect."[12]

By the fourth year, with the cooperative efforts of the CAU, TOBA, and publications such as "The Page," the organizations eliminated many of the undesirable elements in the profession. The CAU continued to vigorously campaign for members through ads in the *Billboard*, the Chicago *Defender*, the Indianapolis *Freeman,* and the Baltimore *Afro-American.* Membership rose above 1,000; but the goal was to get every colored member of the profession in the union. "The Page" listed names of bona fide union members. It was one of the first times any professional black organization had gone so extensively to the press to demonstrate its strength.[13] By this time, the CAU made additional provisions to accommodate the unfortunate. The union helped actors when necessary, by covering their doctor bills or moving them when stranded. The union also planned to build a home for disabled actors and actresses in which they could take refuge in when laid off or ill. Furthermore, it would take care of the burial of those who left no funds.[14]

The National Association of Colored Fairs

Another area of black theatricals that "The Page" helped to organize was the out-of-doors entertainment field. During Jackson's initial tour throughout the country, he talked with more than fifty fairs, fifty-five fair official associations, and visited eight fairs. During the summer of 1921, he met one black carnival owner, heard from four others, saw fifteen black concessionaires working for themselves and found artists working in the concerns of other concessionaires. He visited six parks and discussed the operations of a dozen more. He also met thousands of actors and musicians and over fifty men experienced in the arts of the outdoor business and games.[15]

Owing to his contacts, observations, and the success of the CAU, Jackson felt that if fairs organized, they would assure more efficient management and a more profitable operation. If the fair owners aligned themselves with the National Negro Business Mens' League he thought, they would have a subsidiary body that could place them in direct contact with black business leaders. Jackson recommended that this body be composed of three groups: fair officials and park owners in one group, theater owners and managers in another, and traveling show owners and managers in a third body—all, however, under one unit were concerned with amusement interests as a whole. He believed the association should address the needs of the first group since it was the most pressing; and that they should consider a joint venture because they were too big for individual handling and work together to reap financial rewards, especially since they were losing large profits by delaying organization. Presenting an organized front with the combined attendance figures would mean that the association could secure more exhibits of nationally advertised farm and domestic appliances.

Jackson's proposal attempted to add dignity and prestige to the fairs, increase income, reduce expenses, improve the program of events and methods, and keep more of the profits in the black community. With definite dates and steady employment, the fairs would attract more black showmen during the fair season; in addition, they would offer a wider variety of areas blacks could succeed. In numerous editorials, Jackson urged interested fair owners to get together, to organize an association, to work in harmony, and to cooperate with one another and the National

Negro Businessmens' League. He also compiled a list of the many fairs promoted and patronized by blacks in this country—probably the first such directory ever made. The partial list included Alabama, Kentucky, Louisiana, Maryland, Missouri, North Carolina, and Pennsylvania. Although incomplete, the list awakened the interest of those who appreciate the value of listing their organization and its dates with *Billboard*, and emphasized the growing numbers in this field.[16] In a March 1922 editorial "Growing Importance of the Colored Fair: Officials Rapidly Awakening," Jackson presented attendance figures and financial statistics on successful major fairs: "There were 20,000 in attendance at the North Carolina Negro Fair at Raleigh last October and 16,000 passed the gates on one of the four big days at the Lexington Fair, 50% of the opposite race. The receipts for the four days totaled $40,000 according to a daily newspaper. Not only carnival companies exhibited at Lexington but also manufacturers of both races." Jackson explained that the integrated policy indicated great understanding since the fair operated as an open door for the transmission of a better understanding of blacks and the accomplishments of this underestimated group.[17] His editorials also publicized the importance of these fairs. Oscar Jenkins, a veteran fair concessionaire and operator at Suburban Gardens, in Washington D. C, on a few occasions filled-in for Jackson and reported on "out-of-door doings."

Within a few months of the proposal for a national fair association, Jackson received a number of encouraging responses, in particular from W. S. Scales, Secretary of TOBA, owner of the Lafayette Theater at Winston-Salem, North Carolina, and a Director of the Piedmont Fair. The owner of The Lexington Fair readily saw the value of the idea, if for nothing more than to reduce the detail work of each association. This was the most firmly established fair in the country attracting 16,000 each day. The Secretary J. L. Hathaway acknowledged that "If organized, we will be glad to give it first consideration."[18] Reverend A. W. Hill of Columbia, South Carolina, a progressive man, fully appreciated any effort to attract better publicity and more exhibits to his fair. Oscar Jenkin's letter printed in "The Page" entitled "Colored Fair Improvements: The Views of a Practical Show Person Expressed," stated the only way to get organized was to put two black carnivals in the field.[19] More than twenty letters from secretaries of various fairs also came to the publication in September and October, during the last two months of the fair season, seeking important information on advertising before April 1, the beginning of the Spring season.

Five questions most frequently raised by the dozen fair officials that handicaped the outdoor entertainment industry were how to:

- increase the educational value;
- secure more black amusements and attractions;
- obtain a greater diversity of exhibits of Negro origin;
- obtain advertising matter portraying Negro characters;
- attract exhibits of nationally advertised farm appliances and
   domestic equipment;
- and, to coordinate conflicting fair dates.

"The Page" suggested that acts adjust dates for the many fairs held in the state.[20] The solution to these problems seemed to rest on the future usefulness of the colored fair, Jackson surmised, and that usefulness would determine the degree of success and would encourage the establishment of still more of the type. Jackson saw them as pioneers in an immense field of social and economic service.[21]

Jackson's suggestion for the first query, regarding the educational value of the fairs, was to continuously cooperate with the U. S. Bureau of Extension Work in the Department of Agriculture, and with the local and state representatives. He suggested careful scanning of the Lyceum and Chautauqua[22] fields for the better entertainers of the race and inviting active educational societies such as the NAACP and kindred bodies.

Tangible evidence resulted in *"Billboard* Jackson's" efforts to persuade black fair officials to organize. S. H. Dudley, the wealthiest black in the amusement industry, tentatively provided answers for the second and third questions by the fair owners: "How may they secure more colored amusements and attractions?" and "How may they obtain a greater diversity of exhibits of Negro origin?" Before this time, he was one of the best-known comedians on the American stage, a dominant character in black theatricals, and a substantial business man. At various times he owned several tented attractions; and through his booking office, had connections with many different types of outdoor acts and attractions. Dudley, while accompanying Jackson to a TOBA meeting in Chattanooga, Tennessee, discussed black fairs. He pledged to finance, equip, and put out a Colored Carnival-Circus if fair officials organized in any way, or if they arranged to coordinate their dates and bookings to assure continuous engagement. He suggested it be composed of no less than ten cars, two or more rides, more than six shows, and at least thirty concessions and two free acts, presenting every variety of performance with black artists. Moreover, Dudley stated that if he could secure fair dates to keep the attractions engaged from August 15 until November 15, he could get it on the road by July 1 to play open dates till fair time. He estimated that it would require $90,000 and 250 people to make the show he had in mind for him to be willing to produce the show.[23] Black bands had long been an attraction with the circus side shows, but when Jackson learned that they had invaded the "big top," an achievement he much longed for, it was with "distinct pleasure." Featured with the Patterson Trained Animal Show were: Coy Herndon, the hoop-roller, once with Howe's Great London Show, and Allie Johnson, a wire-walker. They became to the circus world what Bert Williams and Charles Gilpin were, respectively, to musical comedy and drama in theaters. Jackson also knew of at least twenty-eight other acts that could adapt their routines for a circus or carnival. The list included one male and one female aviator, acrobats, aerialists, bicycle riders, calliope[24] players, contortionists, jugglers, magicians, leapers, animal trainers, and a horse exhibitor. The attractions boasted of many excellent musical organizations: P. G. Lowery Band with the Barnum-Ringling Brothers show was the conceded leader. In that class was the Edward Farrel Band with the Albert Barnes Show the season before. Six black comics shared honors with the other group of "Jerrys"[25] in securing laughs with their antics. They were with the Albert Barnes show the previous season. Many bands among the different acts received their training in the field where they had to be good to survive. They were bona fide showmen such as Shell Paris, Oscar Jenkins, W. A. Barclay, Roy Craddock, and J. H. Dixon. Jackson felt that the concert band, which spectators often overlooked for the fairs, could be a big pull. Most were from Nebraska and neighboring states. The Dan DesDunes Regimental Band of Omaha became a standard attraction at the big state fair and at a number of fair gatherings in the State.[26]

The fourth obstacle that handicapped fair owners was the inability to obtain lithographs that illustrated black types. At this time over fifty black fairs had to use advertising matter designed for white fairs and parks. Black customers assumed that it was a white fair being advertised and paid no attention to the show, thus defeating its purpose. Illustrators also needed a guarantee that there will be a need to fully justify the time and expense of producing a black lithograph. They asked concerned persons to show their appreciation to the house that ventured to make this big initial expense in their interest; and to prove to them that they approved of progressive business practices. Two months later, the Fairfax Colored Fair in Fairfax County, Virginia, announced that the directors authorized the use of the new issue of Donaldson's Lithograph paper; and that they designed two lines especially for black fairs.[27] "The Page" displayed no examples of Donaldson's Lithograph paper.

Publicity was Jackson's reply to the fifth question fair officials asked: How then may they attract exhibits of nationally advertised farm appliances and domestic equipment? He cited that some of the problems of fair organizations were the absence of expert advice, poorly placed advertising, or no advertisement at all, except by word of mouth. Publicity obtained was entirely too local in distribution, except for the Lexington, Kentucky Fair, who placed ads as far as Chicago. Jackson also stressed the importance of publicizing long before the fairs open and continue long after they close, so that the promotion departments of exhibitors can remember them at the end of the season and consider them for the next season's program. He further explained that neither the black press nor the papers of more general circulation could afford to ignore a collection of officials representing the purchasing possibilities of 2 or 3 million people, regardless of race.

The matter of conflicting fair dates was the final element of discord that fairs officials felt handicapped the outdoor entertainment industry. "The Page" suggested that acts adjust dates for the many fairs held in the same city and territory. This would also protect association members against the irresponsible promoters—and largely obviate conflicting dates.

Within six-months, Jackson realized his goal to organize black fairs. On August 1922, the manager of the Norfolk, Virginia Colored Fair, and a number of fair officials, shows, and celebrity folks throughout the country met. Present were Mr. J. H. Love, Secretary of the North Carolina Negro State Fair, Henry Hartman, of the Fairfax, Virginia Fair, and Bob Cross, Manager of Norfolk Virginia Colored Fair. They organized as a subsidiary to the National Negro Business Mens' League. They held the meeting at the convention of that organization in Norfolk, Virginia, August 16, 17, and 18, and the National Association of Colored Fairs (NACF) adopted a charter. The new organization's purpose was "to make colored fairs a real asset to the race and to increase the service of these institutions to the people by aggressively going after more and better exhibits and attractions."[28]

The NACF met the next year in Norfolk on February 22, 1923 Washington's Birthday, and wrote that date into the constitution as their annual meeting date. At the meeting thirty-five officials from four different states represented twelve black fairs. Five other fairs sent letters and membership fees. In addition, the Alabama-Tennessee division, an already organized group of six fairs, said they would work in accord with the larger body. Considering NACF was one of fifteen units that comprised the larger body in outdoor entertainment and the short span of time they had to operate as an organization, the first year's activities were impressive.

Within the first year, Jackson's campaign to formulate and nurture both the CAU and the NACF came to fruition. Throughout the life of "The Page," the unions on numerous occasions evidenced the importance of organizing for protection, to realize their potential and to be more effective.

Notes

[1] Jackson, "Our Race and the Equity," *Billboard* 8 July 1921: 18.

[2] Ibid.

[3] Ibid.

[4] Jackson, "As the New Season is about to open by Boots Hope," *Billboard* 3 Sept. 1921: 43.

[5] Ibid.

[6] Ibid., "Lifetime Membership," *Billboard* 26 July 1924: 49.

[7] Ibid., "Unions Card," *Billboard* 8 Nov. 1924: 48.

[8] Ibid., "Dudley Explains CAU Action Against Howard," *Billboard* 30 Aug. 1924: 48.

[9] Ibid.

[10] Ibid., "CAU Official on Tour," *Billboard* 6 Sept. 1924: 50.

[11] Ibid., "Improved Conditions On TOBA Circuit," *Billboard* 28 Mar. 1925: 50.

[12] Ibid., "TOBA Report," *Billboard* 22 Nov. 1925: 48.

[13] Ibid., "CAU Will Conduct Advertising Campaign," *Billboard* 29 Nov. 1924: 50.

[14] Ibid., "CAU," *Billboard* 31 May 1924: 46.

[15] Ibid., "The Growing Importance of the Colored Fair: Officials Rapidly Awakening," *Billboard* 18 Mar. 1922: 71.

[16] Ibid., "Colored Fair Official," *Billboard* 19 Nov. 1921: 47.

[17] Ibid., "Columbia State Fair," *Billboard* 19 Nov. 1921: 63.

[18] Ibid.

[19] Ibid., "Encouragement for Colored Carnival Company—Lexington Fair Offers Option," *Billboard* 18 Feb. 1922: 43.

[20] Ibid., "The Growing Importance of the Colored Fair: Officials Rapidly Awakening to its Possibilities," *Billboard* 18 Mar. 1922: 71.

[21] Ibid.

[22] The annual summer educational and recreational assembly formerly held in the town

of Chautauqua, New York.

[23] Ibid., "Fair Achievements Have Been Accomplished," *Billboard* 21 Jan. 1922: 47.

[24] Calliope: an organ-like musical instrument fitted with steam whistles.

[25] "Jerrys": German soldiers.

[26] Jackson, "Fair Achievements Have Been Accomplished," *Billboard* 21 Jan. 1922: 47.

[27] Ibid, "Fairfax Colored Fair," *Billboard* 18 Mar. 1922: 70.

[28] Ibid., "Negro Fair Officials To Organize under Sanction of National Negro Business Mens' League," *Billboard* 8 July 1922: 42.

VI

Reception and Impact of "The Page"

J ackson's editorials did not have the same kind of monumental impact on black performance as did Jackie Robinson's entry into major league baseball or Arthur Ashe's entry into professional tennis. The question then becomes: What influence did "Jackson's Page" have on African-American performance during the Harlem Renaissance?

Drawing upon the standards set by pioneer theatrical editors in black publications, Jackson wanted to eliminate faults of black performance news reporting and improve the colored entertainment business. His initial objectives were to provide a better understanding of the Negro artist and his problems; to afford a medium for an exchange of views; to enhance the value of the colored artists for those marketing their services; to establish reciprocal relations with the black publications and professional organizations.

"Selling" the Black Performer

To achieve his first objective providing a better understanding of the Negro artist and his problems, Jackson had to "sell" the black performer to the general public. Believing that "understanding begets tolerance and harmony," he wrote sympathetic editorials depicting historical perspectives of blacks, pointing out the obstacles deterring their advancement in American entertainment. By 1922, according to "The Page's" annual survey, the Negro performer made social progress. Jackson proclaimed that from all over the country news had come of a better relationship between the black performer and the public and that there was more general recognition of the performer's personal value to society at large—

most of these reports had to do with big name stars. He talked about the opportunities now open to blacks, but pointed out that "The Negro performer is expected to come into this new estate with precisely the same equipment, the same mental attitude of suspect for his calling, and the same sense of responsibility to the business as prevails with all others who would have its rewards."[1] Jackson also felt that, because of the selfishness, disloyalty, greediness, and the lack of self-respect of a few artists, the society at large measures the black race as a group rather than as an individual. As social barriers lessened and the general public became more amenable to black entertainers, Jackson began to encourage black artists to do something for themselves.

Providing a Medium for an Exchange of Views

To provide a forum to exchange viewpoints, which was "The Page's" second objective, Jackson began identifying problems and airing grievances by professional artists. The key issues throughout were setting standards, improving conditions on the TOBA and organizing outdoor entertainment. Jackson believed that if the black artist were to advance in the entertainment business or to integrate into mainstream American entertainment, he had to "measure up" by improving his standard of conduct. To "clean up" the industry, Jackson directed his editorials to the subject of profanity and broader forms of vulgarity, neatness and appearance on and off stage, contract jumpers, acts breaking up, mountebank promoters, exploitation of performers by local promoters, improper conduct in small towns, and artists not preparing for the future. Within two years, the problem of promoters exploiting artists decreased. Jackson reported in 1923 that "The past two seasons had been very disappointing to the exploiting promoters. . . . The modern performer should not be asked to give away his talent. . . . He takes his business seriously and tries to conserve his strength."[2]

"Smut shooters," however, were the most difficult to control and the most harmful to the industry. Jackson felt that public indignation against indecency of this type creates a prejudice against almost all black acts, and discourages women and children of color from attending. To compound the problem, theater managers and a few spectators expressed approval of suggestive sexual humor and obscenities with loud boisterous laughter that inspired acts to use "blue" material. To Jackson, it seems that far too many acts lack ethical standards. He contends that genuine advance is registered only when a person or group attains higher standards and becomes firmly established in the possession of them. Also joining the column's fight against indecency with positive results were artists, agents, promoters, theater owners, race papers, and the CAU.

Two artists, Harry J. Earle and his wife, owners and principal comedians of A Happy Night in Dixie show, adamantly supported Jackson's campaign against indecency. They thought the language they heard in theaters on State Street in Chicago was appalling: "It was too bad some of them [the acts] couldn't put in a season as they did in the bush playing to white audiences and really learn the value of clean material."³

To make the point that Harry J. Earle and his wife practice what they preach and that the public really does appreciate clean shows, "The Page" printed an extract from an issue of the *Amusement Reporter* of Waterloo, Iowa. The story by theater managers Simon and Heimer, entitled "We Say It is Some Show," said:

> An entertainment given by colored performers has something about it that appeals to the ordinary run of theaters, and Mr. and Mrs. Harry J. Earle have appeared before so many audiences of varied kinds that they have been able to work out a clean, refined program without a single suggestive line of offensive allusion of any sort. They demonstrate conclusively that smut is not necessary to make a performance go . . . not a minstrel, neither is it a concert . . ., it is a cleverly constructed entertainment combining the elements of both.⁴

The black press also joined Jackson's fight for better standards. The Baltimore *Afro-American*, with a readership of over 250,000 within the Baltimore and Washington vicinity, had a few things to say about "smut." William E. Brady, Jr., son of the theatrical reviewer for that paper, in a reprinted article in "The Page," stated, "The paper was not a prude or self-righteous. . ., realizing that in a strictly vaudeville entertainment, a little 'spice' of a varied nature may occasionally be expected, but the downright filth . . . is too disgusting."⁵ Brady also singles out women. He says, "Some of the worst in this are women—the sex from whom is expected to spring whatever is pure and good in any nation or people."⁶

An editorial, reprinted from a Duluth, Georgia daily paper, headed "Smut Shooters, Read This and Weep: Decency Vindicated," also helped validate Jackson's contention that blacks wanted a "cleaner" stage. "The Page" notified producers of modern musical comedies, revues, vaudeville, or just girl shows that they might learn a lesson from their dark-skinned brothers. The article stated:

Duluth witnessed a musical revue last week that was entirely the work of Negroes. It was composed by Negroes, staged by Negroes, and every member of the company and of the orchestra was a Negro. The lesson that these Negro entertainers had to teach was not just the value of spontaneity, although they demonstrated that most effectively, it was not that a modern, popular musical entertainment shouldn't have life, color, rhythm, 'class,' and 'pep,' altho they demonstrated that also, but they did prove to producers whose skin don't happen to be black that it is possible to present the liveliest and most entertaining of revues without the faintest hint of vulgarity.

Many a producer with a white skin will tell you that the public wants smut. We might thank our dark-skinned entertainers for proving that it's a lie, and that good taste and decency can compete with vulgarity and indecency on better than an equal footing.[7]

Jackson added: "Some of our stink-talk stars will not earn that much real praise in the whole history of their career. Imagine the sort of editorial some tabloid shows we know would have inspired in the same paper and the chance any colored show would have to play the town after them."[8]

W. C. T. Ayes, Theatrical Editor for the *Columbus News*, the "lusty young Ohio journal" devoted nearly a full page to theatrical news affirming "cleanliness" in the black entertainment industry. He said: "After seeing wonderful shows like *Shuffle Along, Chocolate Dandies, Follow Me, Smarter Set, Seven-Eleven, Liza, Plantation Days,* and knowing of their success, we wonder why some small shows still bring us smut and low-down comedy."[9]

Preachers also got into the act against indecency. Howard Agnew Johnson, Sr. appealed to the Federal Council of the Churches of Christ in America. He made strong charges against stage morality and appealed for self respecting colored people to help purge the amusement business. Jackson warned the industry that a preacher, "telling the sisters all about the naughty theater, can talk away many a dime from the theater."[10] Clarence Muse, the reputable actor, film director, and journalist, also went on record as a subscriber to "clean" theater. In a reprinted article from the Chicago *Enterprise* under the heading of "The Negro Theater," Muse presented his argument:

It may be the demand of your public that the stage produce obscene productions, but I do not believe it, for at heart we are . . . clean people. A talented play bolstered with smutty scenes, suggestive jokes and immoral costumes put a dent in the better nature of everyone who patronizes it. Why should the Negro theater, as young, so full of potential, start in missing as widely the purpose of the true stage? It is in the power of the Negro theater to uplift, even while entertaining, the morals of a race. The stage, of all things, should be clean and every spoken line and every bar of music should be a tonic and not a sedative to a man's moral nature.

The stage should educate the people up to accepting nothing but clean, wholesome productions. Bend a twig while it is young; that is to say, that while the Negro theater is in its infancy let it fulfill its purpose, that of elevating the morals of the race to a higher and fuller existence. The writer thinks as old-timers always think that clean plays never go begging for patronage.[11]

Another performer, Bill "Bojangles" Robinson, the highest salaried black artist in vaudeville, spoke out against improper standards of conduct. On February 16, 1925, over 100 performers gathered at a midnight meeting at the Comedy Club in New York City. It is an "epoch-making event," proclaims Jackson, "the first . . . effort . . . of colored performers playing on mixed bills to take into their own hands the matter of disciplining those whose conduct is harmful to the Race."[12]

Men and women equally divided the assembly. Among them were many standard acts. For three hours they listened to speeches seriously addressing ways to punish offenders who seem to be beyond redemption, and how to advise the less fortunate and youthful artist. Bill "Bojangles" Robinson, with his wife sitting behind him, gave a forty-minute harangue. He began: "I used to sport, I used to fight and I used to think pleasure more important than business. Time was when I was both indifferent to the future and to my associates, and when I change for the better it's time for every colored performer to try to be an angel."[13] From that point on, he emphasized the need to improve the deportment of the group if it were to retain its place on the American stage. He described conditions that needed improving, named performers who had tarnished the whole group, and mentioned incidents that reflected unfavorably upon all high and low salaried alike. Jackson, invited to speak after Robinson, stated, "for the first time [Robinson] verbally presented the arguments for decency that have so often been sent in the *Billboard* and that to a great extent helped to crystallize sentiments with the performers to the point of leading up to this meeting."[14]

The performers appointed a vigilance committee with power to select ten associate members to investigate the merits of reports against performers; to caution the derelict ones; and to cooperate with managers, agents, and other organizations in disciplinary measures. Jackson was first selected as a chairman of the committee by an unanimous vote, but declined, explaining, "It would be better that such matters be strictly within the hands of the performers themselves."[15] Sam Tolson accepted the position when Jackson offered to serve in an advisory capacity. Jackson stated in the 1995-96 *Negro Year Book*: "There has been a noticeable elevation of the standard of performance submitted to black audiences. Higher salaries now prevail;

and there is a steady tendency toward the elimination of . . . offensive material with which the Negro theater abounded a few years ago."[16] Possibly Jackson's fight to improve standards, and the support of a broad segment of the profession was a factor in the increased attendance figures and acceptance of black artists into mainstream entertainment.

Jackson also tried to improve conditions on vaudeville circuits catering to black patronage. The major concerns by entertainers were unfair treatment by their managers, low salaries, long jumps, and irregular employment. Since "The Page" fought to improve black vaudeville, Jackson was in the best position to evaluate the progress of the TOBA the M. & P. Circuits. In 1922, a little over a year after the restructuring of the TOBA Jackson reported slight improvements in the salaries offered; however, he explained, "not all . . . managers had yet realized that transportation, bread, butter, and the other necessities of life are just as expensive for colored performers as for the other races."[17]

At the annual TOBA meeting in 1922, Jackson submitted twenty-one suggestions for the improvement of conditions. A year later he stated, "they have in the main been approved by the artists and many of the managers to whose attention they were brought. I was gratified to note a tendency in the right direction with most of the suggestions, sometimes a quite decided advance, sometimes a mere gesture in the right direction, but nevertheless right."[18]

In a 1923 editorial, Jackson stated: "he has not always agreed with their methods, but believes in the sincerity of many of the officials." He went on to appraise the conditions on the circuit:

> More tabs have been getting into N. Y., and while there, have been obtaining new material and costuming. More acts have been writing in providing a route of more than just the next week. More theaters have been making a feature of their orchestra, although far from enough of them. Reviews at Birmingham, Shreveport, Cincinnati, Winston-Salem, and Washington show an improvement in the bills so far as variety is concerned; however, much remains yet to be done in the direction.

> Generally speaking, business conditions have greatly improved and the officials are to some extent free from the anxiety that prevailed last year concerning the possibility of keeping business alive at all. Perhaps they will . . . devote more attention . . . strictly to the professional phase of affairs. . . . They might do well to begin by not making the artists the cat's paw in their fights against opposition and we believe that when the inhumanity of it is realized other means of combat will be found.[19]

For the March 28, 1923 meeting in Washington, D. C., when a

committee representing performers met with managers to discuss conditions on the vaudeville circuits, Jackson hailed it "The greatest single advancement in the business since the opening of the colored theaters."[20] They talked about ways to formulate Dudley and Jackson's suggestions of classifying acts; and of designating try-out houses to inspect and censor all acts before presenting them on the circuit. Other subjects covered were: better salaries, sanctity of the contracts, time limit on contracts and its variation, costumes and their attendance, deportment, the vaudeville unit, and the ideal tabloid company. "The Page" functioned as the Chairman of the meeting. Apparently Milton B. Starr, former president of TOBA liked Jackson's idea of designating a "try-out" house to provide a greater variety of entertainment for black patrons. Starr personally conducted a tour of the Andrew Bishop-Cleo Desmond Players through the biggest houses of the circuit.

TOBA took into account suggestions made in "The Page." Many were implemented. For one, they assigned correspondents unknown to actors, managers, or agents to report on the acts as an advisable check on some of the wild press agenting. Two official representatives of "The Page," Wesley Vernell and Billy Chambers, reviewed and classified acts in a few of the TOBA houses. Also, TOBA in its desire to rectify some of the complaints of wrongdoing by the CAU and performers, assigned a press agent, W. R. Arnold, to oversee the houses on the circuit. These new additions provided a better assessment of the economic value of the acts and a first-hand account of conditions on the circuit. The amalgamation of the two major circuits in 1924 insured smoother operations of acts; and it helped obviate the congestion of the two circuits that had often occurred in extreme Southern cities. It also made it easier to attract local investors in black theater. In addition, TOBA permitted theater owners to use attractions that until then had only played to metropolitan audiences. By sending artists to the "provinces," the organizations enhanced the value of all local black theater investments and encouraged the building of numerous theaters in towns that previously had no place of amusement. They were able to offer better routing and resolve many of the problems of long breaks.

A Jackson editorial in 1924 underscored the importance of the circuit to black performance: "Inasmuch as the circuit operates in all the towns and cities that are centers of large black populations; since the officers and stockholders of the association are bona fide owners of the theaters in these communities; and since the colored public is decidedly partial to the vaudeville type of entertainment, the organization [probably] constitutes the backbone of the organized show world."²¹

Although the organization provided bookings for hundreds of black performers, complaints about conditions on the circuit still arose. To these artists, the acronym for the organization became known as "Tough On Black Actors" because of the unfair treatment by theatre managers, poor routing, segregated theatres, and low salaries. The TOBA notwithstanding, the number of minor dissension and the occasional defection of theater owners continued in black vaudeville. The four booking units, combined with the arrangement that prevailed with the Cummings and M. & P. organizations, employed more black talent than all other theatrical concerns combined, and performers with "recognized" abilities were receiving more week's work, higher salaries, better contracts, and a minimum of long jumps.

Jackson's penchant for order manifested in his theme to organize black theatricals for their protection. "The Page" lent assistance to various groups whenever possible and was a voice for their fight against abuses in the industry. The column was influential in the formation of The National Association of Negro Musicians, the Colored Actors' Union, and the National Fair Officials Association. When Bart Kennett, the Chief Deputy for the union, embarked upon his journey around the industry to get accurate information on the profession, Jackson offered the CAU the only complete card index covering the black show world (see Appendices). This index represented an accumulation of five year's correspondence between Jackson and members of the entertainment industry, as well as interviews. In addition, Jackson solicited donations for the building of the Actors' Home and was an "unofficial representative" of CAU in their three meetings with the TOBA.

Evaluating what the CAU represents to the black entertainment profession is the best way to measure its effectiveness. It was a fraternal organization owned and controlled by blacks for the protection of blacks. The union had an Actor's Home where artists could stay at a minimal fee; the union paid hospital bills, moved stranded artists, and worked to safeguard their interest in every detail. With a membership of over 1,000 and a chief deputy monitoring the affairs of black show business, the union had a first-hand account of what was happening in the industry, thus reducing the amount of "smut" and irresponsibility among managers and actors. Classifying acts as "A," "B," and "C." meant better salaries and inspired artists to work harder to become more creative—resolving some of the problems of lack of variety. By refining the acts, the union improved business in theaters and booking offices. More union houses meant that performers and managers had to meet standards set by the CAU. With such a large and strong organization to oversee the industry, both the CAU and TOBA benefited. For the performer it meant better treatment by managers and the possibility of better salaries; and for the theater owners it meant a better caliber of performer, improved material, and ultimately more patrons. Most of all, the union helped not only to clean up the industry, but to dignify the profession.

The greatest economic and community-serving and socially relevant achievement, according to Jackson, was in the outdoors entertainment business and the formation of The National Association of Colored Fairs (NACF). Jackson's editorial in 1922, "The Growing Importance of the Colored Fairs: Officials Rapidly Awakening" revealed attendance figures and the financial success of the major fairs: During the month of October alone, 20,000 attended the North Carolina Negro Fair at Raleigh;16,000 passed the gates on one of the four big days at the Lexington Fair—half were white. According to the local newspaper, receipts for the four days totaled $40,000.[22]

Also in terms of race development, The NACF, allied with two strong bodies, the National Farmer's Association and the National Negro Business Mens' League. The three organizations secured from The Department of Agriculture black fair exhibits for a demonstration that required two thousand square feet. Jackson commented, "It will require years to tell of the immense value to the culture of the country that this organization is and will be responsible for. . . . The value of the Negro farmer . . . to the counties at large, especially to the States where each of the farming depends upon the race, cannot be easily nor quickly determined. . . . It is a direct blow at the oft-mentioned ignorance that has handicapped better crop production of Negro-owned farms."[23]

"The Page's" survey of 1923 showed that advertising and the backing of the national organization boosted the number of black concessionaires and carnival programs. More than two hundred black professionals paid for space that year at black fairs as opposed to a mere dozen two years earlier. The more frequent use of black acts at these fairs encouraged novelty artists previously employed only intermittently. There was also an increase in exhibits by black and white merchants and manufacturers. The fair owners attributed it to the concentrated publicity in "The Page" they obtained for association members and non-members alike. As public awareness increased concerning different commodities, the demand for goods exhibited, also increased. Consequently, opening a wider market helped to stabilize the fairs. "Hence," stated Jackson, "the whole business fabric of the nation is, to some extent benefited . . . the integrated policy indicates great understanding and the fair operates as an open door for the transmission of better ideas regarding Negroes and the accomplishments of a much underestimated group."[24] The chief asset of the National Association was that it reduced the exploitation of acts, although it was not entirely eliminated, but vast improvements were noted.

Enhancing the Value of Black Artists

Did Jackson enhance the value of black artists for better marketability? A comparison between the   progress of African-American entertainment from the time the column started with what happened a few years later will provide some answers. The 1923 report shows a substantial improvement and a remarkable surface progress in sheer numbers. Jackson said: "After a decade of almost complete obscurity the colored group in the show world emerged from a sort of crystal state and the world has for the past three years been almost electrified with successive discoveries of the rich talents with which the acts abound."[25]

In the field of drama, there was nothing quite as spectacular as *Emperor Jones* or Gilpin's rise to fame, but an equal amount of pioneering occurred that year. More blacks portrayed racial characters in dramatic companies and films. Productions by the Ethiopian Art Theater, a R. G. Doggett Company, served to focus the general public's attention upon black artists which played Chicago, Washington, Philadelphia, New York, and the Lafayette Players. Possibly the greatest impact on drama was in the increase of theater houses catering to black audiences. Two more Lafayette Players companies formed; they toured the Northeast, the Midwest, and the South for the first time, stimulating more interest in that field. Howard University began offering credits to students in drama, opening up an area where new natural talent could find direction and be discovered. There was a proliferation of dramatic actors, and numerous community projects sprang up that reflected the nationwide progress toward an appreciation for drama. This explosion of theatrical activity inspired black playwrights to write plays that reflect the essence of the black experience.

In musical comedy, within two years after *Shuffle Along*'s success in 1921, musicals proliferated. Among them were *Put & Take, Bombay Girls, Running Wild, Follow Me, North Ain't South*, and *Dinah*. This indicated that these types of shows were money-makers and that black performers might be able to abandon previous expectation of singing and dancing in humorous renditions of the Cake Walk, Charleston, and Blackbottom.

Another phase of advancement on Broadway in the music field was in the number of talented choreographers, ingenious music arrangers, and clever dance instructors who left an indelible impression upon entertainment on Broadway. The most prolific and prominent composers were Henry Creamer & Turner Layton, James P. Johnson, Qualle Clark, Bern Barbour, Alex Rogers, and Luckeyth Roberts.

In the dance field, instructors such as Frank Montgomery, Leonard Harper, Eddie Green, Lubrie Hill and others set the black's idea of action into vogue. Black publishers Harry H. Pace, W. C. Handy, and Clarence Williams made remarkable progress in the volume of business and in the range of record distribution by black artists. There was a particular rise in women recording artists in the blues field, artists such as Mame Smith and Bessie Smith (no relation), Ethel Waters, Alberta Hunter, Sarah Martin, and Daisy Martin. Department stores and other metropolitan outlets featured in displays black recording artists.

Concert artists also transcended race designations. Some were accepted on merit alone, notably: Helen Hagen, Hazel Harrison, Harry Burleigh, Roland Hayes, Florence Cole, and Cleota Collins. Artists also formed Lyceum circuits. In Grand Opera, Valdo Freeman who conceived, produced, and financed eight grand operas, helped to establish a place for blacks in the musical history of the nation. Bands and orchestras could revel in the notion that musical organizations of every type had grown plentiful. Military, concert, and jazz bands numbering in the hundreds appeared after the war. In New York alone there were more than 170 musical outfits. They were also successful in Paris and England and on the continent.

With the amalgamation of TOBA and the M. & P. Circuit, vaudeville became the largest employer of black talent. There were 350 black vaudeville acts and more than forty outdoor acts that were available for fairs, parks, and circuses. Burlesque performers made the greatest strides attracting positive comments with the Columbia and the Wheel circuits.

Both had black acts galore—an impossibility a few years earlier. Many artists played with good stock companies as added attractions.

The motion picture industry in 1920 launched fifty different projects. There were fewer than twenty in 1923. Jackson explained that more had quit than had entered. The number of theater houses opened was the bright spot. There were 368 as opposed to 285 the year before.

Black outdoor entertainment offered ninety-six different black state, county, and district fairs representing a substantial increase from the mere twenty-five three years earlier. Parks listed increases from nine three years earlier to thirty. Two black carnival companies supplied entertainment for black fairs by the Michael Brothers. The twenty-two tented attractions and minstrels touring the county were profitable. An important advance in that area was the *Hello Rufus* company's Southern tour. There were more indoor bazaars and more members of the race owned and operated steamboats.

In places that dispensed food and entertainment together, artists had successful summer seasons in New York, at the Happy Rhone's Ornate Club in Cleveland and at the Hawaiian Gardens, and clubs in Atlantic City. Out west, the Bungalow and the Alhambra, two exclusive places of character in Seattle, and the Paradise Gardens in Los Angeles employed black entertainers. Several similar places scattered across the country provided comfortable recreation centers for groups, and at the same time, opened another avenue of employment for a big contingent of black performers. Bands also filled engagements at summer resorts that catered to an exclusive clientele in New York and Ohio. Bands and minstrels had a chance to show their stuff on the circus lots, but had to limit their routines to clowning and comedy roles in big acts. A few were helpers for animal handlers. These were the first steps in an open field. In all the areas of black performance in 1923, apart from motion pictures and folk singing, the black performer saw eloquent testament that he had arrived.

As for the black actors and showmen, the first census by "The Page" in 1920 listed 1,095 and 878, respectively, for a total of 1,973. Nearly five years later the survey estimated 3,900 actors and performers. Of these there were 1,200 black vaudeville performers and 2,700 engaged in other types of shows. "Another thousand are in allied lines of work," states Jackson, "There are as nearly as can be ascertained 16,000 musicians in the country. That includes professional and semi-professional workers in bands and orchestras. Show bands, dance orchestras, fraternal bands, clubs and school bands, factory bands, etc., in fact, all who do work for pay as a musician. . . . Considering the cost of musical instruments [and] that many own several different instruments, it represents a tremendous market that spends perhaps a half million annually to meet their needs."[26]

Another area of advancement was in the number of black artists in the Actors' Equity Association. The union reported twelve blacks in the organization. "All the Negroes who appeared with white casts," according to Jackson's survey in the 1925-26 edition of *Negro Year Book*, "have become members of the Actors' Equity Association, and upon the word of the secretary, the door is open to anyone who seeks admission and meets the requirements as to employment in drama, musical comedy, [and] motion pictures. Bert Williams was the first member, Leon Williams and Leigh Whipper both in films were the next."[27]

Reciprocal Relations with the Black Press

Reciprocal relations with black newspapers and organizations was another goal "The Page" achieved. When Jackson joined *Billboard*, Charles T. Magill of the Chicago *Defender* printed a half-column story on Jackson and commended the publication for hiring him. Also, "The Page" received recognition from local and national black newspapers. Jackson, on more than one occasion, acknowledged his indebtedness to the pioneer theatrical writers for their contribution in improving black performance news reporting.

With the proliferation of black newspapers in the early 1920s, Jackson says: "The papers of the race have become a recognized factor in both the economic and the cultural development of the whole race. More than twenty weekly papers of the group maintain theatrical and amusement pages. To our definite knowledge at least 60% of these are very recent developments. Even the big Negro News Service Bureau, the *Associated Negro Press*, has seen fit to establish in New York, Chicago and two Southern cities representatives of a department charged with securing amusement news of their people."[28]

This network of black performance news reporting also meant more exposure and recognition for the black entertainment industry. Often, Jackson's friend and colleague, Tony Langston, editor of the Chicago *Defender* and journalists at many other black newspapers reprinted Jackson's reviews and editorials, and he did not require a fee. "The Page" reciprocated by reprinting articles and reviews from black publications and performers.

A professional working relationship between "The Page" and the black press continued throughout the life of the column. Jackson enthusiastically endorsed the *Messenger* and *Opportunity's* talent contests; the Indianapolis *Freeman's* 50th anniversary; and the promotion of C. T. Magill and Jack Cooper of the Chicago *Defender*. He reprinted reviews and articles pertinent to the black entertainment industry. This practice helped many black critics and artists to gain credibility in a national entertainment trade paper and to legitimize black performance news reporting.

According to "The Page's" survey of 1921, practically every publication in the country was devoting some space to big-name black performers such as Charles Gilpin and Bert Williams and to shows such as *Shuffle Along*. A year later, many "really competent artists" were receiving even more widespread publicity. Jackson commented: "More recognition has been accorded to our group from the general public in every way, especially from the press. Some of the most aristocratic and most conservative publications have favorably discussed the race and its artists. Unkindly designations and caricature references have become so few as to make the occasional use very noticeable. . . . Trade journals that once candidly declared against any editorial consideration of the Negro performer have seen fit to alter this policy of discrimination."[29]

Using the Column for Legitimate Publicity

"The Page" realized its final objective of encouraging organizations to use the column for legitimate publicity. To encourage the groups to use "The Page" to gain exposure was not difficult since Jackson was a member of most groups related to the show business profession. The better known were the National Negro Business Mens' League, the NAACP, National Negro Press Association, The Dressing Room Club, IBPOE (Elks), Clef, CVBA, CT&P, and Mu-So-Lit. The organizations received valuable publicity in "The Page" and profited financially. There was an abundance of talent sent out from the CVBA and the Clef Club by the Deacon Johnson's Exchange in New York. Also, Charles Cooke of Chicago, General Shook of Detroit, Sammie Keechel in Portland and others filled a number of desirable dates.[30] The Urban League and the NAACP also showed more than a passing interest in the show world.

On June 20, 1925, "The Page" disappeared without notice. The next week, Jackson's colleague and friend, Tony Langston, manager of the theatrical column for the Chicago *Defender* headlined a full column that read: "Page Closed: J. A. Jackson, No Longer on Staff of *Billboard*." Langston received a letter from Jackson disclosing that "the removal came solely on account of . . . a lack of the needed advertising for the upkeep of "The Page," and the policy of "The Page" which forbids solicitation . . . three departments were discontinued for the same reason . . . [and that] the *Billboard* through this action reduced its size from 124 pages to an even 100."[31] "The termination was a most regrettable one," asserts Langston, "and [will] be keenly felt by members of the profession everywhere . . . the presence of "The Page" increased readership and attributed to the overall success of the *Billboard*."[32] He states: "When he opened his department there were but few readers of the publication among racial performers aside from those interested in carnivals, circuses, fairs and other out-of-doors-work. In fact, none but actual novelty turns were at all interested in its columns. It was not long, however, before "The Page" carried comprehensive information to all; and the paper's circulation among members grew into a healthy condition."[33] Langston assured readers that *Billboard* afforded all professional courtesies to Jackson: "The letter of notification dated June 12 is a remarkable testimonial of Jackson's ability and that it was sincere is shown by the fact that it was accomplished not only by a check for a full month's salary but by a bonus of a substantial amount, a spirit of fairness and friendliness being evident throughout the transaction."[34] Langston concluded that: "Jackson more than made good as an editor of the department, he never spared an effort in behalf of the performer, he at all times exhibited a keen interest in things uplifting; and conducted his Page with a dignity which demanded the respect of the readers and which elicited the praise of his fellow workers in the newspaper field. There is no need for a man of Jackson's type and ability to go unattached for any great length of time. So there is but little doubt that his forming a new allegiance with one of the bigger and better publishers will be a news item of the near future."[35] With this kind of encouragement, one might assume that Jackson would try to sell "The Page" to another paper, but there is no evidence to support this theory.

Articles in most black publications seemed to concur with Tony Langston's sentiments toward Jackson and "The Page"; however, one black journalist, Romeo Dougherty of the New York *Amsterdam News*, the self-proclaimed "truth teller," had a few uncomplimentary remarks in a July 1, 1925 article. He stated,

> We do not know how true it is, but we'll take a chance and say that it came from a source we consider reliable, and that is the news that J. A. Jackson is no longer writing 'The Page' on the white theatrical weekly known as The *Billboard.* A splendid chap and a brilliant writer, Mr. Jackson will be missed by hundreds of colored performers all over the country. It was a mighty liberal mind that gave him the opportunity to conduct those pages on this weekly magazine. We believe that it has often been said that Mr. Jackson is a writer of 'constructive' tendencies, and it is strange to note that in the retrenchment taking place on The *Billboard,* 'The Page' happened to be among the first to go. Constructive, perhaps, but we have always maintained that those pages lacked the punch to carry any especial appeal.
>
> Jackson, in our opinion, maintained the policy of constantly catering to that old fashioned form of Negro journalism which found it better to go along the line of least resistance and employ the same flowery praise for the worthy and unworthy. Great stuff in the old days, but with the generation in which live such minds as George Schuyler, Theophilus Lewis, J. A. Rogers and the others, whose trenchant pens are making history—the kind which they can very well afford to feel proud in handing down to another generation.[36]

These are strong words indeed by a journalist who frequently reproduced articles by Jackson in his own theatrical column. Given the response by the black press, it appears that the majority did not hold Dougherty's opinion.

Progenitor of Black Performance News Reporting

Jackson may have also been the progenitor of black performance news reporting in a white entertainment paper. Four years after *Billboard* inaugurated the column, the 1925-26 edition of *Negro Year Book* stated: "There are now more than thirty-five Negroes employed on white publications. Harry Earle is a theatrical and sports writer on the Fairmount, Minnesota *Daily Sentinel.* Lester Walton, who has for many years been a writer of theatrical news, is now a reporter and feature writer on the staff of the New York *Age.* Noah D. Thompson is a member of the staff of the Los Angeles *Daily Express* does general work and was one of the staff to cover the 1924 National Political Convention. Edward H. Lawson, a Washington, D. C., School Principal has become a member of the staff of the Washington *Post.* Perhaps the highest salaried and least known is Eugene Gordon, a short-story editor and assistant editorial writer on the Boston *Post.*"[37]

To determine the column's contribution to the development of black performance, an assessment of what happened in this field after the "The Page" closed is useful. The experience with and exposure in "The Page" during the 1920s must have had an impact on black performance. For one it created an audience. With the depression in the 1930s, the Harlem Renaissance came to a crashing halt, as did many aspects of the entertainment profession. When the commercial theater went into a slump, blacks were the hardest hit. The TOBA and the M. & P. circuits, the largest employer of black talent, folded leaving many vaudevillians out of work. *Variety*, the theatrical trade journal, reported that there were "25,000 unemployed theatrical people in all phases of the profession . . . 3,000 of these . . . black."[38] James Haskins, author of *Black Theatre in America*, estimated that this figure includes nearly all the blacks in the theatrical profession at the time. Nonetheless, because of the Harlem Renaissance and the exposure in "The Page," artists with recognizable names and reputations as proven money makers were able to find employment during the succeeding decades. During the Great Depression some worked in the Negro Units of the Works Progress Administration's theatrical program best known as the Federal Theater Project. Beginning in the 1940s to the present, the booming musical comedy field became an avenue for musicians, and former vaudeville and burlesque performers. This was due perhaps in part to the financial success of *Shuffle Along* and other black musicals that were abundant during the 1920s as they have been today on Broadway: *Eubie, Bubbling Brown Sugar, The Wiz, Dreamgirls, Your Arm's Too Short to Box With God, Bring in da Noise, Bring in da Funk*, and *Jelly*'s *Last Jam*. The popularity of black musicals could also be due to the abundance of reputable African-American talent in this field from that era. Even in the 1970s we find Alberta Hunter, Lena Horne, and Ethel Waters and musicians such as Eubie Blake, Cab Calloway, and Duke Ellington.

In the dramatic arts, Charles Gilpin's resounding success in *Emperor Jones* and the reception of the Lafayette Players by black audiences for over twenty years proved to community and professional groups that there was a market for black drama. In the 1960s with the raising of black consciousness, numerous black drama groups mandated many principles adhered to by groups during the Harlem Renaissance. The Negro Ensemble Company in New York and Crossroads in New Jersey are the most obvious descendants of the Lafayette Players.

In the out-of-doors activities, spectators may find blacks not only in the band box, but also performing in three-ring circuses such as Ringling Brothers' Barnum and Bailey, in carnivals, rodeos, fairs, festivals, and on the streets of New York as "break dancers." There are a few traditions, however, that Jackson tried to eliminate from the profession that were not completely left behind. The vulgar and profane "smut shooters" who long plagued the black show business have made their way into American entertainment by way of Richard Pryor, Eddie Murphy, and Martin Lawrence.

Based on this investigation, Jackson had to make compromises working for a white publication whose primary interest in black entertainment was not social but economic. In spite of all of that, "Jackson's Page" contributed to the development of black performance in very important ways. The column was significant both as a progenitor of black performance reporting and as a contributor to the development of black entertainment. It was the first column in a major show business publication to report on and promote the various types of African-American entertainment. It served as a vital line of communication for those interested in black show business and provided a weekly chronology of artists, theatrical productions and organizations that were active during the middle stages of the Harlem Renaissance. The editorials, articles, surveys, advertisements, and photographs drew attention to the activities and interests of the multi-talented black performer. "The Page" reported on the black artist's unique gifts to the American culture: the syncopated jazz sounds; the Charleston and Blackbottom dances; the blues, gospels, and spirituals; the big musicals with their fast pace and partially garbed chorus "girls"; the fledgling motion picture industry; original vaudeville and burlesque acts depicting aspects of black culture such as their peculiar gait, dress, dance, movement, humor, dialect; novelties in the out-of-doors field; and sounds that Broadway producers "borrowed." Jackson was a black voice for the profession at a time when it was desperately needed. He rendered sensitive portrayals of the black performer's predicament in American entertainment as a means of helping the public at large to better understand the black artist, thus relieving many uncertainties. In the process black performers attracted an audience, white and black, and business interests began to realize their rich talent and financial worth. Even today, Jackson remains one of the few who wrote about performance in its truest sense. He was not only a prolific writer on black performance of the Harlem Renaissance, but also a contemporary historian who provided a comprehensive rendering of the profession and the period. He provided an important black voice, and improved conditions in the industry. He gave visibility to black performance, helped raise the level of employment in the industry, and most importantly Jackson legitimized black performance in the American entertainment industry. As a black journalist, Jackson epitomizes what is possible if given the opportunity. What is most impressive is that he achieved these objectives almost single-handedly, illustrating what is possible when one commits to bringing about change.

Notes

[1] James Albert Jackson, "Annual Survey," *Billboard* 5 Dec.1922: 45.
[2] Ibid., "Pittsburgh Squawks, " *Billboard* 4 Apr. 1925: 50.
[3] Ibid., "Practices What He Preaches," *Billboard* 17 Dec. 1921: 47.
[4] Ibid.
[5] Ibid., (17 December 1921) 47.
[6] Ibid., "Public Won't Stand for Stage Filth," *Billboard* 22 Oct. 1921: 45.
[7] Ibid., "Smut Shooters, Read This and Weep: Decency Vindicated," *Billboard* 17 Nov. 1923: 57.
[8] Ibid.
[9] Ibid., "From 'The Columbus News,' " *Billboard* 18 Apr.1925: 51.
[10] Ibid., "Smut Shooters, Read This and Weep: Decency Vindicated," *Billboard* 17 Nov. 1923: 57.
[11] Ibid., "Muse Says Mouthful to Filth," *Billboard* 3 Nov. 1923: 56.
[12] Ibid., "Actions for Bettering Performers Affairs," *Billboard* 28 Feb. 1925: 50.
[13] Ibid.
[14] Ibid.
[15] Ibid.
[16] Ibid., 359.
[17] Ibid., (16 December 1922) 46.
[18] Ibid., "The TOBA Meeting," *Billboard* 27 Jan. 1923: 50.
[19] Ibid.
[20] Ibid.
[21] Ibid., (13 December 1924) 94.
[22] Ibid., "Columbia State Fair," *Billboard* 19 Nov. 1922: 63.
[23] Ibid., "The Year with the Colored Performer," *Billboard* 16 Dec. 1923: 102-106.
[24] Ibid., 86-89.
[25] Ibid.
[26] Ibid. 359-360.
[27] Ibid.
[28] Ibid., "The Present Situation of the Colored Performer," *Billboard* 10 Dec. 1921: 16.
[29] Ibid., "The Year with the Colored Performer," *Billboard* 16 Dec. 1922: 86-89.
[30] Ibid., "The Present Situation of the Colored Performer," *Billboard* 10 Dec. 1921: 16.
[31] Tony Langston, "Page Closed: J. A. Jackson, on Longer on Staff of *Billboard,* " Chicago *Defender* 27 June 1925: 6.
[32] Ibid.
[33] Ibid.
[34] Ibid.
[35] Ibid.
[36] Romeo Daugherty. *New York Amsterdam News* 1 July 1925: 5.
[37] Ibid., *The Negro Year Book: 1925-26*, 361.
[38] Ibid., *Variety* 85.

Appendices

COLORED ACTORS' UNION
Theatrical Guide
BY BART KENNETT
TELLS EVERYTHING YOU WANT TO KNOW

BART KENNETT
Author

1249 SEVENTH STREET, NORTHWEST
WASHINGTON, D. C.

Copyright, 1925

During J. A. Jackson's five years at *Billboard* (1920-1925), he traveled 11,000 miles, conducted numerous interviews and compiled a card index on black performers (possibly the only one of its kind) that he donated to the CAU. Bart Kennett, the CAU's chief deputy, assembled a theatrical guide on the black entertainment industry that includes much of Jackson's data.

The
Colored Actors Union

ARE YOU A MEMBER?
IF NOT   WHY NOT?

———

The Union is doing some Wonderful work

**Ask some of the members
what we have done**

———

Joining Fees To-day Is
$5.00

It will be more soon

———

Officers

Jules McGarr, President   Chinte. Moore Vice President
Paul Carter, Vice President   Talfair Washington, Secretary
Joe Watts, Recording Secretary   Bart Kennett, Chief Deputy
S. H. Dudley, General Manager and Treasurer

Colored Actors' Union Membership

Up to Date, May 1925

Rastus Airship
Jerry Anthony
Spencer Anthony
George Allen
Jerry Allen
Dolly Allen
Evelyne Allen
Almyra Anderson
W. Henri Bowman
Rastus Brown
Bessie Brown
Arthur Boykins
John Berry
Sandy Burns
Odessa Barber
Magrette Brown
Herbert Brown
Billy Bradford
Rosa Brown
Babe Brown
Jimmie Brown
Blondian Brown
Flora Toota Bean
Blanche Banks
Ellen Bosworth
Leo Boatner
Curley Brooks
Mary Bradford
Jessie Brown
Marie Bidding
Arsenia Bowman
Kid Brown
Neliska Briscoe
Harrison Blackburn
William Benbow
Anita Bush
Beulah Benbow
Robert Barge
Ernest Bundy
Hattie Blackley
Charles De Bonita
Leslie Braxton
John H. Bradley
L. Henry Banks
Harry Brock
Thelma Baytop
Joseph Byrd
Clothide Brown
Helen Brown
Rosetta Brannon
John Henry Banks
Laura Bailey
Dora Carr
John Churchill
Perry & Covan
Ed Lee Coleman
Happy Coles
Claude Collins
Dora Bell Collins

Jimmie Cox, (deceased)
Paul Carter
Elsie Carpenter
Wilton Crawley
Pauline Clark
Julian Costella
Lillian Clark
Harry Clark
Kid Curry
Wallace Curtis
Annia May Cole
Mr. Chavers
Mrs. Chavers
Frank Crocket
Joseph Clark
Mary Clark
Catherine Coleman
Mabel Carter
George Cooper
Billy Cornell
Lillian Curtis
Clifford Curtis
James B. Clark
Martha Copeland
Carlyn Carter
John W. Cooper
Charlie Chicken
I. Love Cox
Baby Cox
Evelyn Carter
Lena Corbin
Jack Cooper
Jessie Crump
Joe Carmouche
Henry Coleman
S. H. Dudley
Fred Durrah
Bonnie B. Drew
Barbara Denslow
Boisey Delegge
Florence Delegge
Alfred Dangerfield
Mattie Dorsey
Quenn Dora
Boyd Douneveor
Lattimore Dixon
Charles Davenport
Al Bowman
Mabel Dilworth
Bill Dooley
Austin Drake
Ralph Demond
Juanita S. Davis
Toussaint L'duers
Willard Davenport
Jannie W. Davenport
Nathan Deloache
Billy Delmar
Sidney Easyon

Evie Elliott
Donald Van Epps
George E. Edwards
Billy Ewing
Beulah Ewing
Willie Eldridge
George W. Edwards
John Fox
Jimmie Furguson
Joseph Frazier
Bertna Forbes
M. Tepose Foster
Dusty Fletcher
Robert Ferebee
Andred Fairchild
Cyrill Fuller
Elnora Fuller
Elizabeth Franklin
Annie Gresham
Marion Gresham
Leroy Gresham
Cecil Graham
Pearl Gooden
Margrette Gentry
Sam H. Gray
Lelia B. Grant
James Gillispie
Francis Goins
Bobbie Grant
D. Mose Gaston
Connie Green
D. Piedmout Gaskin
Mathilda Gasperd
Roberta Green
Jim Greene
Mabel Gant
Walter Gray
Candy A. Gray
Leon Sonny Gray
Lee Goldie
Sally Goldie
George Gould
Sammy Graham
Clifford Green
Marie B. Green
Charles Gaines
Albert Gaines
William Harris
Aletta Harris
Hayes & Hayes
Ida Hooten
Eugene Hooten
Bob Hayes
Leroy Herbert
Chas. Hightower
Melvern Hunter
Marion Hughes
Marie Harris
Pearl Howard

Fred Harris
Bobby Henderson
Ethel Hart
Coy Herndon
Jimmy Howell
Estella Herbert
Erma Hollis
Myrtle Hugg
Mildred Holland
Billy Higgins
Boots Hopes
Bud Harris
Jessie V. Hicks
Virginia Hartley
Lucille Heagimin
Catherine Harris
Bobby C. Harris
Leathia Holloway
Emma Hall
Sally Hunter
Kid Holmes
Odell Irvin
Leroy F. Johnson
Beatrice Johnson
Annice Johnson
Esther Johnson
Bell Johnson
Bruce Johnson
Sylvian B. Jordan
Harold H. Jackson
Sol H. Jones
Alonza Johnson
John Idaho Jordan
Seymore Jeter
Celesta James
Hezekiah Jenkins
Dorothy Jenkins
I. W. Dad James
Joseph Jones
Mrs. Bertha Idaho
Nuggie Johnson
Columbus Jackson
Diyaw Jones
Florence Johnson
Lemuel Jackson
Slim Jones
Harry Jackson
Alexander Jackson
Walter Jones
J. Lewis Johnson
Katie Jones
Lizzie Jackson
J. A. Jackson
Emma J. Jackson
Eddie Jackson
Baby Johnson
Beatrice Johnson
Mack Jones
Isabelle Johnson
Fred Jenkins
Lukie Johnson
Lizzie Jones
Edna Johnson
Charles C. Jones
James W. Kennimon

Marie Kitchen
Bart Kennett
Dude Kelly
Luther King
Marie King
Estella Kennedy
J. Ralston Kennan
Capt. May Kemp
Henrietta Lovelace
Jessie Love
Virginia Liston
Hazel Lee
Velma Lindsey
Buster Lee
Boy Lee
Eddie Lewis
Marie Lewis
Johnnie Lee
Tony Langston
Baby Lewis
Johnnie L. Long
Lorenza McLane
Means & Means
Ethel McCoy
Melba & More
Sweetie May
Chintz Moore
Billie Miller
Livingston Mayes
Eugene Martin
Jules McGarr
Billy McOwens
Roscoe Montella
Iris Miller
Billy Mack
Billy Mitchell
Sarah Martin
Edward Madison
Dusty Murry
Ozie McPherson
Kitty Miles
Effie May Moore
Billie McKenzie
Daisey McClennon
Willie McCurry
Loraine McClain
Baby McClennon
Melvern
Buster Miller
Elemore Moore
Bluch McLanian
Charles Mason
James Madison
Ida Madison
Fay Dean McKenny
Eugene Moore
Louis McBride
Gertrude Marshall
Loretta J. Mabley
Thelma Moyer
Harry Miller
Slim Mason
Russel Moppin
Arribelle McCoy
George Motto

Harry Massingake
John H. McLoy
Edgar Martin
Buster Martin
Charles Mason
Gertrude Marshall
Russel Moppin
George McClennon
Baby Mark
Thelma Moyer
Dewayman Niles
Lemmar Oakley
Chane Oakley
Lola Owens
Anna Pace
Rector Patterson
Marvin S. Price
Erline Parker
Alma Perry
Willie Porter
John Pickett
Dorothy Powell
F. F. Peat
Thelma Payne
Clifford Padmore
Alberta Perkins
Thelma Payne
Prince Oskazuma
Hernanz Go Quano
Billie Rochester
Gladys Rhodes
Sam Rhodes
Beatrice Robinson
Amanzie Richardson
Lillian Russel
Johnnie Riddick
Walter Rector
Lillian Radcliff
Marie Robinson
Bob Robinson
Louise Redder
David Roesborough
Tiny Ray
Sammy Randall
Al G. Reed
Virginia Randall
The Robinsons
Clarence Rucker
Fred Redders
Original Rags
Sam Russell
J. Jellyroll Robinson
Sam Robinson
Smith & Smith
Bennie Sparrow
Maud Sparrow
Laura Smith
Brown Singleton
Hettie V. Snow
Gertrude Struffin
Gladys Smith
Dinah Scott
R. P. Smith
Rector Smith
Inez Saunders

William F. Sledge
Emma Simmons
Leeman Smith
Louise Silver
Teddy Smith
Gus Simmons
Mary Sellmon
Irby Smith
W. A. Sullivan
Jimmy Stewart
Jennie Straine
Johnny Stevens
Dancing Sonny
Cress Simmons
Ernest Seals
Doorkey Singleton
Gus Smith
Joe Slats
Julia Shedrick
Lucille Smith
Laurence Simmons
James Sykes
Jolly Saunders
Amanda Scott
Tom Scott
Ernest Session
James Strong
Trixie Smith
Carl Smooth
Lucille Smooth
Lucille Snow
Pauline Stevens
William Sibley
Catherine Simmons
Eulalie Smith
Joy Scott
The Schavers
Mattie Spencer
Travis Tucker
E. Manuel Taylor
Willean G. Thomas
Kid Thomas
Gibson Trio
Bethel Gibson
Elnora Gibson
Corrine Gibson
Albert Gibson
Anconia Turner
Frank R. Taylor
James Towel

Rosa Townsend
George Townsend
Willie Thomas
Kid Talley
Willie Townsend
Richard Perry
Lewis Tally
Pat Tucker
Cherekee Thornton
Lillie Tuck
Skeet Terry
Vader & Vader
Louis Edith
Leroy White
Telfair Washington
Mary Williams
Williams & Williams
The Bird
George Williams
Billy Walker
James E. Worlds
Lew Watts
Cy Williams
A. B. Williams
Hazel Wallace
Garnett Warbington
James Wanza
Johnny Woods
Bessie Walker
Raymond Wooten
Arthur Winn
Wesley Wilson
Clara Walker
Bessie Williams
Viola Williams
Rastus Winfield
Johnnie Wiggins
Elbert White
Billy Willis
May Wade (deceased)
Jules Weaver
Eulia Weaver
Boston Webb
Alonza Webb
Bobbie Woldridge
Pattie Willis Billy
Willis Watts
Alberta West
Jessie Wilson
May Willis

George Wiltshire
Evelyne White
Dan Wiley
John S. Williams
Burch Williams
Leonard Moxey
Bobby Wilson
Baby Rose Whiting
Speedy Wilson
Roy White
John Webb
Annie White
Jimmie Warren
Billy Zeek
Kid Foster
Sonny Thompson
Cyrill Fullerton
Marie Boatner
Inez Jackson
Buddy Morgan
Galle Degaston
Lillie Yuen
Grant Kay
Lonnie Fisher
Younder Sellmon
Alex Kent
Jap Reed
Curey Drysdale
Henry R. Dixon
Onnie L. Jones
Pearl Lee
Corrine Jones
Bill Jones
George Alexander
Charles Doyle
Julius Hall
Jazz Lindsey
Jimmie Dick
Octavia Dick
Ruth Trent
Hester Kenton
Catherine Stanley
Isabelle Dabner
Sarah Veneable
Etta Chatterman
Alex Lovejoy
Elnora Fuller
Elbert White
Kid Holmes

Many Members names are not printed because of lack of space

Excess Baggage Rates For One-Way Railroad Fare

RATES APPLY TO 100 LBS. EXCESS BAGGAGE

When Fare is From	to	Excess is	When Fare is From	to	Excess is	When Fare is From	to	Excess is	When Fare is From	to	Excess is
$ 05	90	15	20 41	20 70	3 45	40 21	40 50	6 75	60 01	60 30	10 05
0 91	1 20	20	20 71	21 00	3 50	40 51	40 80	6 80	60 31	60 60	10 10
1 21	1 50	25	21 01	21 30	3 55	40 81	41 10	6 85	60 61	60 90	10 15
1 51	1 80	30	21 31	21 60	3 60	41 11	41 40	6 90	60 91	61 20	10 20
1 81	2 10	35	21 61	21 90	3 65	41 41	41 70	6 95	61 21	61 50	10 25
2 11	2 40	40	21 91	22 20	3 70	41 71	42 00	7 00	61 51	61 80	10 30
2 41	2 70	45	22 21	22 50	3 75	42 01	42 30	7 05	61 81	62 10	10 35
2 71	3 00	50	22 51	22 80	3 80	42 31	42 60	7 10	62 11	62 40	10 40
3 01	3 30	55	22 81	23 10	3 85	42 61	42 90	7 15	62 41	62 70	10 45
3 31	3 60	60	23 11	23 40	3 90	42 91	43 20	7 20	62 71	63 00	10 50
3 61	3 90	65	23 41	23 70	3 95	43 21	43 50	7 25	63 01	63 30	10 55
3 91	4 20	70	23 70	24 00	4 00	43 51	43 80	7 30	63 31	63 60	10 60
4 21	4 50	75	24 01	24 30	4 05	43 81	44 10	7 35	63 61	63 90	10 65
4 51	4 80	80	24 31	24 60	4 10	44 11	44 40	7 40	63 91	64 20	10 70
4 81	5 10	85	24 61	24 90	4 15	44 41	44 70	7 45	64 21	64 50	10 75
5 11	5 40	90	24 91	25 20	4 20	44 71	45 00	7 50	64 51	64 80	10 80
5 41	5 70	95	25 21	25 50	4 25	45 01	45 30	7 55	64 81	65 10	10 85
5 71	6 00	1 00	25 51	25 80	4 30	45 31	45 60	7 60	65 11	65 40	10 90
6 01	6 30	1 05	25 81	26 10	4 35	45 61	45 90	7 65	65 41	65 70	10 95
6 31	6 60	1 10	26 11	26 40	4 40	45 91	46 20	7 70	65 71	66 00	11 00
6 61	6 90	1 15	26 41	26 70	4 45	46 21	46 50	7 75	66 01	66 30	11 05
6 91	7 20	1 20	26 71	27 00	4 50	46 51	46 80	7 80	66 31	66 60	11 10
7 21	7 50	1 25	27 01	27 30	4 55	46 81	47 10	7 85	66 61	66 90	11 15
7 51	7 80	1 30	27 31	27 60	4 60	47 11	47 40	7 90	66 91	67 20	11 20
7 81	8 10	1 35	27 61	27 90	4 65	47 41	47 70	7 95	67 21	67 50	11 25
8 11	8 40	1 40	27 91	28 20	4 70	47 71	48 00	8 00	67 51	67 80	11 30
8 41	8 70	1 45	28 21	28 50	4 75	48 01	48 30	8 05	67 81	68 10	11 35
8 71	9 00	1 50	28 51	28 80	4 80	48 31	48 60	8 10	68 11	68 40	11 40
9 01	9 30	1 55	28 81	29 10	4 85	48 61	48 90	8 15	68 41	68 70	11 45
9 31	9 60	1 60	29 11	29 40	4 90	48 91	49 20	8 20	68 71	69 00	11 50
9 61	9 90	1 65	29 41	29 70	4 95	49 21	49 50	8 25	69 01	69 30	11 55
9 91	10 20	1 70	29 71	30 00	5 00	49 51	49 80	8 30	69 31	69 60	11 60
10 21	10 50	1 75	30 01	30 30	5 05	49 81	50 10	8 35	69 61	69 90	11 65
10 51	10 80	1 80	30 31	30 60	5 10	50 11	50 40	8 40	69 91	70 20	11 70
10 81	11 10	1 85	30 61	30 90	5 15	50 41	50 70	8 45	70 21	70 50	11 75
11 11	11 40	1 90	30 91	31 20	5 20	50 71	51 00	8 50	70 51	70 80	11 80
11 41	11 70	1 95	31 21	31 50	5 25	51 01	51 30	8 55	70 81	71 10	11 85
11 71	12 00	2 00	31 51	31 80	5 30	51 31	51 60	8 60	71 11	71 40	11 90
12 01	12 30	2 05	31 81	32 10	5 35	51 61	51 90	8 65	71 41	71 70	11 95
12 31	12 60	2 10	32 11	32 40	5 40	51 91	52 20	8 70	71 71	72 00	12 00
12 61	12 90	2 15	32 41	32 70	5 45	52 21	52 50	8 75	72 01	72 30	12 05
12 91	13 20	2 20	32 71	33 00	5 50	52 51	52 80	8 80	72 31	72 60	12 10
13 21	13 50	2 25	33 01	33 30	5 55	52 81	53 10	8 85	72 61	72 90	12 15
13 51	13 80	2 30	33 31	33 60	5 60	53 11	53 40	8 90	72 91	73 20	12 20
13 81	14 10	2 35	33 61	33 90	5 65	53 41	53 70	8 95	73 21	73 50	12 25
14 11	14 40	2 40	33 91	34 20	5 70	53 71	54 00	9 00	73 51	73 80	12 30
14 41	14 70	2 45	34 21	34 50	5 75	54 01	54 30	9 05	73 81	74 10	12 35
14 71	15 00	2 50	34 51	34 80	5 80	54 31	54 60	9 10	74 11	74 40	12 40
15 01	15 30	5 55	34 81	35 10	5 85	54 61	54 90	9 15	74 41	74 70	12 45
15 31	15 60	2 60	35 11	35 40	5 90	54 91	55 00	9 20	74 71	75 00	12 50
15 61	15 90	2 65	35 41	35 70	5 95	55 21	55 50	9 25	75 01	75 30	12 55
15 91	16 20	2 70	35 71	36 00	6 00	55 51	55 80	9 30	75 31	75 60	12 60
16 21	16 50	2 75	36 01	36 30	6 05	55 81	56 10	9 35	75 61	75 90	12 65
16 51	16 80	2 80	36 31	36 60	6 10	56 11	56 40	9 40	75 91	76 20	12 70
16 81	17 10	2 85	36 61	36 90	6 15	56 41	56 70	9 45	76 21	76 50	12 75
17 11	17 40	2 90	36 91	37 20	6 20	56 71	57 00	9 50	76 51	76 80	12 80
17 41	17 70	2 95	37 21	37 50	6 25	57 01	57 30	9 55	76 81	77 10	12 85
17 71	18 00	3 00	37 51	37 80	6 30	57 31	57 60	9 60	77 11	77 40	12 90
18 01	18 30	3 05	37 81	38 10	6 35	57 61	57 90	9 65	77 41	77 70	12 95
18 31	18 60	3 10	38 11	38 40	6 40	57 91	58 20	9 70	77 71	78 00	13 00
18 61	18 90	3 15	38 41	38 70	6 45	58 21	58 50	9 75	78 01	78 30	13 05
18 91	19 20	3 20	38 71	39 00	6 50	58 51	58 80	9 80	78 31	78 60	13 10
19 21	19 50	3 25	39 01	39 30	6 55	58 81	59 10	9 85	78 61	78 90	13 15
19 51	19 80	3 30	39 31	39 60	6 60	59 11	59 40	9 90	78 91	79 20	13 20
19 81	20 10	3 35	39 61	39 90	6 65	59 41	59 70	9 95	79 21	79 50	13 25
20 11	20 40	3 40	39 91	40 20	6 70	59 71	60 00	10 00	79 51	79 80	13 30

THE WORLD OF AGENTS

NEW YORK

A

Abbay Amusement Co., 1482 Broadway.
Aiston, Arthur C., 210 W. 107th.
Amalgamated Vaude. Agency, 1441 Broadway.
Anderson & Weber, 220 W. 48th.
Arganza, Andy, 774 Union Ave., Bronx, New York.
Ashland, Wilfred, 1650 Broadway.
Associated Theatres, 214 W. 42d.

B

Baerwitz, Samuel, 160 W. 46th.
Baker, Bob 160 W. 46th.
Beck, Arthur F., 135 W. 44th.
Becker, Herman, 148 W. 46th.
Benedict, Phil P., 1402 Broadway.
Bentham, M. S., 1564 Broadway.
Beman, Jack, 24 Court St., Brooklyn.
Berlinghoff, Henry, 1493 Broadway.
Bernstein, David, 1540 Broadway.
Bierbauer, Charles, 1607 Broadway.
Binkoff, Harry L., 472 2d Ave.
Bloch, A. L., 502 W. 179th.
Bloch & Barmore, 145 W. 45th.
Bloom, Celia, 1564 Broadway.
Blue, John J., 233 W. 51st.
Blumenfield, Herman, 1579 Broadway.
Bradley, Lillian, 1658 Broadway.
Brecher, Leo, 623 Mad. Ave.
Breed, Charles S., 1564 Broadway.
Browman, George H., 1402 Broadway.
Brill, Sol, 1540 Broadway.
Broadway Varieties Co., 2834 Broadway.
Brooks, Morris & Freeman, 1493 Broadway.
Brown, Miss G. F., 1564 Broadway.
Brown, Jos. K., 313 E. 27th.
Buckley & Sullivan, Inc., 1607 Broadway.
Burke, Bernard, 1581 Broadway.
Burke, Billie, 1495 Broadway.
Bush, Phil, 1493 Broadway.

C

Cantor, Lew, 160 W. 46th.
Carpenter, E. J., 1402 Broadway.
Casey, Pat, Dramatic Agency, Inc., 701 7th.
Choos, Geo., 110 W. 47th.
Claremont Entertainment Bureau, 4141 3d.
Cohn, David, 1493 Broadway.
Collins, H. D., 1493 Broadway.
Connors, Jack, 160 W. 45th St.
Consolidated Theatrical Enterprises, Inc., 1588 Broadway.
Cooper, Irving M., 1416 Broadway.
Cooper, Jas. E., 701 7th Ave.
Cornell, Charles, 1520 Broadway.
Cornell, John, 1520 Broadway.
Cosby, Vivian, 160 W. 45th St.

D

Dandy, Ned, 148 W. 46th.
Davis, Al, 1547 Broadway.
Davis, Frank, 245 W. 47th St.
Davidow, Edward, 1493 Broadway.
Dow, A. & B., 1547 Broadway.
Driscoll, Dave, 500 Astor Bldg.
Duffus, Bruce, 1493 Broadway.
Dunbar, Ralph M., 1564 Broadway.
Dupree, Geo., 1547 Broadway.
Durand, Paul, 1562 Broadway.

E

Eckl, Jos., 1493 Broadway.
Edwards, Gus, 1531 Broadway.
Ehrlich, Paul, 140 W. 42nd St.
Eichner, Manny, 1545 Broadway.
Elliott, Wm., 104 W. 39th.
Evans, Frank, Inc., 1564 Broadway.

F

Fallow, Sam, 160 W. 46th.
Farnum, Ralph G., 1564 Broadway.
Feinberg, A., 160 W. 46th.
Feldman, N. S., Inc., 1493 Broadway.
Fitzgerald, H. J., 220 W. 48th.
Fitzpatrick & O'Donnell, 160 W. 46th.
Flynn, Jack D., 1564 Broadway.
Ford, Max, 1674 Broadway.
Fox, William, 126 W. 46th.
Friedman, John E., 218 Romax Bldg.

G

Garren, Jos., 160 W. 46th.
Gerber, Alex, 1607 Broadway.
Golden, M., 160 W. 46th St.
Golder, Lew, 1564 Broadway.
Grady, Billy, 1564 Broadway.
Grau's, Matt, Agency, New York Theater Bldg.
Grisman, Sam, 1493 Broadway.
Grossman, Al, 160 W. 46th.
Green, Howard, Jr., 110 W. 47th.

H

Hall, Syd, 148 W. 46th St.
Hallett, Louis, 1493 Broadway.
Hart, Jos., 137 W. 48th.
Hart, Max, 1540 Broadway.
Harvey, Charles J., 1402 Broadway.
Hastings, Ben, 160 W. 45th.
Hastings, Harry, 701 7th Ave.
Hathaway, O. S., 1476 Broadway.
Henry, Jack, 1607 Broadway.
Herman, Al, 245 W. 47th.
Hirshfeld, M., 1441 Broadway.
Hockey, Milton, 110 W. 47th.
Hogarty, John E., 200 W. 52d.
Horn, J. E., 1493 Broadway.
Hughes, Gene, Inc., 1562 Broadway.

I

International Variety & Theatrical Agency, Inc., 218 W. 42d.

27

Smith, Patsy, 1562 Broadway.
Smith, Joseph R., 245 W. 47th St.
Sobol, Eddie, 245 W. 47th.
Sobel, Nat, 1579 Broadway.
Sofferman, A., 1493 Broadway.
Solti, David, 417 W. 43d.
Spachner, Leopold, 116 W. 39th.
Stahl, John M., 220 W. 42d.
Stater, Leona, Suite 330 Putnam Bldg., 1493 Broadway.
Stewart, Rosalie, 110 W. 47th St.
Stokes, John, 151 W. 42d.
Stoker, Floyd, 245 W. 47th.
Sullivan, Joseph, 1607 Broadway.
Sun Gus, Booking Exchange Co., 1493 Broadway.

T

Tennis, C. O., 1476 Broadway.
Thalheimer, A., 160 W. 46th.
Thatcher, James, 755 7th Ave.
Thomas, Lou, 1544 Broadway.
Thor, M., 245 W. 47th.
Tilden, Cordelia, 1493 Broadway.
Tishman, Irving, 160 W. 46th St.
Turner, H. Godfrey, 1400 Broadway.

V

Vincent, Walter, 1451 Broadway.
Vogel, Wm., Production, Inc., 130 W. 46th.

W

Walker, Harry, 1674 Broadway.
Weber, Harry, 1564 Broadway.
Weber, Herman W., 1564 Broadway.
Weber, Ike, 701 7th Ave.
Wells, Wm. K., 701 7th Ave.
West, Roland, Producing Co., 236 W. 55th.
White, George R., 220 W. 43rd.
Williams, Sim, 701 7th Ave.
Wilmer & Vincent Theater Co., 1451 Broadway.
Wilshin, Charles S., Inc., 1573 Broadway.
Wilton, Alf. T., 1564 Broadway.
Winter, Wales, 1476 Broadway.
Wirth & Hamid, Inc., 1579 Broadway.
Wolfe, Georgia, 137 W. 48th.

Y

Yates, Irving, 160 W. 46th.

CHICAGO

A

Allen-Summers Theatrical Agency, 145 N. Clark St.
American Theatrical Dramatic Agency, 36 W. Randolph St.
Associated Booking Offices, 54 W. Randolph St.
Athenium-Harvey Thomas Theatrical Agency, 59 E. Van Buren.

B

Barnes, F. M., Inc. (Fairs), 624 S. Michigan Ave.
Baxter, John, 119 N. Clark St.
Bennett's Dramatic & Musical Exchange, 36 W. Randolph.
Benson Music & Entertainment Co., 64 W. Randolph St.
Bentley, John H., 177 N. State St.
Billsbury, John H., Agency, 54 W. Randolph St.
Borthwick, Al, Booking Agency, 22 Quincy St.
Brandt, Alfred D., 22 Quincy St.

C

Carrell's Theatrical Agency, 36 S. State St.
Charette & Valentine, 25 N. Dearborn St.
Coffey, Jee, Amusement Co., 127 N. Dearborn.
Continental Vaudeville Exchange, 160 W. Washington St.
Crowl, Chas., 54 W. Randolph St.

D

Danforth, Harry, Inc., 177 N. State St.
Davidson's Orchestra, 64 W. Randolph.
Davis, Col. W. L., 36 W. Randolph St.
Doll & Howard, 36 W. Randolph.
Doyle, Frank Q., 22 Quincy St.

E

Eagle & Goldsmith, 177 N. State St.
Earl & Perkins Theatrical Agency, 54 W. Randolph St.
Ellis, Charles E., 159 N. State St.

F

Fine, Jack, 159 N. State.
Fine & Willems, 159 N. State.
Fisher Pony Enterprises, 177 N. State St.
Freeman, Jesse, 159 N. State St.
Friedlander, Robert, 180 W. Washington St.

G

Gardner, Jack, 177 N. State St.
Girdeller, Earl, 159 N. State St.
Gladden Booking Offices, 36 W. Randolph St.
Goldberg, Lew M., 54 W. Randolph St.

H

Halperin-Shapiro Agency, 190 N. State St.
Hernian, Sam, 119 N. Clark St.
Horwitz, Arthur J., 177 N. State St.
Howard, Monte, 36 W. Randolph.
Howard & Doll, 36 W. Randolph.
Hubb & Weston, 36 W. Randolph St.

I

International Vaudeville Exchange, 54 W. Randolph St.

J

Jackson, Billy, Agency, 177 N. State St.
Jacobs, Wm., 54 W. Randolph St.
Johnstone, O. H., 36 W. Randolph St.

K

Keith, B. F., Vaudeville Exchange, 190 N. State St.
Keough, Ez, 54 W. Randolph.
Kingston Vaudeville Booking Assn., 106 N. LaSalle St.
Klein, Martin, 129 E. 31st St.
Kraus, Lee, Inc., 177 N. State St.

L

Levey, Bert, Circuit, 54 W. Randolph St.
Loew, Marcus, Western Booking Agency, Suite 604 Woods Theater Bldg.

M

M. & E., Agency, 108 N. Dearborn St.
MacDonald Groff Concert Co., 2828 W. Madison St.
Mack & Gerger, 177 N. State.
Maine, Billy, 36 W. Randolph St.
Marsh, Edward, Amusement Exchange (Fairs), 159 Nl State St.
Matthews, J. C., 300-301 Garrick Bldg.
Morse Theatrical Agency, 159 N. State.

O

Orpheum Circuit, 190 N. State St.

P

Pantages' Vaudeville Agency, 36 S. State St.
Patlin, J., 22 Quincy St.
Powell, Tom, 54 W. Randolph St.
Powell-Danforth Agency, Inc., 54 W. Randolph.

R

Raimund Booking Agency, 22 Quincy St.
Rich, Frank, 177 N. State St.
Roberts, Sam, 177 N. State St.
Rogers Producing Co., 54 W. Randolph St.
Robinson Attractions, Inc. (Fairs), 202 S. State St.
Ruggia, John, 542 N. Wells St.

S

Schallmana Bros., 36 W. Randolph St.
Schuster, Milton, 36 W. Randolph St.
Schuster, Milton, 36 W. Randolph St.
Seymour-Shapiro, 36 W. Randolph St.
Sloan, J. Alex., 624 S. Michigan.
Simon Agency, 54 W. Randolph St.
Spingold, Harry, 54 W. Randolph St.
Sternad Attractions, Inc., 64 W. Randolph St.
Stewart, John R., 36 W. Randolph.
Summers, Allen, 145 N. Clark St.
Sun, Gus, Booking Exchange, 36 W. Randolph.
Suranyi, M. I., 36 W. Randolph St.

Symphony Amusement Offices, 8 S. Dearborn.

T

Taylor, Earl, 159 N. State St.
Temple Amusement Exchange, 159 N. State St.
Thomas, Harvey, Theatrical Agency, 59 E. Van Buren St.

U

United Fairs Booking Assn., 624 S. Michigan Ave.

V

Van, Edward, 159 N. State St.

W

Webster Vaudeville Circuit, 36 W. Randolph St.
Western Vaudeville Managers' Assn., 190 N. State St.
Weyerson, Edw., 22 Quincy St.
Wingfield, James, 139 N. Clark St.
Willems, Charles J., 159 N. State.
World Amusement Service Assn., 624 S. Michigan Ave.

Y

Young, Ernie, 159 N. State St.

Z

Zimmerman, Wm., 106 N. LaSalle St.

BALTIMORE, MD.

McCaslin, John T., Vaudeville Agency, 123 E. Baltimore St.

BOSTON, MASS.

Hub Amusement Co., 230 Tremont St.
Keith, B. F., Vaudeville Exchange, 164 Tremont St.
Quigley, John J., 184 Boylston St.
Timmins & Joyce, 176 Tremont St.
Walters, Louis E., 238 Tremont St.
White Amusement Bureau, 180 Tremont St.

BUFFALO, N. Y.

National Vaudeville Exchange, 617-619 Bramson Bldg.

CINCINNATI, O.

Jones, Morris, Agency (511 Coppin Bldg., Covington, Ky., near Cincinnati).
Middleton, Jack, 21 E. 6th St.

CLEVELAND, O.

Kendall, Norman, Room 302, 919 Huron Rd.
Miller, Muriel W., 417 Newman-Stern Bldg.
Russell, Danny, Booking Exchange, 350 The Arcade.

DENVER, COL.

H. & C. Theatrical Exchange, Room 2, E. & C. Bldg.

DETROIT, MICH.
International Vaudeville Exchange, 2539 Woodward Ave.
Sun, Gus, Booking Exchange, 1504 Broadway.
Zobedie's Theatrical Agency, cor. Broadway and Grand River.

KANSAS CITY, MO.
Consolidated Amusement Co., 415 Lee Bldg.
Feist, Ed F., Gladstone Hotel Bldg.
Hammond, Kathryn Swan, care Coates House, 10th and Broadway.
Kansas City Vaudeville Agency, 716 Chambers Bldg.
Simpson, Karl F., 17 Gayety Theater Bldg.
Western Vaudeville Mgrs. Assn., 211 Mainstreet Theater Bldg.

LOUISVILLE, KY.
Flagler Theatrical Exchange, 201-4 Starks Bldg.

NEW ORLEANS, LA.
Brennen, B. F., 155 University Place.
International Booking and Theatrical Circuit, 419 Catondelet St.

PHILADELPHIA, PA.
Collins & Philips, 1305 Arch.
Consolidated Booking Offices, Market & Juniper Sts.
Donnelly, Frank, Real Estate Trust Bldg.
Dupille, Ernest, Real Estate Trust Bldg.
Griffiths, Wm. T., 1322 Vine St.
Hammond & Harn, 122 S. 13th.
Heller Entertainment Bureau, Keith Theater Bldg.
Jefferies, Norman, Real Estate Trust Bldg.

Keiler Vaudeville Agency, Real Estate Trust Bldg.
Kline Booking Co., 1305 Vine St.
Krause & Shaw, Real Estate Trust Bldg.
Lipschutz & Maser, 507 Schubert Bldg.
McKay Vaudeville Agency, Empire Bldg.
Russell, Mae, Vaudeville Agency, 21 N. Juniper St.
Sablosky, David R., Keith Bldg.
Senator Music & Entertainment Bureau, Hotel Adelphia.
Spring Garden Entertainment Bureau, 819 Spring Garden Street.
Sulzer, Fred Albert, 1714 Chestnut St.
Weil, I., 1322 Vine St.

ST. LOUIS, MO.
Dane, Oscar, Gayety Theater Bldg.
Drisdall Sisters Entertainment Bureau, 620 Chestnut St.
Hagen, Bobby, Gem Theater Bldg.
Missouri Theatrical Exchange, Pineate Bldg., 804 Pine St.
States Booking Exchange, Calumet Bldg.
Thompson, A. A., Amusement Enterprise, 801 United Home Bldg.
United Musical Comedy Exchange (tabloids), Calumet Bldg.
W. V. M. A., Joe Erber, mgr., Arcade Bldg.
Weber, R. J., Entertainment Bureau, Times Bldg.
West, Bobby, Entertainment Bureau, Gem Theater Bldg.

TORONTO, CAN.
Canadian Booking Offices, 3 Dundas St., West.
Ontario Booking Office, 36 Yonge St., Arcade.

Foreign Dramatic and Vaudeville Agents

LONDON
Adacker, W. Scott, 26 Charing Cross Road, W. C. 2.
Actors' Association, St. Martin's Lane, W. C. 2.
Adams' Agency, 122 Shaftesbury Ave., W.
Akerman, May, Agency, 7 and 8 Leicester Place, W. C. 2.
Ashton & Mitchell, 33 Old Bond St.. W.
Arnold, Tom, Sicilian Ho., Sicilian Ave., Southampton Row.
Astley, Reg., 9 Chandos St., W. C. 2.
Baird, Enid, Theatrical and Musical Bureau, 53 St. Martin's Lane, W. C. 2.
Barclay, George. 221 Brixton Hill, S. W.
Bauer, G., Broadmead House, Panton St., Haymarket, S. W.

Barry O'Brien Agency, 18 Charing Cross Road, W. C. 2.
Benet, Harry, 3 Piccadilly, W. 1.
Bentley's, Walter, Agency, 122 Shaftesbury Ave., W.
Berry & Laurance, Ltd., 25 Haymarket, S. W.
Blackmore's Dramatic Agency, 11 Garrick St., W. C.
Bliss, David, 22 Leicester Square, W. C.
Braham, Philip, & Campbell, Ltd., 26 Charing Cross Road, W. C.
Brown, Joe, & Co., Albion House, 61 New Oxford St., W. C.
Bonner, E. J. (in assn. with H. W. Wieland. Zaeo, Agency), 33 Whitcomb St.. W. C. 2.

31

Theatrical Resume

It is certain that theatrical display, at least in some crude shape, existed before the dawn of authentic history. Dates given for the first introduction of theatricals in America: Hon. Charles P. Daly named February, 1733; Dr. Francis named February, 1750; Mr. Dunlap named September 17, 1753.

Alexander Sergewich Pushkin, the most celebrated of all Russian poets, was born in Moscow on May 26th, 1799. His mother was the granddaughter of Abraham Petrovitch Hannibal, a favorite Negro enrolled by Peter the Great, who died February 10th, 1837.

The first American comedy worthy of the name was written by Mrs. Anna Cora Nowatt, was produced at the Park Theatre, New York, in March, 1845, and was entitled "Fashion." Revived in February, 1924, by Provincetown Prayers, Inc., at Provincetown Playhouse.

Negro theatricals, as far as can be obtained, began about 1861 with the Lucca family traveling through the States of the North and West giving concerts in halls and churches. They traveled in a wagon from town to town. Following the Lucca family were the Fisk Jubilee Singers, beginning October 6th, 1871, touring the country immortalizing Negro spirituals.

The first Negro minstrels were introduced by Charles Cruso, a Negro, in the early '70's. He was billed as "The Man Who Talks."

The musical team of Lyles and Lyles played the free and easy variety halls in the early '70's.

"Carry Me Back to Old Virginny," and "In the Evenin' by de Moonlight" written by Jim Bland, celebrated Negro comedian. Sam Lucas wrote "Grandfather's Clock" in the late '70's. Sam Lucas and the Hyer sisters started in underground railroad in 1877.

Bob Kelly introduced first Negro woman to variety halls, with his team of Kelly and Holmes, in the early '80's.

August, 1883, Callender's Minstrels, with Agustav and Charles Frohman as owners and Mr. Welch as Manager, gave a three-months' jubilee of minstrelsy at San Francisco, Cal. Blind Tom, concert artist, thrilled many with his marvelous playing. He is looked upon as one of the pioneers.

When Callender was the rage on the coast, Mme. Selika was in concert, winning favor as the greatest Negro singer the race had ever heard. She is now teaching music and enjoying excellent health. The concert field boasted later of Sisseretta Jones, Black Patti, who won favor in the United States and Europe.

In 1892 Sam T. Jack formed the Creolo Company. This event is looked upon as the acceptance of Negro women on the stage. Heretofore no organization had carried such numbers as this did. The idea of the minstrel part with olio and after piece done by men and women. In 1893 Primrose and West, then the leading minstrel show of the stage, carried out the famous 40 whites and 30 blacks.

The double-necked guitar was inventer by Richard Byron, father of the Byron Brothers, and named the Bryondolin. In 1894 John W. Isham Octroons were formed. In 1895, breaking away from the minstrel show idea and bordering on musical comedy with a finish of opera, Oriental America, a continuation of the Octoroon show, was the first Negro aggregation to play houses other than burlesque. In 1896 vaudeville had supplanted variety, and Negroes were among the headliners. Williams and Walker were among these, and in 1897 there was a deluge of Negro shows. These headliners formed their first company and toured as "The Senegambian Carnival." Black Patti left the concert field and headed "Black Patti's Troubadors." "Oriental America" was in Europe, but the Octoroons continued. In 1898 "The Trip to Coontown" with Bill Cole and the original Billie Johnson made its appearance. This was the first show written for Negroes that was a musical comedy.

Williams and Walker introduced "The Policy Players" in 1899. In this production Williams and Walker worked in 12 of the musical numbers. Ernest Hogan, known as the "Unbleached American" and writer of "All Coons Look Alike to Me," with his minstrel show, sailed for Australia in June, 1899. Williams and Walker produced "Sons of Ham" in 1900. Gus Hill opened "The Smart Set" with Ernest Hogan in 1902. Williams and Walker opened in Dahomey in 1902. In 1903 Negro theatricals were reaching heights that had only been dreamed of. The minstrel shows were on the wane, and each year shows were seeking something new along musical comedy lines. Williams and Walker leaders played the first legitimate engagement given a Negro organization when "In Dahomey" played the New York Theatre at 46th and Broadway for four weeks. Six weeks later there was an engagement at the Shaftsbury Theatre in London which lasted eight months, followed by a six months' tour of the provinces.

In 1904 S. H. Dudley starred the Smart Set Company. In 1905 Ernest Hogan opened in "Rufus Rastus." In 1906 Hogan opened in "The Oyster Man." After a brief tour, the show was forced to close on account of illness of the star. This was his last show.

The spectacular production of "Abyssinia," with Williams and Walker, opened at Park Theatre, New York, in 1907. "Bandana Land" Opened in 1908. "Mr. Lode of Coal," with Bert Williams as a star, opened in 1909. In 1910 Bert Williams entered vaudeville and later joined "The Follies." From 1910 to 1919 the Smart Set Companies 1 and 2 and Black Patti were the only recognized Negro companies traveling with the exception of J. Lubrie Hill's "Darktown Follies," an aggregation that was due every consideration, but lack of finances caused many reverses.

In 1919 Charles Gilpin was given a part with a legitimate drama of the highest type, John Drinkwater's "Abraham Lincoln" was the play. November 1, 1920, Charles Gilpin starred "Emperor Jones" with the Provincetown Players and won favor as the first recognized Negro dramatic star of America. Gussie L. Davis was the first Negro to win distinction as an international song writer. Black Carl was the first Negro theatrical bill poster and stage carpenter, in 1887. Lew Henry, first Negro theatrical carpenter, admitted into the union in 1889.

Pekin Theatre in Chicago, first theatre operated by Negroes in the country, an idea of Flournoy Miller. "To the Goats," a Negro theatrical organization of Chicago, introduced the midnight shows now so popular throughout the country.

FLORENCE MILLS.

Few people from Washington, D. C., who remember the "Bijou" know anything good about it, but when you know it was at this theatre Florence Mills made her debut, you will forget the policy that theatre held for years. The following is a clipping from the "Washington Star" following the professional appearance made by Baby Florence Mills:

"Baby Florence Mills, the peerless child artist who has appeared before the most exclusive set in Washington, delighting them with her song and dances, is appearing this week at the Empire Theatre with the Sons of Ham Company No. 2. An extra attraction is Baby Florence Mills singing 'Hannah from Savannah.' Baby Florence made a big hit and was encored for dancing."

At this time Miss Mills was less than six years old, but held the championship for cake-walking and buck-dancing. Both medals are in her possession now. On one occasion when Baby Florence was entertaining some of the elite of Washington, Lady Ponceforte, wife of the British Ambassador, presented her with a gold bracelet. Her debut brought her many offers for the stage, and one from "Bonita" was accepted; and for years she traveled as one of the picks with Lew Hearn. After leaving that company, with her two sisters—Olivia and Maud—she then formed the Mills Sisters, playing until the trio dwindled to Maud and Florence. She next teamed with Kinky Clark, the team as Mills and Kinky, until she joined the Panama Trio (Cora Green, Adah Smith, and Florence Mills). This trio played from coast to coast for pantages for three consecutive years. After leaving the Panama Trio, she joined the Tennessee Ten, playing all of the big time for four seasons. It was during this engagement she met U. S. Thompson. Then, with the closing of the Tennessee Ten, Miss Mills and Mr. Thompson were to enter vaudeville, but Miss Mills was called to take a roll in "Shuffle Along" that was created by Gertie Saunders; and so pronounced was her success that Broadway demanded her. Lew Lesle, one of the wisest producers in this country, a man wh ɔ never overlooks a good bet, secured her services, placing her at t ɪe head of the "Plantation Revue." The show was such a decided hit that it was carried to London, where it received the same praise that it had in America. I shall quote John Ervine concerning London's view of Miss Mills:

"The coming of Miss Florence Mills to London is looked upon as one of the theatrical events of the season. The success acquired by Miss Florence Mills, the American colored girl playing in 'From Dover Street to Dixie,' is something unequalled by any American playing in here in the last decade. She is by far the most artistic person London has the good fortune to see."

NOBLE SISSLE.

Noble Sissle is considered one of the most accomplished Negro lyric writers in the country. He began to show his musical talent as a boy in Cleveland, Ohio. In 1915 he made his first professional appearance at the Hotel Seven, Indianapolis, which engagement was followed by a trip to Palm Beach with the Royal Ponciana Sextette. On his return he played at Riverside Park, Baltimore, Md., and while there he met his present partner, and the team was formed upon their arrival in New York. The value of the team was at once recognized. Playing vaudeville during this time, they wrote many songs of merit, among them being "Patrol in No Man's Land," "Good-night, Angeline," and many others. While on tour they formed the famous combination of Miller and Lyles, Sissle and Blake. Blake wrote the score to that great success, "Shuffle Along," that ran on Broadway for two years.

EUBIE BLAKE.

Eubie Blake was born in Baltimore, Md., attended the public school of that city and received his musical education there. He might be called a born musician, for music appears to be a natural gift to him. In 1915 he began his song-writing career with his present partner, and in 1919 toured the Keith vaudeville circuit as the team of Sissle and Blake. Together they wrote the score of "Shuffle Along" and also "Elsie," a white musical show for Broadway.

MILLER AND LYLES.

Miller and Lyles received their educatioin at Fisk University, Nashville, Tenn. In 1907 Miller and Lyles got their first professional engagement as playwrights, when they were engaged by ..obert Motts of Chicago to write for the Pekin Stock Company. Their first play was a decided hit, entitled "The Mayor of Dixie," with a capable cast, including J. Frances Moore, Charles S. Gilpin, Laurence Chenault, Miss Lottie Grady, and Lena Marshall. This same play was rewritten and produced years later as that sensational Negro comedy, "Shuffle Along." While at the Pekin Theatre the company made such an unprecedented hit that Mr. Motts decided to send the company to New York. These boys wanted to see the big city and find out how the East was going to accept their plays. Lyles, in order to get to New York, came as Harrison Stewart's valet and Miller came as assistant property man. While in New York they met Ernest Hogan and were engaged to write "The Oysterman," his biggest and his last play.

Miller and Lyles opened in August, 1910, for B. F. Keith and played continuously until 1915, when they went abroad for the first time, playing all the British Isles. After their tour they returned to London and played in a revue named "This and That," produced by Andre Charlot at the Comedy Theatre. Returning to America near the close of the war, they played for B. F. Keith until the forming of the combination of Miller and Lyles, Sissle and Blake, producing "Shuffle Along," which enjoyed an uninterrupted run of three years. They are now the stars of "Running Wild," produced by George White.

LOTTIE GEE.

Miss Lottie Gee is one who worked from a chorus girl to a leading lady. Her stage career began as a chorus girl with the Cole and Johnson Red Moon Company. She then entered the chorus rank of the Smart Set Company, and for two years toured with that company, with S. H. Dudley as the star. Miss Walker had her as one of her dancing girls. While resting in Washington it occurred to her that she might try a single, and was given her first engagement at Ford Dabney's Theatre, where she at once became very popular. It was during this engagement that she formed a trio with Effie King and Lillian Gillam. This did not last long. Then the sister team was formed as King and Gee. This was a team that the race could brag about at that time. They worked together for a number of years, then Miss Gee was engaged with the Southern Syncopated Orchestra. After a short tour of the United States, the company went abroad with Miss Gee as the soloist. With this she toured Europe, winning praise in such countries as England, France, Italy, and Asia Minor.

JOHNNIE HUDGINS IN DECISION WON AGAINST BIG THEATRICAL PRODUCER.

Johnnie Hudgins, colored comedian famed in burlesque as the star of "Chocolate Dandies" and featured now in "The Club Alabam" on Broadway, N. Y., recently was granted a decision in his favor by Judge Mitchell in Part I Special Terms of the Supreme Court of New York. B. C. Whitney, owner of "The Chocolate Dandies" Company, featuring Sissle and Blake, has served notice that he will appeal to the appellate division with a view of restraining Mr. Hudgins from appearing with any other management, which he claims is in violation of a contract with the Sissle and Blake

45

show. The bill of particulars filed by Nathan Burkan, attorney for the plaintiff, sets forth that Mr. Hudgins' services are unique and cannot be replaced. This is the first time that such an allegation has been made with reference to a Negro artist. The appeal gives especial emphasis to the claim Mr. Hudgins is reported to have received $125 with the B. C. Whitney Company and now to be under contract to the Shubert interests via Arthur Lyons, an agent, for approximately $500 per week, with special performance appearances, record privileges, cabaret work all reserved to Mr. Hudgins. In addition the Shubert interests assure him feature publicity, denial of which was the motivating cause for his retiring from the Sissle and Blake organization. Incidentally his defection greatly weakened the show, a fact admitted in the papers filed by the complainants B. C. Whitney. New York papers have recorded in one incident front-page publicity to the incident, and some of them treated it with the sort of comedy effect which they usually adore stories concerning Negroes. This, however, does not alter the value and the distinction that Mr. Hudgins has achieved.

JESSE SHIPP, VETERAN PLAYWRIGHT AND PRODUCER.

He could write a book concerning his experiences in the show world. He started in the '70's with his partner named Dave Simms. This team did not get very far, as Shipp, with his partner, returned to Cincinnati, where he took a job with a laundry as a driver. While working at the laundry a quartette was formed with Hagerman (afterward the first Negro appointed to the police force of that city), Gilbert Fredericks, Ed. Monroe, and Mr. Shipp. They were known as the Beethoven Quartette, playing beer gardens Sunday nights. They were taken from there by a man named Snyder and placed in variety halls. Remaining seven years, they then toured with Draper's "Uncle Tom's Cabin" until the Eureka Minstrels were formed. This aggregation consisted of Jesse Shipp, Griff Wilson, Billy Allen, Billy Windom, Billy Cook, Ed. Monroe, Jim Tyler, and a white band of seven Englishmen. Jacob Litt then formed the Georgia Minstrels, the Eurekas merging with them, with the exception of the band. Charlie Buck and John Chur were with them and later Ben Hunn and Ike McBeard. Mr. Shipp then joined Primrose' and West' "Forty Whites and Thirty Blacks," staying with them until the Octroons, after which he went with the Oriental American Company. With the opening of "The Trip to Coontown" Shipp was with the original company. His work on the book of that company turned him to play-writing, and he wrote "The Policy Players" for Williams and Walker the following year. He joined the Williams and Walker Company after writing the new show, "The Sons of Ham," and remained with the several companies until the end of the producing by these stars. During that time he wrote "In Dahomey," "Abyssinia," and "Bandana Land." The books of the above productions were from the pen of the one

46

and only Jesse Shipp, and we doubt seriously whether there is another who can boast of writing the consecutive hits as he has done. With the disbanding of Williams and Walker Company, Mr. Shipp went to the Pekin Theatre in Chicago, where he produced stock for thirty weeks. He is responsible for the success of "The Tennessee Ten," "The Down Home Ten," and "Dixie School Days" with the Mills sisters. All of these were vaudeville acts.

WILL H. VODERY.

Will H. Vodery was educated in the public schools of Philadelphia. He is a born musician, inheriting his wonderful talent from his mother. While librarian for the Philadelphia Symphony Orchestra he attracted the attention of Heer Louis Koemmennich, of the University of Berlin, afterward a director for Walter Damrosch. Through the courtesy of Mme. Nicholi, Mr. Vodery was sent to study under this great professor and developed into the arranger he is today. At the request of Williams and Walker he came to New York as an arranger for M. Whitmark and Sons. He later went to Chicago as custodian of Theo Thomas Chicago Symphony Orchestra, where he studied symphony under Frederick Stock. He condensed and transcribed "Parsifal" for Henry W. Savage, which attracted much attention. He has arranged "The Follies" several seasons and numerous other productions, including "Aphrodite" and "Town Topics." Mr. Vodery is today considered one of America's foremost arrangers and musical authorities.

PERRY BRADFORD, KNOWN TO HIS FRIENDS AS "MULE."

Perry Bradford, known to his friends as "Mule," was born in Alabama and frankly states so. Mr. Bradford holds the distinction of being the first man to introduce Negro singers on the phonograph records. For years he had tried to induce the big companies to try it, but none could see any advantage in doing so. He managed to get the Okeh to try Mamie Smith, and had her singing his songs for the company. After breaking the way with one company, he had very little trouble to get at least a dozen companies to use colored girls and men. His song "The Crazy Blues," is credited with making over a quarter of a million dollars for the company and himself. He has a publishing house on Broadway—1547 Broadway, New York City.

BOB COLE

Cole, Robert Allen, "Bob" Cole, noted comedian and playwright, was born in Athens, Georgia, July 1, 1868, and died in New York City August 2, 1911. He was one of the most versatile and gifted colored actors that America has produced. A member of the famous Cole and Johnson team and company, he was a pioneer in the effort to have the Negro show an entity in itself, with a plot and

47

atmosphere of its own. Among the plays which he wrote are "A Trip to Coontown,"; "A Shoofly Regiment," and "The Red Moon." Among the songs which he composed are "Lousiana Lize," "I Must Have Been Dreaming," "No One Can Fill Her Place," "Katydid," "The Cricket and the Frog," and "The Maiden with Dreamy Eyes." He and his partner, J. Rosamond Johnson, together wrote "Under the Bamboo Tree," "Big Indian Chief," "Bleeding Moon," and "Oh, Didn't He Ramble."

BERT WILLIAMS.

Bert Williams, most noted of present-day Negro actors. He is a native of New Providence, Nassau, in the British Bahamas Island. When he was two years old his family came to New York. His father was a papier mache maker, which brought him in contact with the theatres. In this way Williams got acquainted with the stage. From New York the family moved to Riverside, California, in which place he graduated from high school and went to San Francisco, intending to study to be a civil engineer. His first experience on the stage was as a member of a little Mountebank minstrel show which played the lumber and mining camps of California. Williams became noted as a member of the famous Williams and Walker Company. For the past several seasons before his death he had been the star of "The Follies," a leading white production.

ANITA BUSH—A LITTLE LIGHT
(By Belfast)

When little Anita Bush, full of life, beauty, and romance in the varied portrayals of comedy and drama, made her first appearance in the Great Metropolis several years ago, although she may not have known it then, she was driving the first wedge into a field in which her people had hitherto been considered as jokes.

Considering things as they are, there is a grave likelihood that she has not been shown the proper amount of appreciation nor given the full credit for all that she has done in drama. She entered a path of thorns that had not a single beaten passage to encourage her own in the performance of that which people said could not be done. She worked hard and strenuously in the face of obstacles that must have caused her to shed tears more than once, and which would have easily dampened the ardor of a little woman with less determination to make her dreams come true. Her work, however, has not been futile. She, unlike the average pioneer, has lived to see it blossom forth like a lovely rose. She has lived to hear it said by others that "Little Anita" was our guiding star.

The dramatic field once closed as rigidly as anything could possibly be against the intrusion of any other race except the one already there began to open and expand with her first appearance. She had swept aside doubt and scipticism, and created conviction.

48

Everybody began talking about the Negro in drama; the Negro broken suddenly away from the old traditional plantation melodies and plantation production of plantation life the laurels of elevated drama. They had been showing the playgoers throughout the world that they could laugh and make fun; had impressed upon another social life the originality of their themes to such an extent that even today the white actor prefers a plantation melody to any other song, and now they wanted to show that they possessed a serious side.

"Let us render unto Caesar that which is Caesar's and unto God that which is God's." Anita was as truly a pathfinder as were Lewis and Clark or any other of the great personalities who have left an indelible stamp on the progress of mankind. The others came after her to pick up where she left off. Before her there had been no "Rider of Dreams," "Simon the Cyrenian," "Granny Maumee," no operatic Faust. All of these wonderful dramatic accomplishments of Negro artists came after her. She was not a great actress by any means. Maybe she was never intended to portray the deep emotional roles which she sometimes attempted. That, nevertheless, alters nothing. Her success and the depth of gratitude which is rightfully due her from all Negroes spring from something infinitely more noble, lasting than merely great acting. It springs from the spirit which was encouched in her heart and soul to broaden places that were narrowest in the show world.

Since her departure from New York the Lafayette Theatre has become an institution. The actresses and actors there who have played everything from Resurrection to Faust, in their every line of speech and action are adding another laurel to the wreath first begun by the Little Light—Anita Bush.

S. H. DUDLEY.

Veteran Producer and Vice-President and Eastern Representative of The Theatre Owners' Booking Association.

Mr. Dudley was born in Dallas, Texas, in 1873. His theatrical career started with a medicine show at Shreveport, La. It was one of those old shows that used to use a guitar and comedian to draw the crowd so as to sell medicine. After this he began to work in the honkytonks and music halls that thrived in the Lone Star State at that time. The first legitimate attraction he was with was "The Nashville Students," in one-night stands in the northern cities.. This show carried eighteen people. New York can put over anything, so Dudley came to New York where opportunities were larger. He appeared with Tom McIntosh and Gussie L. Davis, the latter the greatest ballad writer we ever had.

As a rule actors run through every dime they have. Dudley saw their mistake and profited. He worked as assistant manager of "The Nashville Students" for some time. Then he carried out a show of his own. Adversity attended his efforts, but he kept trying and wouldn't accept defeat. He had twelve members in his company, which opened and closed in Texas. It was known as Dudley and Andrew New Ideal Minstrels. When funds were low they traveled on their baggage. At times they owed the railroad companies for three to five weeks. Mr. Dudley always managed to pay the board bills, even when he couldn't pay the salary and trans- fer bills. No railroad ever lost anything on his shows, however, and he managed to always pay his performers before the season closed. When he closed the show mentioned above in Hempstead, Texas, he had only $16 after paying everybody. Dudley and An- drew received the magnificent salary of $3.50 per week, while the orchestra leader got $4.00. This orchestra leader was Dan Des- dune of Omaha, who now has the greatest band in the West. Dud- ley and Jack Johnson were pals in Texas and were at one time in business together.

Dudley was the first man to ever organize a colored circuit. This was the S. H. Dudley Theatrical Enterprises, the oldest and only successful colored circuit ever organized. This was about the year 1909. He was then starring in "The Smart Set" and saw the passing of the big shows. Four shows were then on the road: Cole and Johnson's "Shoo-Fly Regiment," Williams and Walker's "Ban- dana Land," Ernest Hogan's "Rufus Rastus," and S. H. Dudley's "The Smart Set." It was necessary to get ready for the Negro theatre. At that time he had about twenty-five theatres. They were going fairly well but lacked good attractions to draw and keep their houses. Dudley saw the need, so he opened a booking house in Washington. He did this because the only available theatre. the Minnehaha, was in that city. He leased it and changed the name to S. H. Dudley. Attractions were plentiful and theatres, too. but they didn't know of each other. Dudley brought the demand to the supply.

At first it was hard to show the managers the need of a central agency. So he lost $16,000 the first year by leasing theatres in Newport News, Norfolk, Louisville, Alexandria, and Petersburg, Va., where, by his attractions, he closed the houses of his competi- tors. After he would place a theatre on a paying basis, he would sell it with the condition of use of his circuit service. After that he would go to a manager and offer his service. Upon refusal to use it, he would threaten to open a competing theatre in the city. The Theatre Owners' Booking Association was formed in 1920. Before that time Mr. Dudley had the S. H. Dudley Circuit which controlled bookings of attractions in the East. Martin Klein of Chicago had the Mid-West attractions. Mr. Dudley and E. L. Cum- mings held the controlling stock in the Southern Consolidated, Mr. Cummings (white) being the Southern representative. When the Southern Consolidated disagreed there was a circuit formed called the Colored United Vaudeville Circuit, which was operated by Dud- ley, Klein, and Reevin. There were frequent disagreements which led to the formation of the Theatre Owners' Booking Association.

There are about fifteen stockholders, four colored: Charles Turpin, St. Louis; C. H. Douglas, Macon, Ga.; W. S. Scalls, Winston-Salem, N. C., and S. H. Dudley.

Mr. Dudley has from 200 to 400 people today playing at salaries of $80 to $90 (vaudeville). Those with the little tabloid shows get from $18 to $50 per week. About 500 or 600 different actors in the group. These acts play to the colored theatres exclusively.

Mr. Dudley says that cheap attractions—moving pictures and vaudeville—were the cause of the passing of the big show. About every ten years the show business revolutionizes itself. He thinks the field is greater for colored attractions today than ever before. This, because Broadway has opened to anything the Negro has to offer and any show is a success which can get the New York stamp. However, he does not think the right show has hit Broadway yet. So far, he says, they have been too much like the whites. He believes the hunger of Broadway for attractions was the cause of Miller and Lyle's success with "Shuffle Along." There was a scarcity of real amusing productions on Broadway. His idea of a Broadway show is to get thirty brown skin girls and twenty black men. The black-face comedian furnishes the comedy, but he is funny only when painted up. Bob Cole, he thinks, was the greatest author we ever had, but he didn't think much of him as a comedian. He was a good actor but a poor comedian.

He thinks colored acts are about at an end unless new and most vigilant actors get on the job. There is not enough new stuff, and too much dissipation. To overcome that he has organized a Colored Actors' Union, that the colored actors might have an opportunity of getting together, conversing, noting deficiencies, and classifying acts. As it is now, all acts get one salary, good or bad, with very few exceptions. We are not thinking for tomorrow unless we raise the standard of output service. He is fighting with the T. O. B. A. now for better salaries, etc. He feels someone should make a sacrifice.

Mr. Dudley has accumulated considerable property. Only this year he sold a considerable amount of property in Chester, Pa. He now has property in the District of Columbia and Maryland; a ten-room country home on fourteen acres, with a truck farm and all modern improvements, such as gas, electricity, and hot and cold running water; two beautiful lots in Annapolis, where he can look right into the Naval Academy (both places have cottages for caretakers) ; at 1316 You Street, N. W., Washington, D. C., he has an apartment house with sixteen apartments; at 1223 7th Street, N. W., he has an office and business property; at 1225 7th Street, N. W., a pool room with apartments above; his residence at 1219 Sixth Street, N. W., and a nine-room dwelling at 909 Westminster Street. Just recently he sold out a stable of thoroughbred racers—six horses—among whom was a good stake winner, "Strut Miss Lizzie." As an ex-jockey Mr. Dudley knows the business thoroughly. In addition to the property mentioned above, Mr

Dudley has two cars—a Buick 1923 model, seven-passenger sedan and a Stephens 1922 model, drome sedan.   He carries a $10,000 life insurance.
    Mrs. Dudley is a Georgia girl.   She started working for Mr. Dudley the first year of his business.   They were married last year. He gives her credit for all of his success.

CHARLES H. TURPIN

One of the Leading Theatre Promoters Among People of Color

Like so many people of prominence in these United States, Mr. Turpin was born in the State of Ohio.   To be specific, he hails from Columbus.   When quite young, however, he moved with his parents to Edwards Depot, Miss., where he lived for several years. Then their residence in the famous cotton State suddenly drew to a close.   The elder Turpin was a sort of insurgent and iconoclast, and, as everyone knows, such evidence of an active mentality is not looked upon with favor by the kind, Christian, white-mule consuming gentlemen who sit upon the numerous front porches of the State and fan themselves while the patient Negroes slave away for them.   Hence, to avoid being the only uneasy guest at a lynching— the favorite Mississippi form of amusement—the family hastily withdrew from the rural district and sought the more favorable environment of Vicksburg.   Security in that municipality, however, did not seem to be as great as desired; so the family moved again to St. Louis.

Here Mr. Turpin attended the public schools and graduated well up in his class.   Unlike many of our young men, he was not satisfied when he had completed grammar school; he wanted to go farther.   So he attended the Business College in St. Louis and acquired a good business education.

When he left college his first venture was into the retail grocery business.   Not satisfied with results there, he entered the commission business.   For a time he did a very satisfactory business by buying various products in large quantities and selling them to the retail trade of the community.

Probably every man who ever rose from the bottom to the top has, at one time or the other, shined shoes.   The desire—almost universal where shoes are worn—of wanting to see them bright and shiny has assisted many an energetic and ambitious young man in getting a firm foothold on the ladder of success.   The idea came to him one day of forming all the bootblacks into a union and carrying the price of a shine to ten cents—all the other bootblacks were polishing footgear for a thick nickel.   His ambition to organize and elevate the price to a thin dime was not shared by the other leather rubbers of the city.   He was in a dilemma.   One could hardly form a union with one member and hope for success!   So he tried again, but to no avail.   Like most Americans, his fellow workers were averse to organized effort on the economic field.   Then he did an a union man and all the other scabs, raised his price to ten cents for unusual thing and was quite successful, too. He declared himself polishing the cow hide, and made as high as $7.50 on Sundays. Mr. Turpin maintains this is the only case on record of a one-man union.

It wasn't long before a young man of such promise began to be noticed. This notice came in the form of a positiion as clerk in the Assessor's office. He made good there and at the first opportunity he was given a clerkship in the Recorder's office. Later he became secretary to his brother, who was doing quite well in the wholesale business.

About this time Mr. Turpin's health began to fail and he found it necessary to move to Los Angeles for a while. The salubrious climate of Southern California had the desired effect, and in a short while Mr. Turpin was back on the job in St. Louis. His career from this point is only what one could have expected of an aggressive, industrious, intelligent young man. With only a capital of fifty cents, he started the Booker Washington Theatre in an airdome; then, as winter came on—as winter has a habit of doing, even in Missouri—he covered the airdome with canvas, installed stores, which he rented at a good price, and ran the entire institution through the winter. Today he is lessee of the modern Booker Washington Theatre, 23rd and Market Streets, which he has very successfully operated for ten years. During this time he has developed such well-known artists as Mamie Smith, whom he started at $12 a week; Bessie Smith, whom he started at $15; the Jones Brothers—Jones & Jones; as well as U. S. Thompson, Florence Mills' husband, with whom he worked for a time.

Mr. Turpin's business connections are with the Standard Life Insurance Company, the Standard Service Company, and the Citizens' Trust Company, all of Atlanta, Ga.; the Liberty Life Insurance Company of Chicago, Ill.; the National Benefit Life Insurance Company of Washington, D. C.; and the Douglas Life Insurance Company and the People's Finance Company of St. Louis, Mo.

Apartment houses for Negroes are so great in the Harlem district of New York City that invasion of new territory is constantly being made. In order to assist in meeting this demand a syndicate of Negro business men secured the title to six large modern de luxe elevator apartments constructed at a cost of $1,500,000. These properties are located at 117-135 West 141st Street and 130-148 West 142nd Street. It was stated that the securing of the possession of these apartment houses marked the largest real estate proposition ever undertaken by Negroes in the United States.

Negro Inventions During 1917 and 1918

Charles Stevenson of Amorillo, Texas, invented a glass war bomb.

INVENTIONS BY NEGROES

Benjamin Banneker—noted Negro astronomer—born free November 9, 1731, in Baltimore, Md., received some education in a pay school. Early showed an inclination for mechanics. About 1754 with imperfect tools constructed a clock which told the time and struck the hour. This was the first clock constructed in America.

The first Negro to receive a patent on an invention was Henry Blair, of Maryland, who in 1834 and 1836 was granted patents on a corn harvester. He is supposed to have been a free Negro. A number of inventions were made by slaves. It has been claimed, but not verified, that a slave either invented the cotton gin or gave to Eli Whitney, who obtained a patent for it, valuable suggestions to aid in the completion of this invention.

In 1858 the Commissioner of Patents and the Attorney General of the United States concurred that a slave could not take out a patent on an invention. It is said that a slave of Jefferson Davis in 1862 invented a propeller for vessels that was afterwards used in the Confederate navy.

A Negro slave in Kentucky is said to have invented a hemp brake, a machine used for separating the hemp fiber from the stalk.

Some time after the Dred Scott decision in 1857 the Patent Office refused a Negro of Boston a patent on an invention on the grounds that, according to this decision, he was not a citizen of the United States and therefore a patent could not be issued to him. December 16, 1861, Senator Charles Sumner, on behalf of this Negro inventor, ordered the following resolution in the Senate:

"Resolved, That the Committee on Patents and the Patent Office be directed to consider if any legislation is necessary in order to secure to persons of African descent in our country the right to take out patents for useful inventions under the Constitution of the United States."

The Patent Office, which does not record the race of the patentees, has, by investigation, verified over 800 patents which have been granted to Negroes. It estimated that as many more which are unverified have been granted. The records of the Patent Office show that Negroes have applied their inventive talent of subjects in agricultural implements in wood and metal-working machines, in land conveyances, on road and tractor, wide range of uses in aeronautics, in new designs of house furniture and bric-a-brac, in mechanical toys, and amusement devices.

Joseph Hunter Dickinson, of New Jersey, specializes in the line of musical instruments, particularly playing the piano. He began more than fifteen years ago to invent devices for automatically playing the piano. He is at present in the employ of a large piano factory. His various inventions in piano player mechanism are adopted in the construction of some of the finest piano players on the market. He has more than a dozen patents to his credit already, and is still devoting his energies to that line of invention.

Frank J. Ferrell, of New York, has obtained about a dozen patents for his inventions, the larger number of them being for improvement in valves of steam engines.

Benjamin F. Jackson, of Massachusetts, is the inventor of a dozen different improvements in heating and lighting devices, including a controller for trolley wheel.

Charles V. Richey, of Washington, D. C., has obtained about a dozen patents on his inventions, the last of which was a most ingenious device for registering the call on a telephone and detecting the unauthorized use of that instrument.

Henry Creamer, of New York, has made seven different inventions in steam traps covered by as many patents; and Andrew J. Beard, of Alabama, has about the same number to his credit for inventions in car-coupling devices. William Douglass, of Arkansas, was granted about half a dozen patents for various inventions for harvesting machines.

James Doyle, of Pittsburgh, has obtained several patents for his inventions, one of them being for an automatic serving system. This latter device is a scheme for dispensing with the use of waiters in dining rooms, restaurants, and at railroad lunch counters. It was recently exhibited with the Pennsylvania Exposition Society's exhibit at Pittsburgh, where it attracted widespread attention from the press and public.

Robert Pelham, of Detroit, is employed in the Census Office Bureau. From data sent into the office from the thousands of manufacturers of the country.

John Ernest Matzeliger was born in Dutch Guiana in 1852, and died at Lynn, Massachusetts, in 1889. He is the inventor of the first machine that performed automatically all the operations involved in attaching soles to shoes. Other machines had previously been made, but Matzeliger's machine was the only one then known to the mechanical world. This machine worked automatically and required less than a minute to complete a single shoe. This wonderful achievement marked the beginning of a distinct revolution in the art of making shoes by machinery. Matzeliger realized this, and attempted to capitalize it by organizing a stock company to market his invention, but his plans were frustrated through failing health and lack of business experience. Shortly thereafter he died. The patent and much of the stock of the company organized by Matzeliger was bought up. The purchase laid the foundation for the organization of the United Shoe Machinery Company, the largest and richest corporation of its kind in the world. The United Shoe Machinery Company established at Lynn, Massachusetts a school, the only one of its kind in the world where boys are taught exclusively to operate the Matzeliger type of machine. Some years before his death Matzeliger became a member of a white church in Lynn, called the North Congregational Church Society, and bequeathed to this church some of the stock of the company he had organized. Years afterward this church became heavily involved in debt, and remembering the stock that had been left by this colored member, found upon inquiry that it had become very valuable through the importance of the patent under the management of the large company then controlling it.   The church sold the stock and realized therefrom more than enough to pay off the entire debt of the church, amounting to $10,860.

Official Copy from the Negro Year Book

Negro Towns and Settlements in the United States

Towns that are populated and governed entirely or almost entirely by Negroes:

Towns

Alabama	Population
Cedar Lake (Morgan Co.)	300
Hobson City (near Anniston)	300
Mason City (near Birmingham)	344
Plateau (near Mobile)	1,500
Illinois	
Brooklyn	3,000
Iowa	
Buxton (1,000 white)	5,000
Mississippi	
Expose (Marion County)	700
Des Velente	800
Oklahoma	
Boley	3,000
Red Bird	500
Porter	637
Gayson	411
Taft	352
Tatum	350
Texas	
Independence Heights (near Houston)	300
West Virginia	
Institute (Kanawha County)	600
Michigan	
Calvin Township (Cass County)	800
New Jersey	
Snow Hill (Camden County)	1,250
Ohio	
Long Darke County	500

SPORTS—Pugilism

It is said that Negroes were the pioneers in American pugilism, and the first champion in America was a Negro slave—Tom Molineaux—of Richmond, Virginia, who, in the first part of the Eighteenth century, won his freedom by winning a $100,000 stake for his master, Algernon Molineaux, who had wagered this amount that he could produce a black man who could whip any other slave that could be produced.

Tom Molineaux, after defeating all comers in America, went to England where he was defeated by Tom Gribb, the British champion. The most noted of the Negro pugilists are Peter Jackson (contemporary of John L. Sullivan and James J. Corbett), George Dixon, Joe Gans, Joe Walcott, Dixie Kidd, Joe Jeannette, Sam Langford, Sam McVea, Harry Wills, and Jack Johnson.

Pugilistic Champions

Heavyweight (158 lbs.) Jack Johnson, 1908-1915.
Welterweight (145 lbs.) Joe Walcott, 1901-1904.
Dixie Kid, 1904-1908.
Lightweight (133 lbs.) Joe Gans, 1902-1908.
Featherweight (122 lbs.) George Dixon, 1892-1897, 1898-1900.
Bantamweight (116 lbs.) George Dixon, 189-1892.

NEGRO SYNDICATE TAKES OVER MILLION AND A HALF APARTMENT HOUSES

The demand for high grade apartment houses for Negroes is so great in the Harlem district of New York that invasion of new territory is constantly being made. In order to assist in meeting this demand a syndicate of Negro business men secured the title to six large modern de luxe elevator apartments constructed at a cost of $1,500,000. These properties are located at 117-135 West 141st Street and 130-148 West 142nd Street. It was stated that the securing of the possession of these apartment houses marked the largest real estate proposition ever undertaken by Negroes in the United States.

SUCCESSFUL BUSINESS WOMEN ERECT $250,000 BUSINESS BUILDING, $250,000 RESIDENCE

A number of Negro women have grown wealthy through the beauty culture business. Among the most wealthy and successful of these women are Mrs. A. E. Malone of the Poro Beauty College, St. Louis, Mo., and Mrs. Sarah J. Walker, the head of the Madam C. J. Walker business, formerly of Indianapolis, Ind., and now of New York City. To take care of the growing business of the Poro Beauty College, a five-story $250,000 factory and office building was recently erected in St. Louis. Mrs. Sarah J. Walker, who owned a commodious residence in Indianapolis and a $50,000 home in New York City, gave her New York home to her daughter and erected at Irvington-on-the-Hudson, New York, a residence that was reported to have cost $250,000.

Mrs. Walker died May 25, 1919. She left an estate valued at $1,000,000, of which $100,000 was left to various charities.

G-128512

SPECIAL PAGE

BOOTS HOPES
The King of Them All
Song Writer   Parody Artist

More Acts use Boots Hopes Material
than any other Writer of Negro
Vaudeville Material

BOOTS WAS DISCOVERED BY S. H. DUDLEY IN 1912

He has risen from $6.00 per week to the
highest salaried Monologuist on the T.
O. B. A. Circuit.

*Boots Hopes, born
in Richmond, Va.,
August 16, 1893
Soldier
Lawyer
Grocery Clerk in
Private Life*

*Can speak faster
than machine can
record; at rate of
170 words per
minute.
Test
March 25, 1924*

BOOTS HOPES

SPECIAL PAGE

Don't Forget Our Friend

James A. Jackson

THE PAGE

The Deacon's Club

Of Prince Hall Masons

IN THE

AMUSEMENT BUSINESS

J. A. JACKSON. EXECUTIVE SEC'TY

231 West 140th Street, New York City

An organization designed to frustrate clandestine Masonry and promote Social intercourse between traveling and local Masons

APPENDIX B
A Partial List of Performers, Plays, Theatre Companies, Minstrel Groups,
Film Companies Frequently Mentioned in "The Page" (1920-1925).

Performers
Vaudeville, Musical Comedy, Concert

Charles Gilpin	Bert Williams
Ethel Waters	Jack Johnson
Clarence Muse	Leigh Whipper
Ollie Burgone	Maharajah
Cleo Desmond	Creamer and Layton
Butterbeans & Susie	Ma Rainey
Anita Bush	Lawrence Chenault
Daisy Martin	J. Rosamond Johnson
"Sunshine" Sammy	Evon Robinson
Mamie Smith	Boots Hope
Whitman Sisters	Susie Sutton
Babe Townsend	U. S. Thompson
Harry Fidler	Earle Dancer
G. Paris	Eddie Green
LaRue Jones	Roland Hayes
Gertrude Saunders	W. C. Handy
Prof. Lockwood Lewis	"Ragtime" Billy Tucker
Florence Mills	Sarah Martin
Will Marion Cook	Willie Tyler
Anita Bush	Creamer & Layton
Tim Moore	Chappelle & Stinette
Bob Russell	Bill"Bojangles" Robinson
Bessie Smith	Will Marion Cook
Ollie Burgoyne	Fletcher Henderson
Alberta Hunter	Richard B. Harrison
Rose McClendon	Paul Robeson
Evelyn Preer	Whitney and Tutt

Out-of-Doors Performers

Bessie Coleman—aviatrix, stunt flyer.
Boyd and Boyd—male and female acrobat and contortionist.
Boots Hope—"King of the Liars."
Coy Herndon—hoop roller.
Edwards and Edwards—male and female wire walkers.
Frank Kirk—wire walker.
Harry W. Miller—magician.

Ivan Turner—midget.
Jack Johnson—heavyweight fighter.
Maharajah—magician.
C. Maxwell— ventriloquist, magician.
G. Lowery—bandleader, Ringling Brother's Circus.
Prince Askazuma—mystic.
Prince & Princess Mysteria—mystics.
Princess Sahdo—mystic.
Princess Wee-Wee—midget.
Walter Broadus—magician-mystic.
Wells and Wells—male and female trapese artists.

Motion Picture Performers

Edna Morton
Clarence Brooks
Susie Sutton
Clarence Muse
Ethel Moses.

"Sunshine" Sammy
Anita Bush
Jack Johnson
Noble Johnson
Leigh Whipper

Plays

The Emperor Jones
Business Before Pleasure
The Love of Su Shong
All God's Chillun' Got Wings
Pa William's Gal
Chip Woman's Fortune (Broadway)

The New Negro
White Mule
Mule Bone
Uncle Tom's Cabin
Solome
The Flat Below

Theater Companies

Avenue Association Players
Bradley Theatrical Entertainment Co.
Buddy Austin Players (women)
Checkerboard Players
Dunbar Players

Pekin Players (reunion)
Norfolk Players
Lafayette Players
Howard Players

Minstrel Groups

Southern Exposition Minstrels
Dixie Moon Minstrels
R. H. Harvey's Callender's
Davis' Dixiland Minstrels
Wesley Johnson and Company
Armstead's Minstrels

Main's Georgia Minstrels
Virginia Minstrels
Georgia Minstrels
Harry Dixon's Minstrels
O'Brien's Minstrels
Jack Schaffer Minstrels

Greater Minstrels
Walter's Band and Minstrels
Paris' Minstrels
Herbert's Minstrels
Davis, Rusco & Hockwald's Minstrels

Evan's Minstrels
Sidney Collin's Alabama
Broadway Minstrels
Georgia Minstrels

Film Companies

Micheaux Film Corporation
Lincoln Productions
DelSarte Film Company
Bookertee.Film Corporation
Levy Films
Afro-American Film Distributors
Constellation Film Company
Western Picture Productions

Reol Productions
Maurice Film Company
Muse Enterprises
Comet Films
Norman Film Company
Topeka Film Company
Lone Star Pictures
Leigh Whipper Films

APPENDIX C
A Partial List of Colored Vaudeville Acts Working Steadily with the Keith,
Orpheum, Western Vaudeville and Associated Houses of the Big Circuits.

1921

Bill "Bojangles" Robinson
Chappelle and Stinnette
Clarence "Dancing" Dotson
Fred Rogers
Green and Burnett
Harrington and Tribble
Miller and Anthony
Rosamond Johnson & Co.
Rucker and Winfred
Shelton Brooks
The Tennessee Ten

Austin and Delaney
Farrell and Hatch
Dixie Four
Glenn and Jenkins
Greenlee and Drayton
Jones and Cumby
Moss and Frye
Old Time Darkies
Seymour and Janette
Simms and Warfield

1922

Carter and Cornish
Bill "Bojangles" Robinson
Nasarrol, the Creol Cocktail
Chappelle and Stinnette
The G. Miller Trio
Leroy Smith's Band
The Musical Spiller

Adams and Robinson
Buck and Bubbles
Cooper and Lane
Dancing Dotson
Lee Coates and Company
The Modern Cocktail
Lois and Skeaks

Mason and Bailey
Rosamond Johnson and Co.
The Tennessee Ten
Williams and Taylor
Will Sweatam and Company

Master'sHoliday in Dixie
Seymour and Janette
The Versatile Trio
Tabor and Green

APPENDIX D
*Theatre Houses Playing Vaudeville, Pictures, and Dramas that
cater to Black Patronage ("The Page," 1920-25).*

Theatre / Location / Type / Seating / Manager's Name & Race, if Known
(W: White / B: Black)*

*Vaud.:   Vaudeville or Road Show
Pctrs.:   Pictures
Drm.:   Drama

American, Houston, Tx., Vaud., Frame, 16 X 16, 2 dr. rms., S. 500, C.
H. Cattey, exclusively white operated.
Amusu, Chattanooga, Tn., S. 450.
Attucks, Norfolk, Va., Vaud., Drm., Twin City Amusement Corp, Robert
Cross & Rufus Byars, (B).
Argonne, Baltimore, Md., S. 1,000 Avenue, Chicago, Il.
Bellmont, Pensacola, Fl.
Bessemer, Birmingham, Al.
Bijou, Nashville, Tn., Vaud., M. Starr, (W).
Bon Ami, Opelousas, La., S. 240.
Booker T. Washington, Houston, Vaud. & Pctrs., S. 1,500, stage 20 X 30.,
5 dressing rooms, 4 piece orchestra.
Barrako, Victor Abram (W).
Booker T. Washington, St. Louis, Mo., Vaud., C. H. Turpin, (B).
Booker T. Washington, Texarkana, Ak., S. 500.
Bordeaux, New Orleans, La., Pctrs., Bordeaux and Camp, (W).
Capital, Portsmouth, Va.
Colonial, Norfolk, Va.
Douglas, Baltimore, Md.
Douglas, New York.
Douglas, Macon, Ga.
Dreamland, Opelika, Al., Vaud., (B).
Dunbar, Baltimore, Md. Pctrs., Brown and Steven & Josia Diggs, (B).
Dunbar, Philadelphia, Pa., Vaud., Drm., John T. Gibson, (B).
Ella B. Moore, Dallas Tx., Pctrs., E. B. Moore, (B).
Foraker, Washington, D. C., Vaud., Murray A Ryan, (B).
Fox, Bogaluss, La., S. 350.

Globe, Jacksonville, Fl., Vaud., Pctrs., W. S. Sumter, Dr. J. Seth Hill, & Frank Crowd, (B).
Globe, Cleveland, Oh.
Grand, Chicago, Il.
Greenwich, New York.
Hellinger, San Antonio, Tx, Vaud., Pctrs, S. 550, 5 dr. rooms, 17 sets of lines, Luke Scott, (B).
Howard, Wash, D. C.
Hippodrome, Alexandria, La.
Ideal, Houston, Tx., S. 330, Elmore Martin, owner and manager (B).
Lafayette, New York, Vaud., Pctrs, Murray brothers, (B).
Lafayette, Winston Salem, N. C., Vaud., W. S. Scales, (B).
Liberty, Chattanooga, Tn., Sam E. Reevin, (W).
Liberty, Galveston, Tx., Pctrs., Vaud., S. 400, 4 dressing rooms, 5 sets of lines, orchestra, piano, coronet, and drums, James Brown, owner / mngr, (W).
Lyceum, Cincinnati, O., T. S. Tinley, (W).
Lincoln, Pensacola, Fl., Pctrs., W. S. Sumter, Dr. J. Seth Hills, Frank Crowd, (B).
Koppia, Detroit, Mi.
Liberty, Lafayette, La., S. 400.
Lincoln, Houston, Tx. Pctrs., S. 750, 20 x 24 stage, 18 sets of lines & 2 dressing rooms & gallery, Olen Pullum De Walt, (B).
Lincoln, Louisville, Ky., William Warley, (W).
Lincoln, Washington, D. C., S. 2, 200.
Louisiana, Lake Charles, La., S. 350.
Lyric, New Orleans, La. Vaud., Bordeaux and Bennett, (W).
Maceo, Washington, D. C., V., (B).
Majestic, Hot Springs, Ak.
Mid-City, Washington, D. C., S. H. Dudley, (B).
New Ferguson, Charleston, West Va.
Othello, New Orleans, La., S. 600.
Orpheum, Newark, N. J.
Park, Dallas, Tx, Chintz Moore, (B).
Palace, Memphis, Tn.
Palace, Norfolk Va.
Pastime, Greenville, Tx., S. 400.
Pastime, Houston, Tx., S. 500.
Pershing, Pittsburgh, Pa.
Portsmouth, Portsmouth, Va.
Prince, Lake Charles, La., S. 560.
Princess, Galveston, Tx., Pctrs., S. 500, no gallery, A. B. Lindell, (W).
Regent, Baltimore, Md.
Renaissance, Harlem, NY., William Roach (W. C. Roach Company), (B).
Republic, Washington, D. C.

H. Dudley, Alexandria, Va., Vaud., Pctrs, S. H. Dudley, (B).
H. Dudley, Petersburg, Va, Vaud, S. H. Dudley, (B).
Standard, Philadelphia, Pa., Vaud., John T. Gibson, (B).
Star, Chattanooga, Tx., S. 250.
Star, Galveston, Tx.
Star, Pittsburgh, Pa., Vaud., Charles P. Stinson, (B).
Star, Taylor, Tx.
Steel Curtain, Pittsburgh, Pa.
St Elmo, Houston, Tx., Pctrs., S. 500, owner, H. Shulman.
Temple, New Orleans, La.

APPENDIX E
Musical Comedies: Reviews and Articles, 1921-25

1921

The New American, 1/1/21; *Shuffle Along,* 1/8, 2/20, 3/11-12, 4/15, 4/22,
4/29, 5/6, 5/13, 6/3, 17, 8/12, 8/26, 9/2, 10,21, 10/14, 10/21, 11/4, 9/9,
10/28, 11/4; *The Mayor of Jimtown,* 3/19; *Broadway Rastus,* 4/30; *Creole
Belles,* 5/7; *Bombay Girls,* 6/18; *The New American, Sunkist Southerners,
Strut Miss Lizzie,* 3/26; *Stylish Steppers,* 3/26; *Daffy Dill Girls,* 3/26;
Darktown Scandals of 1921, 4/9; *The Chocolate Brown, Lost in Hawaii,*
4/9; *Strutt Miss Lizzie,* 4/23; *The Chocolate Brown,* 7/30; *Billy King Show,
Cotton Tops, Tim Moore's Chicago Follies, Hello 1922,* 7/2; *Putt & Take,
Broadway Rounders,* 10/8.

1922

Seven Eleven, 1/28; *Broadway Strutter,* 1/28; *Holiday in Dixie, Ku Klux
Blues,* 2/11; *Mutt & Jeff,* 2/18; *Africana,* 2/18; *Taboo,* 2/22, 4/1; *Miss
Green From New Orleans,* 5/6; *Smarter Set,* 5/13; *Creole Follies Revue,*
6/3; *Bombay Girls,* 6/10, 7/22; *Strutt Miss Lizzie,* 6/17; *Jump Steady,* 6/17,
7/8; *Creole Revue,* 6/24; *Business Before Pleasure* 6/24; *Hello Rufus*
7/15; *Step On it,* 7/29, 8/12; *Moonshine,* 7/29; *In Old Virginia,* 9/9; *Bon-
Bon-Buddy Jr.,* 9/23; *Oh Joy,* 9/23, 10/14; *Dumb Luck,* 10/14, 17; *All
Aboard,* 10/7; *Step Along,* 10/21, 22, 11/22; *Seven Eleven,* 11/11; *Follow
Me, Lisa,* 7-11, *Shuffle Along Road Show, Broadway Strutters.*

1923

Seven-Eleven, 4/21; *Salome,* 5/5; *Follow Me,* 5/26, 11/10; *How Come,*
6/23, 4/28, 6/23, 10/13; *Shuffle Along,* 10/10; *Abbie Mitchell in Concert,*
10/13; ; *Plantation Days*; Get Happy, 10/27; *North Ain't South,* 10/20,
12/1; *Grand Opera,* 11/24; *Diana,* 12/3; *The Flolickers,* 12/1.

1924

Come Along Mandy,1/5; *Roseanne*, 1/26; Seven-Eleven, 6/21; *Darktown Bazaar* 5/31; *Struttin' Times*, 6/7.

1925

Salary, 1/3; *Getting Gerties' Garder*, 2/14; *Harlem Rounders*, 3/7/25, *Aces and Queens*, *Dextra Male Chorus*, 4/25/25, *Broadway Rastus*, 3/16/25; *Puddin Jones*, 5/23/25; *The Violin Maker of Creomonia*, 6/6/25.

APPENDIX F
Jackson's Membership in Fraternal Organizations and Clubs

Fraternal Organizations

Prince Hall Masons; Past Exaulted Ruler of West Great Lakes Lodge; Grand Historian, United Supreme Council; board of directors, National Negro Business League; American Marketing Association; Association of Special Agents; Brotherhood of Sleeping Car Porters; NAACP; National Fair Officials Association; Business Men's Exchange; Improved, Benevolent, Protective Order of the Elks of the world (IBPO); League of Teachers in Business Education; American Teachers Association of Business Education; American Marketing Association board of trustees, Pioneer Business Institute, Philadelphia, Pa.; Advisory board, Friendship College, Rock Hill, S. C.

Clubs

The Colored Actors' Union, Dressing Room Club; Associate member, Mu-So-Lit Club, Washington, D. C.; Hiawatha, Los Angeles; Negro Actor's Guild; Florence Mills; Red Caps, Chicago; DePriest fifteen, Wash., D.C.; Tri-Esso, N.Y.C.; Eqilloc, N.Y.

Bibliography

Books

Anderson, Jervis. *This was Harlem: 1900-1950*. New York: Farrar, Straus, Giroux, 1982.

Bergman, Peter M. *The Chronological History of the Negro in America*. New York: The New American Library, 1969.

Bontemps, Arna. *The Harlem Renaissance Remembered.* New York: Dobb, Mead, 1972.

_____. *100 Years of Negro Freedom*. New York: Dobb, Mead & Co., 1961. Brockett, Oscar G. *History of the Theatre*. 6th. ed. Boston: Allyn and Bacon, Inc., 1972.

_____. *The Theatre: An Introduction*. 3rd. ed. New York: Holt, Rinehart and Winston, Inc., 1974.

Clarke, John Herik, ed. *Harlem A Community in Transition.* New York: *Freedomways* Associates, Inc., 1969.

Cripps, Thomas. *Slow Fade to Black: The Negro in American Film, 1900-1942*. New York: Oxford University Press, 1977.

Cisda, Joseph. and June Bundy Cisda., eds. *American Entertainment: A Unique History of Popular Show Business*. New York: Watson-Guptill Publications, 1978.

Daniel, Walter C., ed. *Black Journals of the U. S.: Historical Guides to the World' Periodicals and Newspapers*, Westport, Conn., Greenwood Press, 1982.

Fletcher, Tom. *100 years of the Negro in Show Business*. New York: Burdge and Company, 1954.

Gill, Glenda E. *White Grease Paint on Black Performers: A Study of the Federal Theatre, 1935-1939*. New York, Peter Lang, 1988.

Hartnoll, Phyllis. *The Oxford Companion to the Theatre*. 3rd ed. New York: Oxford University Press, 1967.

Haskins, James. *Black Theater in America*. New York: Thomas Y. Crowell, 1982.

Hatch, James V. *Black Image on the American Stage: A Bibliography of Plays and Musicals, 1770-1970*. New York: Drama Book Specialists, 1970.

_____., and Leo Hamalian. *The Roots of African American Drama*, Detroit, Wayne State University Press, 1991.

_____., and Ted Shine. *Black Theatre, U.S.A.* New York: Free Press, 1974.

Hay, Sam. *African American Theatre: An Historical and Critical Analysis*. Cambridge, Cambridge University Press, 1994.

Hill, Errol. *Shakespeare in Sable: A History of Black Shakespearean Actors*. Amherst, MA.: The University of Massachussetts Press, 1984.

Hogan, Lawrence D. *A Black National News Service: The Associated Negro Press and Claude Barnett 1919-1945*. Rutherford, N. J.: Faileigh Dickinson University Press, 1984.

Huggins, Irvin Nathan. *Harlem Renaissance*. New York: Oxford University Press, 1971.

_____., *Voices from the Harlem Renaissance*. New York, Oxford University Press, 1995.

Hughes, Langston, and Milton Meltzer. *Black Magic*. Englewood Cliffs, N.J.: Prentice-Hall, 1967.

Isaacs, Edith J. *The Negro in the American Theater*. New York: Theater Arts, 1947.

Johnson, James Weldon. *Black Manhattan.* New York: Atheneum, 1995.

Johnson, Boris J., ed., *Who's Who in Colored America 1928-1929.* 2nd ed. New York: Who's Who, 1930.

Kellner, Bruce, ed., *The Harlem Renaissance: A Historical Dictionary for the Era.* Methuen: New York, Routledge & Kegan Paul, 1987.

Kimball, Robert, and William Bolcom. *Reminiscing With Sissle and Blake.* New York: The Viking Press, 1973.

Laistner, M. L. W. *Ancient History.* Boston: D. C. Heath Co., 1928.

Lewis, David Levering, *When Harlem was in Vogue.* New York, Oxford University Press, 1981.

Lincoln, Eric C. *Chronicles of Black Protest.* New York: The New American Library, 1966.

Marshall, Herbert., and Mildred Stock. *Ira Aldridge: The Negro Tragedian.* London: Southern Illinois University Press, Feffer & Simons, Inc., 1968.

McGill, Raymond D., ed. *Notable Names in the American Theatre.* Clifton, N. J.: James T. White and Company, 1976.

Mitchell, Loften. *Black Drama: The Story of the American Negro in The Theatre.* New York: Hawthorn, 1967.

Muse, Clarence, and David Arlen. *Way Down South.* Hollywood, CA.: David Graham Fisher, 1932.

Oak, Vishnu V. *The Negro's Adventure in General Business. Volume II of t h e N e g r o Entrepreneur Series.* Wilberforce, Ohio: Wilberforce University, Antioch Press, Yellow Springs, OH., 1949.

Osofsky, Gilbert, *Harlem: The Making of a Ghetto: Negro New York, 1890-1930.* New York, Harper & Row, 1966.

Papich, Stephen. *Remembering Josephine Baker.* Indianapolis: Bobbs-Merrill, 1976.

Sampson, Henry. *Blacks in Blackface.* Metuchen, New Jersey: Scarecrow Press, 1980.

Schiffman, Jack. *Uptown, the Story of Harlem's Apollo Theatre.* New York: Cowles Book Co., 1971.

Smyth, Mabel M. *The Black American Reference Book.* Englewood Cliffs, N. J.: Prentice-Hall, Inc., 1933.

Southern, Eileen. *The Music of Black Americans: A History.* New York: W. W. Norton & Co., Inc., 1971.

_____. *Readings in Black American Music.* New York: W. W. Norton & Co., Inc.,

Sterns, Marshall, and Jean Sterns. *Jazz Dance, The Story of American Dance.* New York: MacMillan, 1968.

Tanner, Jo A. *Dusty Maidens: The Odyssey of the Early Black Dramatic Actress.* Westport, Connecticut, Greenwood Press, 1992.

Toll, Robert C. *Blacking Up.* New York: Oxford University Press, 1974.

Waters, Ethel. *His Eyes are on the Sparrow.* New York: Doubleday, 1951.

_____. *To Me it's Wonderful.* New York. Harper, 1972.

Wittke, Carl,. *Tambo and Bones.* Durham, N. Y.: Duke University Press, 1930.

Wolseley, Roland E. *The Black Press, U.S.A.* Iowa: Iowa State University Press, 1971.

Woll, Allen, *Black Musical Theatre: from Coontown to Dreamgirl.* Baton Rouge, Louisiana, Louisiana State University Press, 1989.

Dissertations and Theses

Belcher, Fannin S. "The Place of the Negro in the Evolution of the American Theatre, 1797-1940." Ph. D. dissertation, Yale University, 1945.

Bond, Frederick W. "The Direct and Indirect Contribution which the American Negro Has Made to the Drama and the Legitimate Stage, with Underlying Conditions Responsible." Ph. D. dissertation, New York University, 1938.

Buchanan, Singer. "A Study of the Attitudes of the Writers of the Negro Press towards the Depiction of the Negro in Plays and Films: 1930-1968." Ph. D. dissertation, University of Michigan, 1968.

Davidson, Frank C. "The Rise, Development, Decline and Influence of the A m e r i c a n Minstrel Show." Ph. D. dissertation, New York University, 1952.

Dixon, Bessie L. "The Negro Character in American Drama." M.A. Thesis, H o w a r d University, 1926.

Ellington, Mary David. "Plays by Negro Authors with Special Emphasis upon the Period from 1916-1934." Fisk University, 1934.

Fletcher, Winona L. "Andrew Jackson Allen: Internal and External Costumer to the Nineteenth Century American Theatre." Ph. D. dissertation, Indiana University, 1968.

Hardwick, Mary R. "The Nature of the Negro Hero in Serious American Drama, 1919-1964." Ph. D. dissertation, Michigan University, 1965.

Hinklin, Fannie Ella. "The American Negro Playwright 1920-1964." Ph. D. dissert a t i o n, University of Wisconsin, 1965.

Holt, Frances E. "The Negro Character in the American Drama from 1914-1934." Ph. D. dissertation, Fisk University, 1934.

Jeyiflous, Biodun. "Theatre and Drama and the Black Physical and Cultural Presence in America: Essay in Interpretation." Ph. D. dissertation, New York University, 1975.

Kuhlke, William. "They Too Sing America (1918-1930)." M. A. thesis, Adams State College of Colorado, 1952.

Lawson, Hilda H. "The Negro in American Drama." Ph. D. dissertation, University of Illinois, 1939.

Luck, James William. "The Contribution of the Negro to the Legitimate Theatre in America." M. A. thesis, Emerson College, 1953.

Miller, Althea Ann. "The Negro in American Drama." M. A. thesis, University of Oklahoma, 1958.

Monroe, John G. "Charles Sidney Gilpin: The Emperor Jones." M. A. thesis, Hunter College, 1974.

Pembrook, Carrie D. "Negro Drama through the Ages." Ph. D. dissertation, New York University, 1946.

Pettit, Paul B. "The Important American Dramatic Types to 1900: A Study of the Yankee, Negro, Indian, and Frontiersman." Ph. D. dissertation, Cornel University, 1943.

Pinkett, L. Louise. "Folk Elements in American Drama, 1870-1936." M. A. thesis, Howard University, 1936.

Quaranstrom, Isaac Blaine. "Harmount's Uncle Tom's Cabin Company: A Study of a

Twentieth Century 'Tom' Show." Ph. D. dissertation, Ohio State University, l967.

Richards, Sandra. "Bert Williams: His Stage Career and Influence on American Theatre." Ph. D. dissertation, Stanford University, l973.

Sandle, Floyd L. "A History of the Development of the Educational Theatre in the Negro College and Universities, 1911-1959." Ph. D. dissertation, Louisiana State University, l959.

Smith, Allington E. "The Negro Actor in Legitimate Plays, with Special Emphasis on the Period from 1900-1934." M. A. thesis, Fisk University, 1934.

Thompson, Sister Francesca. "The Lafayette Players: 1915-1932." Ph. D. dissertation, University of Michigan, 1972. Westmoreland, Beatrice Fultz. "The Negro in American Drama." M. A. thesis, University of Kansas, 1937.

Periodicals

Jackson, J. A. "J.A. Jackson's Page," *Billboard* (1920-25) Billy Rose Theatre Collection, Lincoln Center Library, New York.

_____. "Steps toward the Negro," *Crisis*, N. 215 Sep. 1922: 66-68.

Rauch, Laurence Lee. "Triple-Threat Artist: Clarence Muse," *Opportunity* N.17 Sept. 1939: 38.

Schechner, Richard. "One View of Performance Studies," *Performance Studies, A Newsletter of the Department of Performance Studies*, Vol. 3 N.1 Fall 1982: 4.

Williamson, Harvey M. "The Gilpin Players," *Crisis*, N. 42 July 1935: 42.

Other Resourses

The *Amsterdam News*	The *New York Age*	*Opportunity*
The *Freeman*	The *Star*	*Theatre Guide*
The Chicago *Defender*	*Variety*	*Theatre Arts*
Crisis		

Interviews

Joseph Bailey, Mariotte Hotel, Woodland Hills, CA., March, 26, 1995.

Dick Campbell, The National Conference on African American Theater at the Day's End Hotel, Baltimore, Md., April 10, 1987.

Taped Interviews: Hatch-Billops Archives

Eubie Blake	Clarence Muse	Anita Bush
Eddie Hunter	Abram Hill	Noble Sissle
Bob Schiffman and Frank Schiffman	Leigh Whipper	Willis Richardson

Index

Dr. Anthony D. Hill earned his Ph.D. from New York University in the Department of Performance Studies in 1988. Currently he is an assistant professor in the Department of Theatre at The Ohio State University in Columbus, Ohio. He has taught at the University of California at Santa Barbara, Vassar, Queens, and Bellevue Colleges. His work has concentrated extensively on marginalized theatre practices, African American and American History, and Performance theory/criticism. Among his publications are two articles each in *Billboard Publications, African American Review* (formerly *Black American Literature Forum*), and *Elimu*, in addition to a review in *The Journal of the Southern Central Modern Language Association.*